OPPOSITION
TO THE
SECOND WORLD WAR

OPPOSITION

TO THE

SECOND WORLD WAR

CONSCIENCE, RESISTANCE AND SERVICE IN BRITAIN, 1933–45

JOHN BROOM

Pen & Sword
MILITARY

AN IMPRINT OF PEN & SWORD BOOKS LTD.
YORKSHIRE – PHILADELPHIA

First published in Great Britain in 2018 by
PEN & SWORD MILITARY
an imprint of
Pen & Sword Books Limited
Yorkshire – Philadelphia

Copyright © John Broom 2018

ISBN 978 1 52671 664 4

The right of John Broom to be identified as author of this work has been asserted by him
in accordance with the Copyright, Designs and Patents Act 1988.

A CIP catalogue record for this book is available from the British Library.

Typeset in Ehrhardt MT & 11/13.5
by Aura Technology and Software Services, India

Printed and bound in England By TJ International Ltd.

Pen & Sword Books Limited incorporates the imprints of Atlas, Archaeology, Aviation,
Discovery, Family History, Fiction, History, Maritime, Military, Military Classics, Politics,
Select, Transport, True Crime, Air World, Frontline Publishing, Leo Cooper, Remember
When, Seaforth Publishing, The Praetorian Press, Wharncliffe Local History, Wharncliffe
Transport, Wharncliffe True Crime and White Owl.

For a complete list of Pen & Sword titles please contact

PEN & SWORD BOOKS LTD
47 Church Street, Barnsley, South Yorkshire, S70 2AS, England
E-mail: enquiries@pen-and-sword.co.uk
Website: www.pen-and-sword.co.uk

Or

PEN & SWORD BOOKS
1950 Lawrence Rd, Havertown, PA 19083, USA
E-mail: Uspen-and-sword@casematepublishers.com
Website: www.penandswordbooks.com

Contents

Acknowledgements

I would like to thank the family of Reverend Rupert Godfrey for permission to quote from his sermons; the family of Oliver Postgate for permission to quote from *Seeing Things* and for the reproduction of the picture on page 13 of the plate section; and Anne Wickes of the Second World War Experience Centre in Wetherby for the provision of material on John Bishop, John Hick and Maurice Beresford.

Thanks also to the family of Harold Hitchcock for permission to reproduce the picture on page 14 of the plate section. Staff at the University of Sheffield Special Collections were extremely supportive in helping me gain access to the Miller Pamphlets and the Sorby Research Institute Collection.

Linne Matthews has guided me through the editing process with skill and thoroughness.

And, as ever, my wife Dawn.

Glossary

APF	Anglican Pacifist Fellowship
ARP	Air Raid Precaution
ATS	Auxiliary Territorial Service
BPF	Baptist Peace Fellowship
BUF	British Union of Fascists
CBCO	Central Board for Conscientious Objectors
CO	Conscientious Objector
CPFLU	Christian Pacifist Forestry and Land Units
CPGB	Communist Party of Great Britain
ELAS	Greek People's Liberation Army
FAU	Friends' Ambulance Unit
FBU	Field Bacteriological Unit
FoR	Fellowship of Reconciliation
FRS	Friends' Relief Service
FSC	Friends' Service Council
FWVRC	Friends' War Victims Relief Committee
GEC	Germany Emergency Committee (of the Religious Society of Friends)
ILP	Independent Labour Party
IVSP	International Voluntary Service for Peace
LCC	London County Council
LFLCC	London Friends' Local Conscription Committee
LNU	League of Nations Union
NCC	Non-Combatant Corps
NCF	No-Conscription Fellowship
NPC	National Peace Council
MPF	Methodist Peace Fellowship
MSTU	Medical Supply and Transport Unit
NMWM	No More War Movement
OTC	Officers' Training Corps
POW	Prisoner of War
PPU	Peace Pledge Union
PSU	Pacifist Service Unit
RAMC	Royal Army Medical Corps
RAOC	Royal Army Ordnance Corps
RNAS	Royal Naval Air Service

UFCPF	Unitarian and Free Church Peace Fellowship
UNRRA	United Nations Relief and Rehabilitation Administration
WAAF	Women's Auxiliary Air Force
WRNS	Women's Royal Naval Service
USAAF	United States Army Air Forces

Introduction

The popular perception of the Second World War is that of a 'good war', one in which the British people stood resilient against evil aggressors in Europe and the Far East. Disaster was averted at Dunkirk and victory eventually wrenched from a position of near-defeat. Winston Churchill is frequently portrayed in films and elsewhere as a popular leader who inspired the nation with his speeches. Party political differences were put aside as the Conservative, Labour and Liberal parties shared power in a coalition government. Men and women gave mutual support in the face of the blitz on British cities and there was a comradely spirit in the armed forces. Britain emerged victorious from the war and the era is often thought of as our 'finest hour'.

However, there is an alternative narrative, one frequently overlooked in the films, novels and documentaries that portray the 1940s. That is of the hundreds of thousands of people who opposed Britain's participation in the war, many of whom refused to be conscripted into the war effort. In Parliament, the government was persistently challenged by a small band of MPs who argued for a swift end to hostilities and for a cessation of the bombing campaign over German cities. This opposition can be traced back to the 1930s and beyond, a period in which a significant pacifist movement was formed in the United Kingdom. One of the defining moments in the articulation of pacifist sentiment occurred during a debate in the Oxford Union in February 1933.

On 30 January 1933, Adolf Hitler was appointed Chancellor of Nazi Germany. Ten days later, on 9 February, the Oxford Union debated and carried the motion 'that this House will in no circumstances fight for its King and Country'. The decision to debate the motion was taken by the president of the Oxford Union, Frank Hardie, and its text written by the union's librarian, David Graham. Because they thought that the motion would receive minimal support, and therefore not be a worthwhile one to discuss, they took the unusual step of inviting an outside speaker to propose it. The man chosen to do it, after some other rejections, was C.E.M. Joad, a regular contributor to the BBC's *Brains Trust* programme, who was serving as head of the Department of Philosophy at Birkbeck College, London. He had been a conscientious objector during the First World War and a member of the Independent Labour Party (ILP, see Chapter 4) for many years before leaving in 1932 due to its endorsement of violence in pursuit of revolutionary aims.

Joad, therefore, was an exponent of absolute pacifism. The dignitary selected to oppose the motion was Quintin Hogg, a former president of the union, who later had a long and distinguished political career as a Conservative cabinet minister and party grandee. The first speaker in favour of the motion was Kenelm Digby, who stated that 'to fight for "King and Country" was a sacrifice of wealth and happiness to the selfish wishes of a class.' He argued that the Great War had been the war to end all wars, and the motion was an affirmation of that fact. The people of the world, he claimed, were far ahead of the statesman in desiring peace. This was a fateful moment for Digby, who would find this speech and its outcome held against him throughout his subsequent legal career.

Responding to the motion, Keith Steel-Maitland, the son of a Conservative MP, stated that he was proud to defend his king, and focused on the inherent contradiction in the Labour supporters' position of believing in class war whilst claiming to love peace. The second speaker to support the motion was its author, David Graham, who dismissed the idea that war was international police work, and that international reconciliation was both superior and necessary. In response, Quintin Hogg argued that pacifism would make war more likely, whilst a strongly armed Britain would be a force for peace. A Britain with no military capability would be unable to exert any influence on European or world affairs.

Next came Cyril Joad, who recalled similar arguments being put before the Oxford Union prior to the Great War, and that in that war his best friend had spent twenty-four hours strung out on barbed wire with his entrails hanging out, begging to die. Joad paraphrased the motion as: 'that this House will never commit murder on a huge scale whenever the government decided it should do so'. He predicted the horrors of mass aerial bombing for civilians and argued for a passive resistance should Britain be invaded. Joad's emotional, eloquent and excoriating speech was credited with carrying the day for the motion. At 11.35 pm the debate ended and the votes were counted; the motion carried by 275 votes to 153.

Initially the result received little press attention, but on Saturday, 11 February, an outraged letter appeared in the *Daily Telegraph*, under the title 'Disloyalty at Oxford: Gesture towards the Reds'. It described the 'shame and disgust' that thousands of Oxford students and graduates must have felt at the result and was 'an outrage upon the memory of those who gave their lives in the Great War'. This letter provoked further controversy, with accusations of communist cells operating at Oxford, and Lord Beaverbrook's *Express* newspapers were quick to wade into the fray. On Monday, 13 February, the *Daily Express* published an attack on 'the woozy-minded Communists, the practical jokers and the sexual indeterminates of Oxford'. This milieu was contrasted with the Mayor of Oxford and his wife 'sitting in front of a log fire reading their Bibles together in their little home'.

The *Evening Standard's* A.A. Baumann averred, 'I suspect upon analysis half the majority would turn out to be foreigners and half "non-ascripts" [*sic*].' He went on to claim there were deeper forces at work in undermining the backbone of the country:

No one but a sand-blind partisan can ignore the fact that there is a confederacy of internationalists which at this moment is remarkably successful in mudding the wells of truth, under the patronage of the polyglot League of Nations, assisted by some of the doctrinaires of the London School of Economics and last, but not least, the BBC.

Some life members of the union, including three ex-presidents, put their name to an open letter drawn up by Randolph Churchill, stating:

> The ephemeral undergraduates who permitted this disgraceful motion to be carried constitute but a tithe of the Oxford Union: they are merely temporary trustees, and they have lamentably failed in their trusteeship. Consequently, we propose to go down to Oxford on Thursday, March 2nd, and to move the adjournment of the Union, and if possible, to expunge the motion from the records of the House. We appeal to you to assist us in this project.

The letter was published in the *Daily Telegraph* of 15 February and circulated to life members of the union. On the same day, a box containing 275 white feathers, the traditional emblem of cowardice, one for each supportive vote, was delivered to the union. The following day, as the union met for its next debate, a group of twenty students walked in, seized the minute book, and tore out the pages that recorded the 'King and Country' debate. The union's committee met and suggested that the minute book not be taken to the next meeting. It was also noted that some of those who had torn out the minutes were professed fascists.

During the interlude between the original passing of the motion, and 2 March, the date it was due to be challenged, the controversy continued to be discussed across Britain. Winston Churchill spoke of the 'abject, squalid, shameless avowal [by the] callow, ill-tutored youths' of Oxford and compared them unfavourably to Germany's 'splendid, clear-eyed youth demanding to be conscripted into an army, burning to die for their Fatherland'.

The *New York Times* later speculated that, far from preventing the war, some of the pacifist activity during the 1930s would actually make it more likely. The respected newspaper could not:

> help wondering to what extent Hitler's political policies have been influenced by a conception of the British temper based on episodes like the Oxford Pledge and bigger manifestations like the English peace plebiscite somewhat later. Prominent among the 'activists' who have egged Hitler on is von Ribbentrop, who used to be Ambassador in London, and who assured his Fuehrer that England would not fight.

Winston's Churchill, who had condemned the Oxford Pledge soon after its passing, wrote after the war that, due to this 'ever shameful' motion, 'in Germany, in Russia, in Italy, in Japan, the idea of a decadent, degenerate Britain took deep root and swayed many calculations.' Churchill's claim was amplified by Erich von Richthofen, who had served on Hitler's General Staff in 1933, in a letter to the *Daily Telegraph* three decades later when the Oxford Union debated a modified form of the motion. He wrote:

> I am an ex-officer of the old Wehrmacht and served on what you would call the German General Staff at the time of the Oxford resolution. I can assure you, from personal knowledge, that no other factor influenced Hitler more and decided him on his course than that 'refusal to fight for King and Country' coming from what was assumed to be the intellectual elite of your country.

Although the validity of this letter has been disputed by historians, there is no doubt that the Oxford Union debate did articulate an impression of the cream of Britain's youth as challenging traditional notions of patriotism and military masculinity. It set the tone for debates and controversies throughout the 1930s and beyond, into the war years, of what methods, if any, should be used in opposing fascism, and caused splits in political parties, the churches and within individual families.

Chapter 1

The International Situation

Pacifism embraces a wide spectrum of views, individuals and groups. For some people, it is the belief that international disputes can and should be resolved peacefully, whilst for others it is the notion that the possession of weapons and a standing army, navy and air force is morally wrong. Others object to war on the basis that the government takes physical control of an individual's body to insist on them performing violence on others. For an absolute pacifist, there can never be any ethical grounds that can justify resorting to war. Therefore, for a pure pacifist the ends, however desirable they may seem, can never validate the means of waging war.

Between the two world wars, there was a large body of opinion in Britain that tended towards what Martin Ceadel, the eminent historian of the British peace movement, described as pacificism. This term described those who, though not pacifists, regarded the prevention of war as an overriding political priority because it was an irrational, inhumane method of solving international disputes. During the 1930s and 1940s, as totalitarian regimes were installed in many European countries and Japan committed acts of aggression in the Far East, people who renounced war as a means of settling international disputes faced stark moral challenges and choices. The goal of defeating Hitler, and stopping the spread of his terrible Nazi regime, had to be set against the carnage that such a struggle would entail. *Opposition to the Second World War* examines the responses of people who tried to work towards a negotiated peace in the world. This introductory chapter will provide an outline of the succession of international crises that characterised the 1930s and provided the context for the growing anti-war movement in the United Kingdom.

There were five main causes for the pacifist and pacificistic opposition to war in the 1930s. Firstly there was widespread recognition that the Treaty of Versailles of 1919 had been unjustly harsh on Germany. The demand for crippling war reparations of £6.6 billion, the removal of territories that included German-speaking peoples, and the drastic reduction in Germany's military capabilities had created poverty and misery in that country. There was an impression that the treaty was discredited and in need of revision. The War Guilt clause, ascribing all the blame for the war on Germany, had divided nations into the innocent and guilty, instead of asking nations to reflect on their own part in the arrival and conduct of war.

German actions in reversing the more punitive terms of the treaty were therefore met with a mixture of indifference or sympathy. The remilitarisation of the Rhineland and the annexation of Austria and the Sudetenland could be seen to be in line with the principle of national self-determination. Until Germany's invasion of Czechoslovakia in March 1939, most British people were willing to interpret Hitler's expansionist actions in central Europe as the redressing of legitimate grievances arising from the Treaty of Versailles.

Secondly, there was a determination that the horrors of the First World War should not be repeated, and that another war, with improved weaponry and the development of aerial warfare, would prove even more destructive. Stanley Baldwin (Plates, page 1), who would serve as Prime Minister from 1935 to 1937, told the House of Commons on 10 November 1932 that:

> I think it as well also for the man in the street to realise that there is no power on earth that can protect him from being bombed. Whatever people may tell him, the bomber will always get through. ... The only defence is in offence, which means that you have to kill more women and children more quickly than the enemy if you want to save yourselves.

Winston Churchill predicted in the Commons on 28 November 1934 that a heavy bombing of London would create between 30,000 and 40,000 casualties within a week. Baldwin reported to the Peace Society in October 1935 that 'We live under the shadow of the last war and its memories still sicken us. We remember what war is, with no glory in it but the heroism of man.' H.G. Wells's 1933 novel, *The Shape of Things to Come*, foresaw the imminent prospect of a situation in which Europe was devastated by a major war involving the aerial bombing of civilians and the development of weapons of mass destruction. Elements of the novel were made into a popular film, *Things to Come*, in 1936. Pablo Picasso's great painting *Guernica* (1937), depicting the destruction of the Spanish town by the German Luftwaffe, gave a stark message about the horrors of modern war, of dismembered civilians and psychological terror. (Plates, page 2)

Most British cities, towns and villages had their war memorial, which served as a daily reminder of the sacrifice of so many young men and women. Many workplaces, social clubs, schools and chapels had their own memorials to those who never returned. Also, a number of great public monuments were erected, including the Cenotaph in Whitehall, meaning the Great War dominated the psychological landscape of the 1920s and 30s. A determination that there should be no repetition dominated the politics, religious life, literature and films of the

1930s. In the world of academia, the Cambridge Union followed the lead of their Oxford counterparts in passing a motion condemning the idea of another war.

Thirdly, a belief in the rational nature of humanity dominated thinking in the 1930s. The League of Nations was based on the premise that all disputes between nations could be settled by diplomatic negotiations or international arbitration. Many commentators believed that another war was unthinkable, because it was illogical. This revealed an understandable lack of awareness about the full depth of Nazi brutality and evil. Prime Minister Ramsay MacDonald told the German ambassador in April 1933 that he had never believed reports of Nazi excesses, and as late as June 1937, Sir Neville Henderson, newly appointed as British ambassador to Berlin, told dinner guests that too many people in Britain had an 'erroneous conception' of Nazism. Therefore, pacifism was a rational approach to take. Wars could be stopped by discussion.

Fourthly, there were significant elements in British society that were sympathetic to European dictatorships, which created a greater space for appeasement and pacifism to flourish. As British politicians struggled unsuccessfully to combat the unemployment and misery that many faced during the 1930s, the idea of a strong leader seemed increasingly attractive. Hitler was commended for slashing unemployment in Germany. In addition, a strong Germany under Hitler was seen as a bulwark against the threat of communism spreading from the Soviet Union westwards across the continent. A seam of anti-Semitism ran through many parts of British society, thus creating a narrative of understanding for some people of why Hitler was reducing the influence of Jews in German society. In 1935, the British Legion sent delegates to Germany who met with Hitler, who emphasised to them the importance of ex-soldiers from both countries collaborating for peace. Lloyd George, British Prime Minister from 1916 to 1922, praised Hitler as the 'greatest living German'.

Fifthly, the Christian churches remained hugely influential in British society throughout the inter-war period. Many Christians across Europe felt guilt at having fought each other during the Great War. As international co-operation between European churches increased during the 1920s and 1930s, this spirit of international brotherhood was given expression through the work of Church leaders in advocating negotiated settlements, and from many clergy who emerged as leaders of the pacifist movement during the 1930s, such as Charles Raven, Donald Soper and Dick Sheppard.

Nevertheless, despite the widespread revulsion at the prospect of another war amongst much of the British public during the 1930s, by 1939 the country was once again engaged in a European – later to become a world – war, one that would prove even more destructive than the first one. The vociferous anti-war movement of the 1930s had fizzled out into a tiny handful of men refusing to be conscripted into the armed services. Political and religious opposition to war became confined to a small group of sincere but marginal voices. However, for many of these people, adherence to conscience and principle meant seeing through the logic of their beliefs no matter what the external circumstances. This book traces their stories, and how the beliefs and actions were mediated by the events of the 1930s and 1940s. To understand the context in which anti-war groups were operating throughout the 1930s and 40s, it is first necessary to understand the unfolding events which shook the European settlement brokered at Versailles in 1919, and of the emerging threats to peace elsewhere in the world.

The League of Nations

An international League of Nations was an idea mooted by US President Woodrow Wilson at the Versailles Peace Conference of 1919. As Germany and the other defeated powers – Austria–Hungary, Turkey and Bulgaria – were excluded from the conference, the initial impression was that it was a 'League of Victors'. One immediate weakness for the League was the fact that the US Senate voted, on 19 November 1919, not to join. When the League was set up in January 1920, Germany was not included due to the fact it was seen as the primary aggressor during the First World War. In addition to the absence of the USA and Germany, another world power, Soviet Russia, was initially excluded as its newly installed Bolshevik government was yet to be internationally recognised, thus further weakening the moral authority of the conference. Although Germany was permitted to join in 1926, as it had become, according to the League of Nations Council, a 'peace-loving country', it withdrew in 1933 once Hitler had assumed power.

The League was based on the idea of collective security. This required nations to act together to address instability and conflict around the world. In practice, for many reasons, this proved unworkable. The League's neutrality tended to manifest itself as indecision. It required a unanimous vote of nine, later fifteen, council members to enact a resolution; hence, conclusive and effective action was difficult, if not impossible. This problem mainly stemmed from the fact that members of the League of Nations were not willing to accept the possibility of their fate being decided by other countries, and by enforcing unanimous voting had effectively given themselves veto power.

The Mukden Incident, also known as the 'Manchurian Incident', was a decisive setback for the League that increased international tension because its members refused to tackle Japanese aggression, but what ineffective actions were taken led to Japan withdrawing from the League. Japan, under the pretext that Chinese soldiers had sabotaged a railway, occupied all of Manchuria in September 1931. They renamed the area Manchuko and set up a puppet government under the leadership of Pu Yi, a former emperor of China. Only Italy, Spain and Germany recognised this government, with the rest of the world considering Manchuria to be still part of China. The League of Nation's response was futile. They sent a team of observers to the region and produced the Lytton Report in October 1932. Japan was declared to be the aggressor and was ordered to return Manchuria to China, a finding backed by a vote of 42–1 in the League of Nations Assembly in 1933. Japan was the only country to vote against the findings of the report, and withdrew from the League in protest. Thus, the idea of collective world security had taken a severe blow. The other nations were either unwilling or unable to enforce economic sanctions. America, Japan's main trading partner, was not a member of the League, and Britain did not want to weaken her economic interest by enforcing sanctions. No one suggested military intervention, for fear of escalating tensions in the area.

The next major crisis to beset the League occurred in October 1935, when Italian dictator Benito Mussolini sent 400,000 troops to invade Abyssinia, modern-day Ethiopia. Marshal Pietro Badoglio, who led the campaign from November 1935, ordered bombing, the use of chemical weapons such as mustard gas, and the poisoning of water supplies against targets that included primitive undefended villages and medical facilities. The well-equipped Italian Army defeated the poorly armed Abyssinians and captured the capital, Addis Ababa, in May 1936, forcing Emperor of Ethiopia Haile Selassie to flee his country.

Once again, the League of Nations condemned the aggressor, but this time imposed economic sanctions on Italy in November 1935. However, these were ineffective as they did not ban the sale of oil or close the Suez Canal as a trade route. League of Nations countries feared an attack by Italian forces if they tried to enforce harsher sanctions. Stanley Baldwin told the House of Commons that collective security had failed in this instance:

> because of the reluctance of nearly all the nations in Europe to proceed to what I might call military sanctions. ... The real reason, or the main reason, was that we discovered in the process of weeks that there was no country except the aggressor country which was ready for war. ... If collective action is to be a reality and not merely a thing to be talked about, it means not only that every country is to be ready for war; but must be ready to go to war at once. That is a terrible thing, but it is an essential part of collective security.

Although America limited exports of oil to Italy, the League's sanctions were lifted on 4 July 1936. By then, Italy had gained control of Abyssinian cities and the country had fallen. The British Foreign Secretary, Samuel Hoare, and the French Prime Minister, Pierre Laval, had attempted to broker a settlement in December 1935 by proposing to partition the country into Abyssinian and Italian sectors. Although Mussolini was prepared to be compliant with what was known as the Hoare-Laval Pact, when news leaked out both the British and French public were appalled at what appeared to be a sellout of Abyssinia. Both Hoare and Laval were forced to resign. In June 1936, despite no longer being leader of his country, Haile Selassie spoke to the League of Nations Assembly, appealing for help in protecting his country. The Abyssinian crisis had once again highlighted how the countries in the League of Nations tempered their actions by self-interest. In addition, an issue with one country had to be placed within a wider geopolitical context, with a fear that harsh sanctions against Italy would provoke an alliance between Mussolini and Hitler.

A further international crisis occurred in 1936, when the Spanish Army, under the leadership of the Fascist Franco, launched a coup against the democratically elected government of that country. The Spanish Foreign Minister, Julio Álvarez del Vayo, appealed to the League of Nations in September 1936 for arms to defend Spain's territorial integrity and political independence. In this instance, not only did the League of Nations refuse to intervene in what was conveniently seen as a domestic affair, but it stood by as Hitler and Mussolini poured in resources to support Franco's Nationalists.

In February 1937, the League half-heartedly banned foreign volunteers from taking part in the conflict, although this was largely a futile gesture and many on the left joined the International Brigades fighting for democracy. This included around 2,500 volunteers from the UK and Ireland, 526 of whom were killed in the conflict.

On 7 July 1937, Japan launched a full-scale invasion of China. On 12 September, Wellington Koo, the Chinese representative to the League of Nations, appealed for international intervention. However, despite admiration for the Chinese struggle, particularly the defence of Shanghai, a city where many Europeans lived, the League offered no practical support.

Underpinning all the above failures of the League of Nations to address acts of aggression during the 1930s was the issue of disarmament. Article 8 of the League's Covenant gave it the task of reducing 'armaments to the lowest point consistent with national safety and the enforcement by common action of international obligations'. Many governments were unsure that such disarmament was realistic, or even worthwhile. The victorious Allied powers from the First World War had an obligation, under the Treaty of Versailles, to work towards achieving for themselves the armament restrictions imposed on Germany. This was envisaged to be the first step towards worldwide disarmament. To that end a special commission had been established in 1926 to prepare for a World Disarmament Conference, which would run from 1932 to 1934. The work of the commission was far from straightforward. France, having been invaded twice by Germany within the past sixty years, was reluctant to reduce its armaments without a guarantee of military assistance should this occur again. Poland and Czechoslovakia both felt vulnerable to attack from Germany or the Soviet Union and wanted a more robust plan from the League to address acts of aggression before they began to disarm. These fears were heightened following Hitler's accession to power in 1933, with his promises to reconstruct German military power and his ideology of *Lebensraum*, or living space, for the German people.

The World Disarmament Conference met in Geneva in 1932, under the chairmanship of British Foreign Secretary Arthur Henderson, with representatives from sixty countries. President Roosevelt of America sent a message of support:

> If all nations will agree wholly to eliminate from possession and use the weapons which make possible a successful attack, defences automatically will become impregnable and the frontiers and independence of every nation will become secure.

It was proposed that nations impose a one-year moratorium on the expansion of armaments. However, countries found it difficult to agree on what constituted offensive and defensive weapons. Germany was growing increasingly aggrieved at the length of time that had elapsed since the end of the First World War, when other countries, especially France, were permitted a far higher level of armaments than they were. France, as noted above, was reluctant to reduce its armaments without security guarantees from the UK and USA. Therefore, the talks broke down and Hitler withdrew Germany both from the conference and the League of Nations in October 1933. Ultimately, the World Disarmament Conference failed to halt the military build-up in Germany, Italy and Japan during the 1930s.

As the 1930s progressed, the League of Nations unravelled. Japan and Germany had left in 1933, Italy and Spain resigned from the League in 1937, and the Soviet Union was expelled in December 1939 after its invasion of Finland. Efforts to maintain international peace and security had failed. The League of Nations lacked its own armed forces to implement its decisions. It also lacked the membership of the strongest military power in the world, the USA, and other significant powers such as Germany and the USSR. The two most powerful members, Britain and France, were reluctant to use their own military to enforce League policy. As this book will demonstrate, this was partially due to a feeling of revulsion against war felt across much of society in the 1920s and 1930s. The League had an illogical stance, advocating at the same time disarmament for its main powers alongside collective security that could only be applied by military force. The words of Maurice Hankey, the Cabinet Secretary during the First World War, were prescient:

> It [a League of Nations] will only result in failure and the longer that failure is postponed the more certain it is that this country will have been lulled to sleep. It will put a very strong lever into the hands of the well-meaning idealists who are to be found in almost every government, who deprecate expenditure on armaments, and, in the course of time, it will almost certainly result in this country being caught at a disadvantage.

Underpinning the failure of the League of Nations to achieve resolutions to the problems in China, Abyssinia and Spain was the increasing disregard shown by Hitler for the terms of the Treaty of Versailles. German rearmament had already begun in secret during the time of the Weimar Republic. Leading politicians, including Chancellor Hermann Müller, believed that the Treaty of Versailles amounted to an economically anti-competitive measure enforced on Germany by France and Britain to remove a rival in terms of global economic competition and empire building. Once Hitler came to power in 1933, the German rearmament programme became more aggressive.

Hitler's government proposed military rearmament, claiming that the Treaty of Versailles was an embarrassment for all Germans. Rearmament became the topmost priority of the German government, spearheading one of the greatest expansions of industrial production and civil improvement that the world had seen. Money was borrowed to finance the programme, and covert organisations were set up to train pilots for the future Luftwaffe. One benefit of this policy was near full employment for men in 1930s Germany. By March 1935, Hitler was openly flouting the Treaty of Versailles, formally announcing a rearmament programme and the reintroduction of conscription.

The Spanish Civil War provided an ideal testing ground for the efficacy of Hitler's new weapons, and new techniques such as dive-bombing were perfected by the Condor Legion on territories held by the Republican government. By September 1938, Hitler could boast, 'we rearmed to an extent the like of which the world has not yet seen.' Western governments took no action against this flouting of the Treaty of Versailles, partly because Hitler was seen as a powerful potential bulwark against Soviet Russia.

This leniency towards Hitler's actions was also apparent in the lack of response to Germany's military aggrandisement from 1936 onwards. Under the Treaty of Versailles, the Rhineland area of Germany that bordered France was meant to be an area free from German troops. However, on 7 March 1936, Hitler sent German forces into the area. France, feeling threatened, lodged a protest with the League of Nations, but took no military action against Germany. British Prime Minister Stanley Baldwin said that Britain did not have the forces to back up its guarantees to France. Furthermore, much of British opinion thought that Germany was only putting troops into its own territory, which was entirely reasonable. Hugh Dalton, Labour's spokesman on foreign affairs, said that the party would not support military action or economic sanctions in this case. In the League of Nations, only the Soviet Union proposed sanctions against Germany.

Hitler took the view that the international community would not resist him and the lack of action over Manchuria, Abyssinia and Spain provided a space in which his ambitions could be realised. With the resignation of Baldwin in 1937, Neville Chamberlain became Prime Minister and pursued a twin-track policy of appeasement and rearmament. The first episode his government had to address was that of Austria. The country had been created from the Austro-Hungarian Empire, which was broken up in 1918, with the majority of the population being German-speaking and wishing to become part of a Greater Germany. This was forbidden at Versailles but was particularly important to Hitler – who was Austrian by birth and supported the idea of a Greater German Reich, which he set out in 1924 in his autobiographical *Mein Kampf*.

Hitler stirred up political unrest in Austria in order to manoeuvre a Nazi – Arthur Seyss-Inquart – into power. Although the British ambassador in Berlin registered a protest with the German government against the use of coercion against Austria, the sitting Austrian Chancellor, Kurt Schuschnigg, resigned in favour of his rival, realising that neither Britain nor France would offer any practical support. On 12 March 1938, German troops crossed the border, meeting little resistance and being greeted by crowds of cheering Austrians. The country became the German province of Ostmark, and a plebiscite was held on 10 April, with a reported vote of 99.73 per cent in favour of the new arrangement.

Although the union of Austria and Germany was forbidden by the Versailles Treaty, no action was taken against Hitler. Chamberlain told the House of Commons that 'The hard fact is that nothing could have arrested what has actually happened [in Austria] unless this country and other countries had been prepared to use force.' The lack of physical reaction led Hitler to conclude that his aggression would not be checked by the international community for now.

The country of Czechoslovakia had also been created at Versailles from a patchwork of nationalities. It included the areas of the Czech Crown lands, Bohemia, Moravia, Slovakia and the Sudetenland, an area with a German-speaking majority. In April 1938, the Sudeten Nazis, led by Konrad Henlein, threatened direct action to bring the area within the frontiers of the Reich if demands for greater autonomy were not met. Both France and Britain advised Czechoslovakia to accede to the request, but the Czech government refused. Lord Runciman, a former Liberal Cabinet minister, was despatched to Prague by Chamberlain to mediate. Meanwhile, Hitler had escalated the tensions, stationing 750,000 troops on the German-Czech border, and the German press carried apocryphal stories of Czech atrocities on Sudeten Germans. At a Nuremburg Rally on 12 September 1938, Hitler made a speech attacking Czechoslovakia, and Sudeten Nazis attacked Czech and Jewish citizens.

Chamberlain himself flew to Berchtesgaden on 15 September to talk with Hitler, who now demanded not just self-government for Sudeten Germans, but the absorption of the territory into the German Reich. The British PM feared that a refusal would lead to war, as only an invasion of Germany could prevent them from attacking Czechoslovakia. Therefore, Britain and France told the Czech president, Edvard Beneš, that all territories containing a majority of German speakers should be turned over to Hitler. Meanwhile, a Sudeten German paramilitary organisation had been established, which carried out terrorist attacks on Czech targets.

Chamberlain returned to Germany on 22 September, agreeing that Hitler should take the Sudetenland into Germany. Hitler responded by demanding the complete breakup of Czechoslovakia. Now he had consolidated Germany's military power through rearmament, Hitler was ready to extend the Third Reich into territories bordering Germany. Both Britain and France mobilised their armed forces. Chamberlain, in a wireless broadcast on 27 September, reacted to the Czechoslovak refusal to accept Nazi demands to cede territory: 'How horrible, fantastic, incredible it is that we should be digging trenches and trying on gas masks here because of a quarrel in a faraway country between people of whom we know nothing.' He then flew once again to meet with Hitler, meeting in Munich on 29 September 1938. This was the Four-Power Conference, involving Britain, France, Germany and Italy (but not Czechoslovakia itself nor the Soviet Union). (Plates, page 1) All four countries agreed that the Czechs should cede the Sudetenland, and if the country resisted, it would stand alone. Hitler signed a peace treaty between Germany and the United Kingdom, and Chamberlain returned to Heston Aerodrome to wave the agreement in front of the newsreel cameras, famously promising 'Peace in our time'.

Czechoslovakia was then broken up, and in March 1939 Germany moved to occupy areas not controlled by Hungary or Poland. At this stage, Chamberlain was still pursuing a policy of appeasement, mooting the possibility of a disarmament conference involving France, Germany, Italy, the USSR and the UK. The Home Secretary, Samuel Hoare, commented, 'These five men, working together in Europe and blessed in their efforts by the president of the United States of America, might make themselves eternal benefactors of the human race.' Chamberlain ultimately accepted all of Hitler's demands because he believed Britain and Nazi Germany were 'the two pillars of European peace and buttresses against communism'.

To many in Britain, Chamberlain returned as a hero, having apparently averted another hugely destructive European war. To others, including Churchill, Czechoslovakia had been betrayed and Hitler's demands would conceivably not end there. The German Führer spoke to his commanders-in-chief:

> Our enemies have leaders who are below the average. No personalities. No masters,
> no men of action. ... Our enemies are little worms. I saw them in Munich.

On 1 September 1939, German forces invaded Poland, and finally Britain and France declared war on Germany. After the fall of Norway in May 1940, Chamberlain was forced to resign and was succeeded as Prime Minister by Winston Churchill. When Chamberlain died shortly afterwards in November, Churchill paid him this tribute:

> Whatever else history may or may not say about these terrible, tremendous years, we can be sure that Neville Chamberlain acted with perfect sincerity according to his lights and strove to the utmost of his capacity and authority, which were powerful, to save the world from the awful, devastating struggle in which we are now engaged.

The vast majority of the British people in the 1930s were sincerely opposed to the prospect of another war. However, most accepted its inevitability at some point between 1933 and 1939 as the events described above developed. Nevertheless, there were individuals and groups whose renunciation of war went further than supporting the British government's efforts at diplomatic solutions to problems in Europe. This book will examine the myriad ways in which their opinions were formed, in which their arguments were put forward, and the extent to which they were prepared to argue for their ethical standpoint, right through the course of the Second World War and beyond.

Chapter 2

The League of Nations Union

The League of Nations Union was formed on 13 October 1918 in the United Kingdom to promote international justice, collective security and a permanent peace between nations based upon the ideals of the League of Nations. It sought to move away from the balance of power theory, in which war had been supposedly prevented by the distribution of military capability between states, thus causing them to form defensive coalitions. This theory had been smashed to pieces by the events of July and August 1914, as the powers of Europe mobilised for war to honour their commitments under the balance of power treaties.

The LNU became the largest and most influential organisation in the British peace movement between the wars. It had a quarter of a million members by the mid-1920s and just over 400,000 by 1931. (Plates, page 3) It was thus one of the largest voluntary associations of its day. Based in Westminster, the work of the LNU was overseen by a General Council, which met twice a year to formulate policy. The Executive Committee met fortnightly to co-ordinate campaigns and educational programmes and to oversee the work of local branches. The LNU was successful in bringing together trade unions, the British churches, much of the political mainstream and the principal newspapers to support its work. In that regard, it had the broadest backing of those organisations working to preserve international peace during the 1930s.

The idea of an international League of Nations, a body that would arbitrate in disputes between sovereign nations and ensure world collective security, had been mooted by Lord Robert Cecil, a Parliamentary Under Secretary of State at the Foreign Office and a committed Christian. (Plates, page 2) The idea was endorsed by the British Cabinet and Cecil was sent as a delegate to the Paris Peace Conference of 1919, where, after negotiations and general support from US President Woodrow Wilson, a League of Nations was established.

On returning to the UK, Cecil threw his energies into the work of the League of Nations Union, seeking to ensure that the work of the international League of Nations remained at the heart of British foreign policy. The LNU was closely associated with the Liberal Party, with its first president being Edward Grey, Foreign Secretary during the First World War, and another leading light being Geoffrey Mander, Liberal MP for Wolverhampton East. The LNU was successful in recruiting some high profile Conservatives, such as Austen Chamberlain, although many in the party were suspicious of its support for pacifism and disarmament. Therefore, it drew most of its following from Liberal and Labour Party supporters. It also had more support in England than in Wales or Scotland and was particularly well supported by the Free Churches. Winston Churchill, rarely one to mince his words, said in the House of Commons about the leading members of the LNU: 'What impresses me most about them is their long-suffering and inexhaustible gullibility.'

Robert Cecil's contention was that 'the war [had] shattered the prestige of the European governing classes' and that their disappearance had created a vacuum that needed to be filled if disaster was to be averted. His solution to this was the construction of a European order based on Christian morality, with a machinery of legal conciliation that could avoid the aggrandisement and tensions of the pre-war system. Free trade was to be another aspect of this world order. The League would not only secure peace between nations, but civilisation and prosperity within each nation. Domestically, the LNU would strive to ensure that the point of view of the international League would permeate party politics.

Cecil regarded 'class war, whether the class attacked be landowners or Labour, [as] the most insidious form of national disintegration'. To this end, he wished for the creation of a centrist party led by Lord Grey, the former Foreign Secretary, and the removal of Lloyd George as Prime Minister. This party would not be anti-working class and would include 'the best of the Liberal and Labour people [and] some of the old landowning Tories'. However, this plan did not come to fruition. Cecil went on to serve in successive governments of the 1920s as the minister responsible for British activities in the League of Nations. In 1927 he resigned from the cabinet over a disagreement regarding a reduction in navy cruisers, causing the breakdown of an international conference in Geneva in 1927. Cecil then turned his attention to mobilising public support for the League of Nations. He founded the International Peace Campaign, an Anglo-French organisation also known as 'Rassemblement universel pour la paix'.

Throughout the 1930s, the League of Nations was faced with a series of challenges that demonstrated many flaws inherent in its composition. The Japanese invasion of Manchuria in 1931 was not militarily opposed by the League. At the Geneva Disarmament Conference of February 1932, due to domestic disarmament, Britain was powerless to stop Japanese aggression. The dislocation between arguing for British disarmament and then urging for military action to deter the aggression of one nation against another was becoming apparent. Prime Minister Baldwin noted:

> The very people like Bob Cecil who have made us disarm, and quite right too, are now urging us forward to take action. But where will action take us? ... If

you enforce an economic boycott you will have war declared by Japan and she will seize Singapore and Hong Kong and we cannot, as we are placed, stop her.

Cecil and the policy of appeasement

Despite the setback over the lack of effective action against Japan, and the appointment of Hitler as Chancellor of Germany in January 1933, Robert Cecil still hoped for further international disarmament, including the abolition of naval and military aircraft and what he termed 'aggressive arms'. As the Geneva Disarmament Conference continued, Cecil argued for other nations to have similar restrictions placed on their armaments as had Germany at the Treaty of Versailles. Cecil did not approve of the Stresa Front of 1935 between Britain, France and Italy as it excluded Germany. He wrote to Baldwin stating that Hitler should be given a chance to sign a disarmament treaty. Should he fail to do so, which was likely, that would be the time to contemplate 'economic and financial measures which might be applied to a state endangering peace by unilateral repudiation of its international obligations'.

By June 1935, Cecil believed that a 'collective threat from the League or a breach of British friendship' would prevent the Italian invasion of Abyssinia. Later that year, Cecil used the LNU to pressure the government into League action against Italy. He also supported oil sanctions and the closure of the Suez Canal (even if this breached international law). He became increasingly sympathetic towards the Labour Party's attitude to foreign policy and in August he contemplated joining it. At the general election held in November, he favoured the Union's policy of advising electors to vote for the candidate most likely to support the League. The Hoare-Laval Pact of December met with Cecil's disapproval because it would mean that 'as between the League of Nations and Mussolini, Mussolini ha[d] won' and that Samuel Hoare, the British Foreign Secretary, had set back the only hope of showing that aggression did not pay. Cecil believed that French suspicion of Germany was the main cause of the Pact and that Britain should offer France co-operation against Germany in return for French co-operation against Italy.

The year 1935 was the high watershed of influence of Robert Cecil and the LNU. Thereafter both went into sharp decline. The remilitarisation of the Rhineland in March 1936 was to Cecil the 'most dangerous crisis since 1914', but it could not be resolved, and Germany was let off the hook. In April, Cecil believed that as Italy had to subdue Abyssinia quickly, Britain ought to favour not only existing sanctions but increased sanctions against Italy. When Abyssinian resistance collapsed in May, Italy should have been expelled from the League in order to demonstrate that 'an effective system of collective security' was possible. Otherwise it would become obvious that the League was a 'failure', the Union was 'bankrupt' and that collective security was a 'farce'.

Cecil tried to prevent Conservative politicians from withdrawing support from the LNU by presenting it as 'an almost ideal machinery' for the preservation of the Empire. However, the Union further swung to the left and received complaints from Prime Minister Neville Chamberlain and the Conservative Central Office about the left-wing tone of Union propaganda. In May 1938, Cecil complained that the government had 'allowed the League to disintegrate' and in August that their 'ambiguities and timidities' were failing to ensure that Hitler understood that further aggression would be a breach of international relations. The LNU was becoming increasingly disengaged from the centre of power in the United Kingdom.

Cecil was squarely opposed to Chamberlain's policy of appeasement. In May 1938 he said in a letter that German diplomacy had never in history been founded on honest dealing:

> The Germans really conceive of their country as always under war conditions in this respect. No one expects a belligerent to tell the truth and, to the German mind, they are always belligerent. The Germans take the view that war is only intensified peace.

Cecil was a critic of the Munich Agreement, writing to Foreign Secretary Lord Halifax on 20 September 1938 that he 'had not felt so bitterly on any public question since the fall of Khartoum' in 1885. The conduct of the government had completely alienated Cecil from the Conservatives.

In his memoirs Cecil wrote that Mrs Beneš (wife of Czech President Edvard Beneš) telephoned him on behalf of her husband and asked for advice on the crisis:

> I felt forced to reply that, much as I sympathised with her country, I could not advise her to rely on any help from mine. It was the only reply that could be made, but I have never felt a more miserable worm than I did when making it. To me and many others the transaction was as shameful as anything in our history. ... Nothing was more painful in the whole of these ... negotiations than the constant threats of the Germans to enforce by arms any of their demands which were resisted, threats to which we instantly submitted.

Cecil wrote a letter to the *Manchester Guardian* denouncing Munich:

> But supposing there is a German guarantee, of what is its value? It is
> unnecessary to accuse Germany of perfidy. Not only the Nazi government
> but all previous German governments from the time of Frederick the Great
> downwards have made their position perfectly clear. To them an international
> assurance is no more than a statement of present intention. It has no absolute
> validity for the future.

Cecil's hopes of peace through collective security were in tatters and war had
become inevitable.

Educational and propaganda activities

By the early 1930s, with falling membership and a decline in the circulation of
Headway, the LNU's magazine, from 100,000 in 1930 to just 60,000 by 1932,
LNU leaders re-examined the effectiveness of their publicity efforts. They
employed a publicity expert, Sir Charles Higham, who advised the organisation to
use lively advertisements in the press, cinema and on radio. Further advice was to
make LNU meetings less formal and stuffy, and revamp *Headway*. Therefore, an
energetic programme of summer schools, films, books and children's camps was
organised to reach a wider audience.

The history classroom was the focal point of the LNU's educational work. This
was to address the tendency for the subject to be taught in a narrow, nationalistic
manner, rather than educating young people to be citizens of the world. The LNU
sought to have textbooks rewritten and teaching schemes revised. It encouraged
the study of international relations and social history to demonstrate to pupils the
interdependence of nations. During the 1920s and 30s, the British school system
was decentralised, with the choice of what to teach and how to teach it frequently
left to individual head teachers, or even teachers. Therefore, it was this group
that the LNU had to convince; summer schools and conferences were organised
for them, and resources in the form of pamphlets, visiting lecturers, films and a
lending library were made available.

The LNU central leadership in London worked with the Historical Association
to issue a list of 'approved' books for teachers to use. It also liaised with publishers
to advise them to update their books to include a chapter on the League of
Nations. Accounts of the previous war that laid all the blame on Germany for
its inception also needed to be rewritten. Over a million schoolchildren saw
documentary films produced by the LNU in co-operation with the Historical

Association. Many Local Education Authorities were co-operative with this work. The London County Council arranged for mass meetings of teachers to hear talks by Robert Cecil. In Yeovil, Somerset, teachers were instructed to spend at least one afternoon each month teaching about the League of Nations, and in Bolton, Lancashire, an essay competition on the League was established to further children's interest.

Board of Education inspectors found that many teachers were LNU members, particularly those teaching the crucial, in this context, subjects of history and geography, and many schools had junior LNU branches organised by these staff. One survey conducted for the LNU in 1931 found that 'even the apathetic teacher who follows textbooks automatically will find himself encouraged to give League instructions, whether he mentions the fact in his syllabus or not.'

Education of children on the LNU was not confined to the classroom. The organisation encouraged public libraries to have a League of Nations shelf in their collections. Pageants and plays were organised. Junior branches of the LNU met after school, and prepared assemblies as well as organising study circles and competitions. The LNU headquarters distributed plays that could be performed. One of these was *Banish the Bogie*, which sought to show how armaments manufacturers played nations off against each other in order to increase their order books. It was performed throughout the country, being described as a 'morality play' by the *Sunderland Daily Echo* on 9 November 1932, when it reported on a performance at the Church Street Methodist School at Seaham Harbour. A LNU fete held in Chelmsford, Essex in June 1934 featured a production of the play. The *Chelmsford Chronicle* reported:

> [Alderman] Thompson played the leading part, which was that of an armament manufacturer. The other characters represented different nations who came to him for arms. The nations fight, realise their folly, and all ends happily with the banishment of the armament manufacturer in a Court trial scene.

Another play, *How the Cake was Shared*, claimed to be 'an amusing analysis of the League of Nations budget, symbolised by a cake'. One production received extensive coverage in the *Coventry Evening Telegraph* of 26 March 1934:

> Stoke Junior Branch of the League of Nations Union presented the play 'How the Cake was Shared' at Stoke Congregational Schoolrooms, on Saturday. In the afternoon there was a large and appreciative audience of children who thoroughly enjoyed the play. There was an evening performance for adults, who equally appreciated the concert.

The Mayoress (Mrs Councillor Thomson) was present for part of the evening performance, and during the interval she spoke to the audience on the subject of 'Peace'. She emphasised the fact that without the security that was the outcome of peaceful relations, no improvement in the social services could be of any lasting use to the nation. Every nation was arming to-day, not because it wished to be an aggressor, but from a false conception of security, and there was the same danger of an armament competition to-day as there was in 1914. It was essential, she said, that the children who, of course had no personal recollection of the horrors of the last war, should be trained into thinking that real national security came from goodwill and understanding among the nations, and that the piling up of armaments could only lead to the unspeakable disaster of war and the probable collapse of civilisation. She reminded her listeners that the only way to combat this tendency was to work whole-heartedly for the League of Nations, which was the only effective peace organisation, and to further the work of international understanding and co-operation as far as they possibly could. ...

The play, 'How the Cake was Shared', deals with the distribution of the national revenue among the various national services. The Junior Branch were extremely fortunate in securing the services of Mr H.H. Warnke, a member of the Stoke Senior Branch of the League of Nations Union, who had constructed a large cake made of plywood, with slices detachable, so that the various characters representing the different services could be given their proportionate shares. 'War' received over three-quarters of the cake while all the other services, education, police, housing, pensions, unemployment etc. received the remaining quarter, the League of Nations receiving an almost infinitesimal portion.

Scholars from the following schools took part in the play: Stoke Council Boys' School, Stoke Council Girls' School, Stoke Heath School, Frederick Bird Girls' School and Frederick Bird Boys' School. All these scholars entered into the spirit of the play with sincerity and enthusiasm.

The *Scottish Milngavie & Bearsden Herald* described a 1933 production given by Class IIIb at Milngavie School, led by their teacher, Miss Morrison. It 'illustrated in bold relief the amount of money that was spent on the social services in this country in comparison with the vast sums that went to pay for the implements of war. The need for disarmament was never more succinctly put.'

The LNU co-operated with other youth organisations such as the Boy Scouts, Girl Guides and the Boys' Brigade in supplying literature and lecturers. It also set up its own Scout-type group, the Nansen Pioneer Corps, named after the

Norwegian explorer Fridtjof Nansen, who was a League of Nations official. Young people aged from thirteen to sixteen would spend a fortnight on a camp, looked after by staff who could explain foreign affairs from the perspective of the League of Nations. The participants would also learn the importance of working with other members to ensure the well-being of a community, and extrapolate this into national and international affairs.

For those too old for the LNU junior branches, a Youth Section was established in 1927. Social activities were arranged, and branches were set up in universities and training colleges. By the early 1930s there were 7,000 members in these institutions, with the 1,000 members at Cambridge University and the 600 at Oxford making them the largest societies at these establishments. However, as the work of the LNU in general became more politicised during the 1930s in response to the international crisis, some educators began to question the prominent role that it was playing in education.

Lieutenant Colonel A.H. Burne wrote to *The Spectator* magazine in June 1936, in response to an article about the LNU in a previous issue:

> SIR – In your last issue you say that it is most important at the present moment that the aims of the LNU should be understood by the public. Would you inform your readers what particular aims and teaching of the LNU the public is still ignorant of? I should have supposed that we were just about impregnated with these teaching – to the edge of risk or over the edge. As an old reader of *The Spectator* I would ask you, Sir, whether it is not time that we say up and rubbed the scales from off our eyes? The words of wise old Bacon are eternally true: 'When a warlike State grows soft and effeminate they may be sure of a war. For commonly such States are grown rich in the time of their degenerating, and so the prey inviteth, and their decay in valour encourageth a war.' ...
>
> Most profoundly do I hope that *The Spectator* will be true to its traditionally sane policy, and come out wholeheartedly and unequivocally in favour of a strong British Empire – in the interests of peace.

The editor of *The Spectator* replied:

> One fact regarding the League of Nations Union of which a large part of the public appears to be still ignorant is that the Union (like the League) does not stand for unilateral disarmament, but for reduction *pari passu* by international agreement. What we said, however, was not that the aims of the LNU needed to be understood, but that 'never did public opinion need educating in the aims and purposes *of the Covenant* more.'

The 1938 Headmaster's Conference warned that it would break its ties with the LNU and junior branches would then fold if this politicisation continued. Gilbert Murray, one of the LNU's leaders, argued that this was due to the unrest of the world reaching classrooms, not to any desire on the LNU's part to be overtly political. The Education Committee of the LNU was made independent from the rest of the organisation and a new Council for Education in World Citizenship was established, which operated through the war years.

Despite all the earnestness, the enthusiasm and intellectual depth of the educational work of the LNU faded as the League of Nations collapsed in the late 1930s. However enlightened and internationalist British schoolchildren had been brought up to be, they were about to emerge into an adult world engaged in an unprecedentedly destructive war.

The Peace Ballot

Another huge initiative organised by the LNU to raise awareness of the international situation and to get the British public to reflect on its attitude to issues of war and peace was the Peace Ballot. Carried out from November 1934 to June 1935, this was a referendum that attracted the votes of 11,640,066 individuals, an estimated 38.2 per cent of the British electorate, making it the largest privately organised vote in British history. In some areas the turnout was even higher; for example, 62 per cent of the Welsh electorate took part. The results suggested that Britons had a broadly pacifist outlook and discouraged successive governments from carrying out an energetic campaign of rearmament. Robert Cecil's purpose in organising the ballot was to demonstrate that the British people were behind moves to approve an extension of the authority of the League of Nations.

The setbacks in international relations in the early 1930s had encouraged some voices in the Conservative Party, such as Leo Amery, to call for Britain to loosen its ties with the League and follow a more isolationist policy and concentrate on the Empire. Others like Lord Beaverbrook, proprietor of Britain's largest selling daily newspaper, the *Daily Express*, advocated Britain leaving the League altogether. The Labour MP Major J.R. Bellerby MC argued in the *New Statesman* that 'a referendum should be taken on complete unilateral disarmament in the British Empire.' Disagreements between France and Germany made Britain wary of getting drawn into further problems between the two nations, and therefore isolationist sentiments were expressed from both the left and the right of the British political spectrum. The Labour Party conference of 1934 passed a motion to 'take no part in war'.

The organisers of the Peace Ballot feared that Britain's isolationist stance would see it withdrawing from the already compromised League of Nations. The World Disarmament Conference had been making slow progress and there were fears that Britain would downgrade its commitment to the League of Nations, sending a signal to aggressive foreign powers that she might not fulfil her obligations under the League's Covenant. Therefore, the ballot was a bid to revive popular internationalist feeling by giving all citizens a chance to state their faith in the League.

A mini ballot of 26,000 voters in Ilford, Essex in early 1934 revealed that nearly 85 per cent of respondents wanted Britain to stay in the League of Nations, 80 per cent wanted the manufacture of private armaments to be prohibited and only 24 per cent supported the intervention of Britain in the event of France or Germany attacking each other, as required under the Locarno Treaty. After further local polls in Yorkshire and Lincolnshire, it fell to the League of Nations Union to organise a full national ballot, in order to prove that the encouraging results represented opinion across the country. With very little infrastructure allocated to the scheme, an army of half a million volunteers walked the streets delivering the ballot forms and explaining the process to householders. They also had to make follow-up calls to encourage people to post off their answers. One of these volunteers was Noreen Branson, who later recalled:

> It meant calling at houses where the house-holder shouted at you and looked as though he might throw things at you, and at houses where the people were totally indifferent and apathetic. It meant having discussions with people who had strong opinions, and giving explanations to those who were puzzled. In rural areas it meant long journeys on foot to collect forms from isolated farms and villages.

The forms the volunteers handed out contained five questions:

1. Should Great Britain remain a Member of the League of Nations?
2. Are you in favour of an all-round reduction of armaments by international agreement?
3. Are you in favour of the all-round abolition of national military and naval aircraft by international agreement?
4. Should the manufacture and sale of armaments for private profit be prohibited by international agreement?
5. Do you consider that, if a nation insists on attacking another, the other nations should combine to compel it to stop by (a) economic and non-military measures? (b) if necessary, military measures?

It is notable that the emphasis of the questions was on multilateral disarmament as a means of achieving peace, as Germany remilitarisation was well under way by this time. However, the implicit attack on private arms manufacturers did force the National Government into setting up a Royal Commission into the trade in November 1934.

The ballot papers were distributed with an accompanying leaflet stating its purpose, asserting:

> In this Ballot you are asked to vote only for peace and war – whether you approve of the League of Nations or not, whether you are in favour of international disarmament or not. And by voting for the League of Nations you are helping not only your country, but the other countries of the World to maintain Peace and abolish war with all its horrors.

In order to raise its profile, the organisers of the ballot recruited an array of prominent people to express public support. These included the Archbishops of Canterbury and York, the Chief Rabbi, Joseph Herman Hertz, and the leaders of the main Nonconformist churches. From the entertainment world there were endorsements from Sir Cedric Hardwicke, Sybil Thorndike, Miles Malleson and Diana Wynyard. Historians H.A.L. Fisher and J.B.S. Haldane expressed support, as did the greatest English cricketer of the age, Jack Hobbs.

Collectively, the churches issued a pamphlet titled *Religion and the Peace Ballot*, which urged voters to send a message that 'there shall be no more war'. Around 500,000 volunteers were involved in canvassing for the ballot, which was not viewed upon favourably by the National Government. Sir John Simon, the Foreign Secretary, attacked the League of Nations in Parliament on 8 November 1934, accusing it of having a socialist bias. Even Anthony Eden, an enthusiastic supporter of the League of Nations, decried the fact that complex questions of international diplomacy were being reduced to yes/no answers.

The *Daily Express* ran a campaign to discredit the ballot. On 25 October 1934 it declared 'the League of Nations, a moribund institution which is a convenient instrument of ambitious and unscrupulous powers in Europe'. On 17 November it urged readers to 'Tear up the ballot paper. Throw the pieces in the waste-paper basket. Turn away from Europe. Stand by the Empire and Splendid Isolation.'

The results of the ballot were announced on 27 June 1935, as follows:

1. Should Great Britain remain a Member of the League of Nations?
    YES   11,166,818 (95.9%)   NO   357,930

2. Are you in favour of an all–round reduction of armaments by international agreement?
   YES   10,542,738 (90.6%)   NO   868,431

3. Are you in favour of the all–round abolition of national military and naval aircraft by international agreement?
   YES   9,600,274 (85.2%)   NO   1,699,989

4. Should the manufacture and sale of armaments for private profit be prohibited by international agreement?
   YES   10,489,145 (90.1%)   NO   780,350

5. Do you consider that, if a nation insists on attacking another, the other nations should combine to compel it to stop by (a) economic and non-military measures? (b) if necessary, military measures?
   (a) YES   10,096,626 (94.1%)   NO   636,195
                                       (862,707 Abstentions)
   (b) YES   6,833,803 (58.7%)   NO   2,366,184
                                       (2,381,485 Abstentions)

This represented a resounding endorsement for the League of Nations and its principles. Winston Churchill later noted:

> The Peace Ballot seemed at first to be misunderstood by Ministers. Its name overshadowed its purpose. It of course combined the contradictory propositions of reductions in armaments and forcible resistance to aggression. It was regarded in many quarters as part of the Pacifist campaign. On the contrary, Clause 5 affirmed a positive and courageous policy which could at this time have been followed with an overwhelming measure of national support. Lord Cecil and other leaders of the League of Nations Union were, as this clause declared, and as events soon showed, willing, and indeed resolved, to go to war in a righteous cause, provided that all the necessary action was taken under the auspices of the League of Nations. Their evaluation of facts underwent considerable changes in the next few months. Indeed within a year I was working with them in harmony upon a policy which I described as 'Arms and the Covenant'.

Philip Noel–Baker, who had been instrumental in the establishment of the League of Nations and who intermittently served as Labour MP for Coventry and Derby in the 1920s and 30s, reported:

> The votes cast in favour of the League and World Disarmament were more than the largest number that had ever put a Party Political government in

power. ... The Peace Ballot proved beyond a doubt that the British people understood the policy of World Disarmament and the collective security of the League.

Certainly, there were huge regional variations in turnout across the country. Whilst many areas of Wales and the north of England recorded a turnout of over 70 per cent, it was below 15 per cent in some London boroughs. In addition, only a small proportion of returned forms had any additional comments on them.

The new Foreign Secretary, Sir Samuel Hoare, found that the Peace Ballot provided an unhelpful backdrop to the Abyssinian crisis. His suggestion of a compromise whereby Abyssinia would be partitioned and the Italian Duce financially compensated for the remaining part would have meant condoning the aggression of one country towards another, something that had become politically inexpedient in the light of the Peace Ballot results. Hoare later wrote:

> The so-called Peace Ballot emphasised the already obvious fact that the country stood for peace. The questions had, however, been so worded that they had no bearing on the actual state of the world. They gave the impression that we could depend on collective security when four of the Great Powers stood aloof, and they kept discreetly in the background the need for British rearmament. The real question that should have been asked: 'Do you support British rearmament in the interests of peace?' was carefully avoided. The result was the strengthening of all the pacifist influences at a time when peace was being threatened, and an encouragement to the complacent in their belief that no special effort was necessary to strengthen British defences. ... The Opposition at once exploited the situation for an attack on the Government for increasing the Air Force and for failing to make quicker progress in the disarmament discussions in Geneva.

Despite these later analyses, members of all three major political parties expressed support for the League of Nations during the general election campaign at the end of 1935. This was despite the opposition of the National Government to the ballot, claiming it to be politically biased and misleading, giving people the impression that they could have collective security and disarmament at the same time. Some historians have interpreted the process and results of the ballot as the origins of appeasement, as evidence of pacifist attitudes to rearmament among the British public. Others have seen the results as a vindication of Britain standing by her international obligations through collective security. Martin Ceadel saw the complexity of British public opinion showing support for a problematic 'middle way between isolationism and militarism'.

Despite the fact that, four years after the ballot, the League of Nations had failed and Britain would be entering a ghastly global war, the ballot can be seen to have provided an example of the mass-mobilisation of public opinion in the area of foreign policy. Women's associations, churches, educationalists and youth groups took part in a national conversation about Britain's role in the world. The LNU found itself as a subsidiary of Churchill's calls for rearmament after the Munch Crisis. In October 1938, the LNU's monthly journal, *Headway*, had been taken over by a group of anti-appeasers known as the 'Focus' group. A group emerged within the LNU arguing for a more federal structure, that collective security could only be ensured by creating a federation whereby individual states would have no say in their defence and foreign policies, these matters being decided centrally.

The LNU limped on through the Second World War, but much reduced in size. In 1940 there were only 100,000 subscriptions and a budget of just over £10,000, meaning that the staff was cut to seventeen – about a sixth of its former size. Gilbert Murray and Robert Cecil were well into their seventies. The international League of Nations was moribund, having failed to prevent a world war. It did expel the Soviet Union in late 1939 for its invasion of Finland, but its general ineffectiveness meant that the LNU turned to trying to define what Britain's war aims should be. The statement on 'World Settlement After the War' stated that economic prosperity and social justice were as important to future world peace as was political security.

Like many people on the home front and in the armed forces, the rank and file of the LNU reckoned that war would only be justifiable if it were to usher in a period of considerable social change. The statement also set out that any future disagreements between nations that could not be settled by negotiation be referred to a third party for judgement. Thus, the use of force would only be permissible under international authority.

Moves towards the end of the war to establish a United Nations organisation meant that the inter-war League of Nations became obsolete. A United Nations Association was formed in October 1945, with the organisational structure and the LNU staff transferred into the new body. On 8 April 1945, Robert Cecil declared, 'The League is dead. Long live the United Nations.' A new era of collective security was born.

One expert on the LNU concluded that it 'appeared to be very much a middle-class do-gooder movement, high-minded and respectable, basically moral in content and attractive to "liberals" of all parties'. However, its cautious and respectable approach, designed to keep in touch with those in power, rendered it ineffective.

LNU leaders hoped that the failure of appeasement and the need to use collective force to defeat fascism would lead historians to judge them favourably. The establishment of the United Nations, they thought, proved the need for an internationally guaranteed security that they had argued for since 1918. Nevertheless, the LNU had advocated disarmament, and it has often been included in accounts of popular pacifism, despite it arguing for a controlled arms limitation, by international agreement, rather than a budget-led reduction of armaments, which occurred during the 1930s. Historian Correlli Barnett wrote, 'a constellation of moralising internationalist cliques ... successfully imposed on governments their pretension to represent public opinion at large.' The advice of men such as Cecil and Murray was influential on successive British governments, and was 'intimate, insidious, bigotedly certain', and Britain was disarmed 'materially and spiritually' as a result.

Others disagreed. Churchill, although often a critic of the LNU, wrote:

> war could easily have been prevented if the League of Nations had been used with courage and loyalty by the associated nations. Even in 1933 and 1936 there was a chance, by making an armed Grand Alliance under the aegis of the League, to hold in subjection the rising furies in Germany or at the very least to enter into armed conflict on terms more favourable than those eventually forced upon us.

The LNU cannot be blamed for the failures of the 1930s, but it can be criticised for not placing enough emphasis on the point that a medium term peace could only be brought about when backed up by the threat of force. The mass support that it built proved to be its undoing as its message lacked clarity, which ultimately meant that it became an increasing bystander as war approached.

Chapter 3

Pacifist Organisations – the No More War Movement and the Peace Pledge Union

The No More War Movement was founded by the Labour MP for Sheffield Brightside, Arthur Ponsonby, in 1921, proclaiming itself 'the one pacifist organisation that offers unqualified opposition to participation in war'. The organisation believed that disputes could be settled by diplomacy, that Britain could create confidence between nations by disarming unilaterally, and 'there is no risk our nation can take for peace as great as the risk of war'. The NMWM was chaired by Independent Labour Party MP Fenner Brockway, with other notable members including Wilfred Wellock, Leslie Paul, A. Barratt Brown, Leyton Richards, W.J. Chamberlain and Monica Whately. The movement also received messages of support from several international figures, including Albert Einstein.

At its height it had ninety-four branches across the UK and numbered some 3,000 members. In 1926, one member proposed the creation of a white poppy, in the style of the British Legion's red poppies, but with a message of hope for an end to all wars. The group did not pursue the idea but it was later taken up by the Women's Co-operative Guild and the Peace Pledge Union.

On 17 March 1927, Ponsonby moved a resolution in the House of Commons to have the Royal Air Force abolished. The speech was powerful, and included a section bemoaning the futility of the war that had ended less than a decade previously. Ponsonby proclaimed:

> The existence of armaments is a menace to civilisation. The governments of the world seem to have learned nothing by the great failure of force from 1914 to 1918. I think that the people realise and know that, after all that great display of violence and force with the tragic losses that it involved, no one single object for which we were told we were fighting was achieved. It was not a war to end war, because war has been going on ever since 1918, and we are preparing for war now. It was not a war to make the world safe for democracy, because we know that half a dozen dictatorships have grown up since the war. It was not a war for small nationalities, because small nationalities have suffered considerably since 1918, and one of them Montenegro, was wiped off the map

by the Treaty of Peace itself. It was not a war to give homes to heroes, because our heroes are still without those homes. Four years were spent in a desperate effort to beat down Germany to her knees, and, when we had succeeded, we spent the subsequent eight years in straining every nerve to set Germany on her feet again. Could imbecility go further than that? I want to make it perfectly clear that I am not a 'turn-the-other-cheek pacifist'. I am often asked: 'What would you do if a man with a knife came along and wanted to murder your wife?' My answer is perfectly simple, 'I should knock him down.' [HON. MEMBERS: 'Hear, hear!'] I thought that would draw cheers, because hon. Members opposite are deluded by the entirely false analogy between an individual criminal and a nation. There is no analogy between the two.

Ponsonby was challenged by Commander Charles Burney, MP for Uxbridge, on what his position would be if criminals were in charge of a nation. He responded by pointing out that criminals had been revealed to the British public in the last war:

> The criminals were Ludendorff, Hindenburg, Bethmann-Hollweg and the Kaiser. Did we touch any of them? Not one! Bethmann-Hollweg has died since; Hindenburg is the President of the Republic of Germany; Ludendorff is alive; and the Kaiser is 'married and living happily ever after'. You did not touch these criminals. Your four years were taken up in massacring innocent men, women and children—the flower of our youth was massacred, and at the end we see that absolutely nothing has come from it.

Other high publicity NMWM activities included exploding a miniature bomb at the Admiralty Theatre, Wembley. A 1928 newsletter stated, 'We pacifists are much too dull. Our propaganda is all alike. There is no variety, no music, no colour, no appeal, except to cold logic and reason, and man is mainly unreasonable and illogical in his thoughts and actions.' Another publicity stunt, presented as two tableaux, suggested by the writer, was:

1. A lawn surrounded with flower beds, in the corner a hammock with sleeping child, children playing while a nurse in the background looks after the wants of each. Slogan 'Disarmament means health, happiness and comfort.'
2. A backyard with a rubbish heap in the corner, dirty unkempt children playing with mud or a heap of ruins with a wall on one side, debris with an arm, leg or head protruding. Slogan, 'Armaments mean poverty, unemployment, starvation or death.'

Ponsonby wrote a Peace Letter to Prime Minister Stanley Baldwin and managed to acquire 128,770 signatories who would refuse to 'support or render war service'. The letter warned, 'we have drifted back into the old rut of war preparation, and engines of destruction are being invented, manufactured, prepared and supplied, not only for our own use, but perhaps to be used against us.' Baldwin dismissed Ponsonby's arguments, stating that an unarmed country would be impotent to resist hostile forces. In addition, the League of Nations would collapse without British military support. Ponsonby replied to Baldwin, insisting that 'unprovoked aggression is a war myth', and that he did not believe in collective security with the sanction of force as its ultimate guarantee.

In 1929, several prominent British intellectuals signed a statement, 'Why I Believe in the No More War Movement', supporting the NMWM's aims. The group published two journals: *The New World* and *No More War*. In 1932, Ponsonby outlined plans for a Peace Book, a riposte to the government's War Book, which contained detailed plans for British society in the event of total war. This would include a list of contacts who would help to counter war preparations, including an emergency officer in every town and village, assistants, recruitment officers and public meetings organisers. In the event of war being declared, each street in the country would have a 'Street Captain', who could canvas residents and announce public meetings. A general strike would be called, and supporters of peace would refuse to pay rents and taxes, boycott large firms, occupy common land and appeal to the police and military to destroy weapons.

In 1935, the movement issued *The Roots of War: A Pamphlet on War and the Social Order*, written by eight members of the Friends' Anti-War Group and the No More War Movement. The lack of concrete progress in building an effective pacifist movement was evident, with individualism not translating into a widespread collective action that would end the prospect of war.

> We may find encouragement in the thought that there is undoubtedly a widespread pacifist feeling, which perhaps deserves to be called a 'movement'; but we are deceiving ourselves if we are not bitterly disappointed by its practical ineffectiveness. We may well ask ourselves whether anything so far attempted will bring peace. Gone is the thrill of the individual refusal to take part in war; we must face the fact that it has not developed into a world conquering crusade and that it offers little more hope in the next war than it did before.

The pamphlet went on to argue that it was not enough to oppose war on moral, ethical and religious grounds, but that an intellectual appreciation of the origins of war was needed to argue the case for peace.

It is vitally important to realise that, at the present day, the root of war is in the system by which the world is ruled and that the conflicts which produce war are, at bottom, conflicts between systems and classes.

Pacifism was, for the authors, intrinsically linked with the building of a socialist revolution.

A working-class mass movement, based upon the overthrow of capitalism, can make war as much a thing of the past as the crudities of the Druids and the barbarisms of Nero. But no other movement can fight war with the faintest hope of success.

The best means of judging the success of the pacifist stance was provided by Fenner Brockway, who wrote in the *War Resister* of September 1934:

The Pacifist must be judged not by the purity of his principles but by the degree to which he lessens by his contribution to life the amount of violence and bloodshed in the world.

However, by this stage the NMWM was declining in influence. After Brockway resigned in 1929, and secretaries Walter Ayles and Lucy Cox left in 1932, the group lost momentum. Members began to drift towards the communist British Anti-War Movement and the New Commonwealth Society. Anarchists were increasingly prominent, but became disillusioned after the movement refused to support the Republican side in the Spanish Civil War, and in 1937 the organisation formally merged with the Peace Pledge Union.

The Peace Pledge Union

In October 1934, just as preparations for the LNU's Peace Ballot were well under way, a more strident voice for peace made itself heard. Canon Dick Sheppard (Plates, page 2), the former Dean of Canterbury and active peace campaigner, wrote a letter to the press. *The Times* refused to publish it, but the *Manchester Guardian* carried it:

The main reason for this letter, primarily addressed to men, is the urgency of the present international situation, and the almost universally acknowledged lunacy of the manner in which nations are pursuing peace. ... It seems essential to discover whether or not it be true, as we are told, that the majority of thoughtful men in this country are now convinced that war of every kind, or for any cause, is not only a denial of Christianity, but a crime against humanity, which is no longer to be permitted by civilised people. ... Would those of my sex who, so far, have been silent, but are of this mind, send a postcard to me within the next fortnight, to say if they are willing to be called together in the near future in support of a resolution as uncompromising as ... 'We renounce war, and never again, directly or indirectly, will we support or sanction another'.

Sheppard was overwhelmed by the response. Over 2,500 postcards arrived within the first two days. (Plates, page 3) Eventually over 135,000 men signed the pledge, becoming members of the Peace Pledge Union. Sending a postcard was the only action required to join the PPU, with Sheppard's aim being to use the weight of numbers to influence government policy. However, this necessarily meant that the PPU was a broad coalition of members, many of whom held widely differing views. A Quaker member might hold an absolute refusal to condone or take part in war, whatever the circumstance, whilst someone opposed to war on political grounds might alter their stance should the political situation change.

The Peace Pledge Union was formed on the basis of this initial response. Originally membership was only open to men, but this was soon altered in June 1936. The first mass meeting of the PPU took place at the Royal Albert Hall in London on 14 July 1935 and was addressed by Sheppard, the war poets Siegfried Sassoon and Edmund Blunden, and the female preacher Maude Royden. The prominent writer Vera Brittain, author of *Testament of Youth*, joined after hearing Sheppard speak in public. Other figures from the artistic world who joined included the novelist Rose Macaulay, the artist and sculptor Eric Gill, and the philosopher Bertrand Russell. Other well-known figures who spoke in support of the PPU (even though they weren't members) included Cyril Joad, George Bernard Shaw and Virginia Woolf. The Methodist Church was represented by Leslie Weatherhead (Plates, page 10) and Donald Soper, and Labour Party leader George Lansbury also joined.

The PPU rented offices in Regent Street, before purchasing its own headquarters in Bloomsbury. There were volunteers and paid staff numbering up to forty, and funds were raised to publish a weekly paper, *Peace News*. Initially an eight-page publication, it was extended to twelve and built its circulation up to 22,000, being placed in over 400 libraries across the country. The PPU's campaigning methods included letters to the press, posters, mass meetings, rallies and demonstrations at military events such as the annual RAF air display.

In Chester, 20,000 leaflets were handed out within a four-day period to crowds attending a military tattoo, and in the summer of 1937, the Leeds Anti-Tattoo Committee handed out over 100,000 leaflets. Films were produced, and a lending scheme was set up so local branches could borrow a projector, sound equipment and a small van.

In order to operate more effectively, the membership was divided into local groups; initially 183 in October 1936, then over 300 by December that year, rising to over 500 by March 1937. The sponsors of the PPU appointed an Executive Committee, which met weekly. The PPU did not seek to co-operate with the LNU but referred to it as a 'whited sepulchre', as PPU leaders thought that collective security was not only a euphemism for war, but impractical in an age of aerial warfare and provided a diplomatic cloak for aggression. The PPU even criticised the LNU's advocacy of economic sanctions as they often resulted in starvation of the innocent, whilst the guilty leaders of the errant states did not suffer. The PPU wished to see an international League of Nations that directed its efforts exclusively to the prevention of war, not the punishment of aggressors once war had broken out.

The PPU believed that the Treaty of Versailles had been unduly harsh on Germany, and its members made great efforts to try to understand German foreign policy aims. Sometimes letters to *Peace News* showed callous disregard for the victims of Nazism, although from 1938 the paper did appeal for its readers to sponsor Jewish refugees during the time they were in London. Mass meetings were held. In November 1936, large rallies were organised in Glasgow, Birmingham and London; 4,000 people attended the Birmingham rally, whilst in London the Royal Albert Hall was filled, with Kensington Town Hall having to be used to accommodate the overflow. Donald Soper addressed meetings on Tower Hill, where a police officer was assigned to note down the contents of his speech, and Soper would sometimes pause to inquire if he was going too fast for the officer to record everything.

The first budget of the PPU was £4,320, but this grew to £10,860. Although some rank and file members wished to set up a distinct pacifist political party, the sponsors were reluctant to do this, so nothing came of the suggestions. In 1937, the No More War Movement formally merged with the PPU, with George Lansbury, former Leader of the Labour Party and chair of the NMWM, serving as president of the united organisation until his death in 1940.

Unfortunately for the future harmony of the PPU, on 31 October 1937, Sheppard died unexpectedly, aged 57, from a heart attack. Vera Brittain later wrote of him:

the feeling that the sun had gone down. … To all of us who cared for spiritual values, the shock of Dick Sheppard's death to his own country was comparable to the blow dealt to India a decade later by Gandhi's.

For two and a half days the people of London passed by Sheppard's coffin at St Martin-in the-Fields. Police held up the traffic as his funeral procession moved along the Thames Embankment to St Paul's Cathedral. At the time of Sheppard's death, the PPU's membership numbered 118,000, with the monthly circulation of *Peace News* at 15,000.

In 1938, George Lansbury launched the PPU's first manifesto and peace campaign. The campaign argued that the idea of a war to defend democracy was illogical and that 'in a period of total war, democracy would be submerged under totalitarianism.' One development that caused considerable discord within the PPU was the Spanish Civil War. Most pacifists rejected civil war and class war as strongly as they did conflict between nations. Thus, opposition to military involvement in Spain was a logical consequence of this stance. However, many PPU members saw the conflict as one between the forces of darkness, represented by Franco and his nationalists, and the forces of light, represented by the democratically elected republican government. Nevertheless, *Peace News* ran editorials against British involvement in the war, and Arthur, now Lord, Ponsonby, one of the PPU's sponsors, spoke in favour of Chamberlain's policy of non-intervention. Warnings were issued that, even if the Republican government were to emerge victorious against Franco's insurgents, Force, not Justice, would be the victor, and an imposed peace would harm the country's future. The PPU sponsored a house in Essex in which sixty-four Basque children, refugees from the Spanish Civil War, were cared for. (Plates, page 3) Dorothy Plowman provided a description in *Peace News* of 12 June 1937:

Five miles out of Colchester on the Ipswich Road a fine old oak in the middle of a grass triangle marks a turning on the left leading to the hamlet of Langham. This local landmark is known as the Langham Oak. Following the turning (and bearing first right then left) for about half a mile, the traveller comes on a solidly built, comfortable-looking house of grey stone standing in finely-kept grounds and called 'The Adelphi Centre'. … Now the whole house is being surrendered to the family of 29 Basque girls and 24 Basque boys for which the PPU has recently made itself responsible. Before it became the Adelphi Centre … the name of that house was – and in the locality still is – 'The Oaks'. As you approach it you realise why: for in front of the house and overshadowing the road is one of the most majestic oak trees I have ever seen. So it seems strangely fitting that these little Basques, whose own ancient oak was one of the few things left standing in Guernica, should have come to Langham; and that the house which is to be their temporary home should link in its name the Basque and the English tree.

Another contributor to *Peace News*, Bella Hooper, described her visit in the 28 August 1937 edition:

> The most striking thing to a visitor or a newcomer to Basque House is the friendliness of the children here. Every visitor is welcomed with smiles and waves of the hand, and the parting guest has a royal send-off, with 'Goodbye, goodbye' from all sides. With complete unselfconsciousness the children accept strangers and, with a natural charm which far exceeds any art, make them welcome. They are almost unfailingly cheerful and always ready to help with any work to be done. Some of them indeed are so zealous that we have to take care that they get a fair share of all the pleasures going, otherwise they would spend too much time helping with the cooking, washing and cleaning.

The Peace Pledge Union and the Nazi threat

Although it was possible to reach a position that satisfied most PPU members and supporters on the question of Spain, it was less straightforward to reach agreement on what should be done about Nazi Germany. Many leading PPU members, including George Lansbury, felt sympathy with the aims of German foreign policy in the aftermath of the harsh terms of the Treaty of Versailles. Although Hitler and his regime were distasteful, it was thought that the German nation had genuine grievances. In 1938, Clive Bell wrote a pamphlet titled *Warmongers*, which was published by the PPU, in which he stated, 'I see no reason why Germany should not have colonies and hegemony too [and] we welcome the idea of a United States of Europe, even though that Europe be policed by Germans.' Bell also argued that Germany should be allowed to absorb France, Poland, Belgium, Holland and Luxemburg, as well as the Balkan states. This was criticised by other prominent PPU figures such as Vera Brittain and Andrew Stewart. However, *Peace News*, under the editorship of Humphrey Moore, and then John Middleton Murry, argued that Hitler should be given control of mainland Europe.

The PPU supported the British government's appeasement policy, believing that Nazi Germany would cease its aggression if the perceived territorial iniquities of the Treaty of Versailles were reversed. It backed Neville Chamberlain's Munich Agreement of 1938, ceding the Czechoslovakian Sudetenland to Germany. However, there were some ill-judged articles in *Peace News* during August and September that disparaged the Czech people and state. One such article argued that the German government had a 'moral case' for taking back control of the Sudetenland, and that the boundaries of Czechoslovakia were unjust. Hitler was praised for his efforts to bring about peace and argued that Germany's contribution to trying to avert war should be appreciated. Little sympathy was shown for the democratic state of Czechoslovakia in its attempts to stand up to the Nazi tyrant who had shown scant regard for minorities in his own country.

Peace News of 8 October 1938 expressed 'unfeigned thankfulness' that the Munich Settlement had been reached and that 'an act of justice' had been performed with the Sudetenland. The Sudeten Germans 'had their traditions of fighting for freedom'. The 22 October edition called Czechoslovakia a 'magpie state' and President Edouard Beneš a 'procrastinator'. A more measured response was issued by Stuart Morris, Chairman of the PPU, recognising the sacrifice Czechoslovakia had made for peace, and calling on other countries to do similar. Lord Ponsonby stated that war had been averted 'because each statesman knew that he was representing the heartfelt and desperate abhorrence of war in the people of his own country and of other countries'.

As Poland became the next focus of Hitler's policy of Lebensraum, *Peace News* continued to see European affairs through a German prism. On 7 April 1939, Humphrey Moore wrote an editorial in which he accepted that Germany was being encircled by hostile powers. On 5 May he wrote sarcastically of scare stories, 'with Hitler as the villain of the piece'. Rose Macaulay, a prominent PPU supporter, said, 'Occasionally when reading *Peace News*, I (and others) half think we have got hold of the *Blackshirt* by mistake,' referring to the British Union of Fascist magazine. In addition, she complained that some pacifists gave 'an impression of partiality on this Nazi business, of condoning or minimising cruelty'. Letters published in *Peace News* during the ensuing weeks showed that many agreed with her points.

However, the main body of the paper continued with its support for Hitler's approach to Poland. Two columns, titled 'The Plain Man' and 'A Pacifist Commentary', took the view that the Poles were too aggressive in defending their national sovereignty, that Germany had a better claim over the disputed lands and that Poland could drag Europe into a war by insisting on defending its territory. In these analyses, Hitler was not ascribed any blame for the situation.

In May 1939, a *Peace Service Handbook* was issued, selling 165,000 copies. (Plates, page 4) Contained in it were suggestions by which members could help the cause of peace. The slim 48-page handbook was prefaced by a quote from St Augustine:

> Peace is the end sought for by man,
> For every man seeks peace by making war,
> But no man seeks war by making peace.

An outline was given of the situation facing Britain in 1939: £630,000,000 to be spent on armaments as part of a five-year programme costing over £1,500,000,000, whilst money on social services was being curtailed. Conscription had been reintroduced for young men aged 20, which was 'undemocratic and anti-social' as they did not then achieve the vote until 21. The pamphlet went on to claim that nobody wanted war – neither dictators nor democratic leaders. However, peace was not something that would happen merely by hoping for it. It had to be prepared for and worked for.

The armaments race was creating a political and economic situation in which tensions were growing and countries would be left with two alternatives: economic collapse through military spending, or the gamble of war to recoup the money spent on armaments. Threats to democracy come from within, not without, it was argued. Fascism abroad was a result of the failure of democracy, and Britain was creating an 'instrument of modern violence' that bent the rights of individuals to the service of war. This meant regimentation and totalitarianism in Britain, 'a loss of all our ideals in the tyranny which must follow the break-up of civilisation which another war would mean'. Fascism could not be destroyed by destroying fascists; therefore another way had to be found to be 'the right means to the right end'.

The pamphlet advocated a programme of 'constructive peacemaking'. Examples of successful non-violent resistance were cited – the Hungarians against the Austrians in 1866, by William Penn against the native American Indians, and by Gandhi in India: 'Truly the best way to disarm your adversary is to be yourself disarmed.' A new League of Nations needed to be created, with violence eliminated from its Covenant. The individual who desired peace needed not to volunteer for Territorial or ARP service, but peace service. In an accusatory tone, the pamphlet declared: 'Nothing is truer than that, if war comes, it will be because individuals like yourself have failed to make a renunciation of war and failed to follow up that renunciation with constructive work for peace.'

There then followed an extensive list of organisations through which individuals could contribute to the building of a society devoted to peace.

These included groups that distributed pacifist literature, such as the National Peace Council and the Council of Christian Pacifist Groups, and discussion groups held by organisations such as the National Council of Labour Colleges and the Women's Co-operative Guild. It was recommended that such meetings be held at regular weekly or fortnightly intervals, usually in people's houses, and should not exceed fifteen people so that everyone could contribute. Next came a list of groups that organised public lectures, conferences and summer schools.

Next, advice on spreading pacifist propaganda was given, 'not a question of forcing cut-and-dried ideas and dogma down people's throats, but of placing before them a true picture so that they may think the matter out for themselves'. Propaganda should appeal to sane reason, and there was a variety of ways suggested in which pacifist information could be spread: arranging public meetings, street sales of *Peace News* (Pic 9), distributing leaflets and pamphlets in busy places such as cinemas showing war films or military recruitment events. Suggestions continued: visiting local guilds, churches and debating societies, running a Peace Shop selling literature, or holding meetings, poster parades, peace pageants at local fairs, home-to-home canvassing, acting peace plays, holding film shows and persuading local libraries and bookshops to stock *Peace News* and other PPU literature.

Such activities often placed the pacifist in the line of public disapproval. The *Hull Daily Mail* of 7 March 1940 reported on a public sale of *Peace News* outside Birmingham Town Hall, where a meeting was being held that was to be addressed by Prime Minister Neville Chamberlain. A Councillor Sale said that he saw in the street at every 10 or 25 yards a young man of military age 'with rather long hair selling *Peace News*. It was a nauseating sight, and he wondered whether it was possible to tackle them for obstruction.' The Chief Constable, Mr C.H. Moriarty, said that there were 'about fifty cranks selling that day. They were mostly weak-minded people.'

On occasions the objections could go beyond words. The *Surrey Advertiser* of 1 June 1940 reported the case of John Boswell Chapman (26) of Hill Court, Surbiton, who was fined £2 with five guineas' costs for causing an obstruction on Kingston Market Place, with a charge of insulting behaviour being dismissed. A Police Sergeant Bragg stated that Chapman was surrounded by a hostile crowd, and some people threatened to throw him into the river. Chapman, a PPU member, had been selling *Peace News* when he had been approached by a man with a stick, who tore a poster he was holding.

A more successful outcome for *Peace News* propagandists had come in Bradford, with a reversal of the Council's Libraries, Art Gallery and Museums

Committee's decision not to recommend the provision of the publication in their newsroom. The *Yorkshire Post and Leeds Intelligencer* of 11 May 1938 reported that Mrs Kathleen Chambers (Labour) had asked whether there was any relationship between this prohibition and the authorisation given for the display and circulation in libraries of poster and handbills advertising a Royal Command Tattoo to be held in Leeds. Herbert Smith, the chairman, denied any relationship between the two. Mrs Chambers responded pithily, 'You withdraw peace and circulate war.' Smith responded that he did not think *Peace News* a significant publication, as he had only found it available by private subscription. Mrs Chambers was supported by two ILP councillors, Alderman A. Tetley and Mr A.L. Brown. The amendment in favour of carrying *Peace News* was narrowly carried by thirty votes to twenty-five.

The *Peace Service Handbook* also listed several peace and goodwill groups, including one known as 'The Link'. This group had been established in July 1937 as an 'independent non-party organisation to promote Anglo–German Friendship'. It produced a journal, the *Anglo–German Review*, which reflected the pro-Nazi views of Admiral Sir Barry Domvile, an ex-naval officer and noted anti-Semite. Domvile had attended the Nuremburg Rally of September 1936 as the guest of the German ambassador, Joachim von Ribbentrop. During the Hythe by-election held on 20 July 1939, he supported St John Philby, the anti-Semitic British People's Party candidate (and father of Kim Philby), and during the war Domvile was interned as a danger to the state. Later in life, Domvile served on the national council of the fascist National Front party.

At its height, The Link boasted a membership of around 4,300, and was opposed to war between Britain and Germany, seeing many commonalities between the people of the two nations, hence its inclusion in the *Peace Service Handbook*. However, when the handbook was seen by the *Daily Telegraph* and *News Chronicle*, both newspapers published articles accusing the PPU of supporting Nazism. This forced Canon Stuart Morris to write to them, stating that there was no connection between the PPU and The Link, and that the PPU did not support German demands for more colonies, or peace at the expense of other nations. The *Peace Service Handbook* was withdrawn from publication and the PPU issued a letter to its group leaders, dissociating it from The Link. As an after note, the Nazi-supporting The Link was investigated by Maxwell Knight, head of counter-subversion at MI5, and was closed shortly after the start of the war, and Domvile was interned as someone who might 'endanger the safety of the realm'. It was then alleged that it was resurrected in 1940 by Ian Fleming, the future author of the James Bond books, in order to entice German Deputy Führer Rudolf Hess to a meeting in Britain in May 1941.

Apart from Morris, other prominent PPU members expressed disquiet at the controversy. Max Plowman stated that The Link's purpose was to provide sympathy and support to the Nazi regime. National Group Organiser John Barclay said that it could not pass the test of wanting true friendship among all peoples. Andrew Stewart, a *Peace News* staff member, argued, 'Let us make sure that we are not, out of excessive sympathy or sheer obstinacy, involving ourselves fatally with a body whose ultimate aim is the very antithesis of our own.'

Therefore, an administrative oversight in failing to fully check the credentials of every organisation in the handbook was the initial cause of the controversy, but underlying the whole furore was a growing perception amongst the general public that the pacifist movement in general was prioritising the wishes of fascist governments above those of other countries in Europe. The PPU appeared to have failed to persuade the public that it had an unequivocal opposition to Hitler and Nazism.

This was unfortunate as the PPU's primary focus was on the attainment of world peace, economic justice and racial tolerance. Pro-German statements were driven by an idea to treat all nations in an even-handed manner. Whilst it is easy with the benefit of hindsight to dismiss the PPU's various statements about Germany as naïve, it is true that there was not a full awareness of the shocking events unfolding under the Nazi regime. To suggest, as many did, that the Sudetenland, Danzig, the Polish Corridor and other territories would be handed over to the Nazis to prevent a war was a superficially commendable position, but often sought to distract attention from the desire for a lasting peace, which was the sincere wish of most PPU members.

Another issue that is now associated with the PPU, and which can sometime cause press controversy in the twenty-first century, is the distribution and sale of the white poppy. This emblem of peace, designed to be worn in the run-up to Armistice Day, was introduced in 1933 by the Women's Co-operative Guild. Immediately concerns were raised in various quarters. On 30 October 1933, British Legion officials in Northamptonshire voiced strong opposition to the suggestion that another emblem should be sold in competition with the Flanders poppy, and threatened to hold a demonstration unless the proposal was withdrawn. In response, Mrs Robinson, an official of the Wellingborough Women's Co-operative Guild, stated that it was hoped that the sale of the peace emblem would be additional to that of the Flanders poppy and that both emblems would be worn by the public. However, Mr W.J.L. Gotch, a Legion official, condemned the suggestion as ridiculous: 'There is no need for a peace emblem in addition to our poppy. Not only does it stand as a memory of the sacrifice of millions, but also as evidence of the determination of those who fought and still live to do all possible to prevent a future war.'

Sister Dora Henson of East Cliff, Dover wrote to the *Dover Express* on 31 October 1933, articulating the hope that the suggestion of selling white poppies on Armistice Day would be suppressed. Her rationale was that:

> Armistice Day is essentially the one out of 365 set apart in this life of rush, for quiet remembrance of the men who served our country in the Great War, and although the Nation desires peace, surely this one day can be kept in peaceful remembrance of all the brave men who have given their lives for King and Country. To have any other sale but the red Flanders poppy on November 11th would appear to be an insult to the Flanders poppy and all it stands for.

Members of the Women's Guild were forced to explain their position. In November 1934, Mrs S. Morrissey of the Burnley Central Co-operative Women's Guild wrote to the *Burnley Express* stating, 'There is no competition whatever with the British Legion. They were given the order last year for many thousands of white poppies, the profits to go to their fund. At the last moment – for reasons best known to themselves – they turned the order down.' Mrs Morrissey went on to defend the Guild against accusations of dishonouring the war dead:

> The Co-operative Women's Guild in this country has a membership of over 70,000 women, many of whom lost husbands, sons and brothers in the Great War. It is an insult to accuse those women of forgetfulness. In wearing our white emblems we are proclaiming that we will not tolerate for ourselves or our children the horrors that are anticipated in the event of another war. We are opposing the menace of both Fascism and war, and are building up that spirit of national and international co-operation which is the very foundation of our movement.

The white poppy was the focus of a large demonstration or support in Bristol in April 1935. The *Western Daily Press* reported on a 2,000-strong rally in the city, starting with a procession from the Rope Walk to the Colston Hall. The symbol was worn by representatives of many groups, including the Youth Section of the Labour Party, the Youth Trades Council, Comrade Circles and Sunday school teachers. These groups marched under a banner that stated they were 'United Against War'. Next came groups marching under 'Peace Means Progress', including the Free Church Federation and the Council of Christian Churches. Finally came a banner imploring the government to 'Save Civilisation', under which marched the National Union of Railwaymen Silver Prize Band and representatives from the building, engineering, printing and transport trades.

There were also people from the Liberal, Labour and Communist parties, and those representing the unemployed.

The Peace Pledge Union in wartime

Once war was declared, some prominent public figures and PPU supporters who had previously campaigned for pacifism shifted their position. Author A.A. Milne, creator of Winnie-the-Pooh, wrote in 1940 that he had changed his mind since writing a book titled *Peace with Honour* in 1934. His original stance had been that:

> Nations fight in order to bring about the complete surrender of the conquered to the will of the conqueror. That surrender is obtained by deliberate 'slaughter and ruin'. The last war involved women and children and the accumulated wealth of civilisation in slaughter and ruin. The next war will involve them in a much greater slaughter and ruin. This seems to be a good reason for making the next war impossible. It does not seem to be a good reason for saying: 'Can't we agree to make the next war a nice war like the last war?'

His new book, *War with Honour*, explained his thinking. Whilst he still rejected the idea of war as had previously been fought – that is, as a competition between countries to secure material advantages – Hitler was threatening 'all Christian and civilised values', and had to be resisted. He wrote, 'I am still a pacifist, but I hope a practical pacifist. I still want to abolish war.'

Cyril Joad, who had successfully argued for the 'King and Country' motion at the Oxford Union in 1933, was another who had renounced absolute pacifism and placed his support behind the British war effort. (Plates, page 6) He wrote an article in the *Evening Standard* in the summer of 1940, during the early stages of the Blitz, commenting that the things he loved about England, 'the free mind and the compassionate heart, the love of truth ... of respect of human personality', were in danger as a German victory would herald a new Dark Age in Europe. 'The Nazi regime fetters the spirit, muzzles the tongue, puts the mind in prison and hands over to the Dictator the keys of the cell. ... Future historians will see in it the greatest single setback to humanity that history records.'

In January 1940, Joad offered his services to the Ministry of Information and was selected to take part in a BBC radio discussion programme on the Home Service, *The Brains Trust*. However, he still continued to argue the case for conscientious objection and opposed the continuation of conscription into peacetime.

Philosopher Bertrand Russell was another who had moved from opposing rearmament against Nazi Germany to support for the war against Hitler. He had written in 1937, 'If the Germans succeed in sending an invading army to England we should do our best to treat them as visitors, give them quarter and invite the commander-in-chief to dine with the Prime Minister.' However, by 1940 he had concluded that defeating Hitler was of greater importance than avoiding a full-scale war. Whilst being opposed to war in general, he wrote:

> I found the Nazis utterly revolting – cruel, bigoted, and stupid. Morally and intellectually they were alike odious to me. Although I clung to my pacifist convictions, I did so with increasing difficulty. When, in 1940, England was threatened with invasion, I realised that, throughout the First War, I had never seriously envisaged the possibility of utter defeat. I found this possibility unbearable, and at last consciously and definitely decided that I must support what was necessary for victory in the Second War, however difficult victory might be to achieve, and however painful in its consequences.

With the outbreak of war in September 1939, the key questions for the leadership of the PPU became what role pacifists should play in wartime. How could an individual pacifist reconcile the demands of their conscience with the duty they felt towards the community as a whole? Three broad positions were adopted, a new '3Rs': Relief, Resistance and Reconstruction.

The 'Relief' advocates, such as Philip Mumford, advised pacifists to co-operate with government war measures such as civil defence and conscription, and aim to undertake humanitarian relief work. In *Peace News* on 1 January 1938, he argued that pacifists should seek to soften the blows of war by helping to alleviate the suffering of its victims. The Pacifist Service Corps, later to become the Pacifist Service Bureau, was established by the PPU to assist those who wanted to undertake positive and constructive work not directly associated with the war effort. For example, in Manchester a branch of the bureau helped with youth clubs and gave assistance to those in air raid shelters. The 'Resistance' strain advocated active resistance to all war measures. Relief work was not objectionable in itself, but the prime duty of a pacifist was to resist war, rather than to find a relief role within it. This group advocated a political settlement to the war, based on negotiation, and later in the war campaigned for an armistice, rather than the complete surrender and humiliation of the Axis powers.

Finally, the 'Reconstructionists' saw themselves as taking a longer view, avoiding engagement in short-term protests, and seeking to act as a redemptive minority, being standard bearers of a renewed society based on communal living. John Middleton Murry saw pacifists as the 'raw material of a new Christian Church ... the nucleus of a new Christian society'. Whilst all three philosophies were given column space in *Peace News*, the magazine's driving forces, John Middleton Murry and Wilfred Wellock, were associated with the Reconstructionists, creating a supplement to the magazine, titled *Community*, to raise awareness of community run along pacifist and socialist lines.

When war broke out the PPU was balanced between a politically minded 'Forward Movement' of young pacifists campaigning for immediate peace, and a 'Forethought Committee'. Once France fell in 1940, the latter group gained the upper hand in the PPU. Its composition was mainly religiously minded advocates of community living, and included John Middleton Murry, Max Plowman, Vera Brittain and Mary Gamble. Plowman moved into a pacifist community named the Adelphi Centre in Langham, Essex in October 1939, acting as the centre's warden. (Plates, page 6)

Plowman expounded his view of the role of the pacifist in wartime in an article in *The Adelphi* in December 1940. The nature of pacifism placed social obligations on the individual. Social sacrifice and social effort had to be made towards the creation of a co-operative or socialist community. The pacifist had to try to stop the war, whilst recognising that in doing so they were dissociating themselves from the majority opinion in society. Voicing anti-war sentiments would not end the war, 'particularly in the case of a nation of persons fighting most reluctantly and only under a sense of moral compulsion'. In the opinion of Plowman and other leading pacifists, Britain was not in the grip of a blood lust, but support for the war was driven by opposition to the Nazi regime. Therefore, there was not a binary polarity between those supporting the war and those opposing it.

As the pacifists could not end the war by words or actions, it was beholden upon them to demonstrate that humans could live in creative harmony and co-operation rather than cruel competition. As those who agreed to fight were undergoing some degree of sacrifice, so too those deciding not to fight had to demonstrate sacrifice. Plowman cited the Quakers as sacrificing their time in social service and relief work. He acknowledged that any form of service in a society organised for total war might be construed as supporting the prosecution of war: 'Logically the pacifist must commit suicide to be totally non-co-operative in war-time.'

Plowman had written in *Peace News* of 1 March 1940 to put forward the benefits of community living. He argued that the war would be a very hard task to achieve, as modern society had been constructed to make war an inevitability:

> What pacifists have got to understand quite clearly is that war is the normal activity of the society to which they belong, and that this country is not so much engaged in a war as in fulfilling the conditions of a system of society whose basic economic working puts us in a perpetual condition of war.

For pacifism to be worthwhile, it needed to demonstrate a constructive renunciation of war, rather than just resisting its current iteration. Therefore, pacifists should seek to reform society from within. This strain within the PPU was in marked contrast to the Forward Movement faction, which was, by January 1940, publicly urging the PPU to be more active in stopping the war.

The current, and future, wars would involve mass mobilisation of the peoples of all combatant nations, with the resultant curbs on civil liberties. Writing to his colleague Wilfred Saunders after the passing of the Emergency Powers Act of May 1940, which allowed for the requisitioning of land and property for military use and detention without trial, Plowman noted:

> Yesterday tolled the knell of personal liberty as we have understood it for a century at least. ... We shall, as I think Murry has well said, have to discover the means of living within the interstices of a totalitarianism that will be like chain mail & handcuffs to freedom of thought.

Whilst those like Murry and Plowman advocated a purist retreat into model communities, other members strove to maintain the structure of a functioning campaigning organisation. The PPU experienced difficulties in the production and distribution of *Peace News* during the war. Initially, the period of the Phoney War up to spring of 1940 had seen sales rise to 40,000. However, concerns were expressed in Parliament about the effect of this publicity for the pacifist cause. On 11 April 1940, Lieutenant Colonel Sir Arnold Wilson, MP for Hitchin, asked the Home Secretary whether he was aware that W.H. Smith's railway bookstalls were stocking *Peace News*, and requested that the Minister of Transport discuss Defence Regulations with the company, and the wider public interest in them stocking the title. Sir John Anderson replied that W.H. Smith's were quite within the law to stock it.

Nevertheless, the fact that the issue had been raised in the Commons caused the existing printers to refuse to print the newspaper due to its advocacy of pacifism, and the wholesalers refused to distribute it. New printers were found in the form of Eric Gill, and then the Brock Brothers, who managed to produce around 20,000 copies by 1941, with volunteers stepping in to do the distribution. This voluntarism ensured that *Peace News* ran at a profit through the war.

One *Peace News* seller was Ernest Goldring, a solicitor who had joined the PPU in 1936. Goldring was an advocate of the 'Relief' approach, not claiming an absolute objection to any war work and undertaking ARP duties. Goldring's pacifism was based on the feeling that Nazism was an evil, but that war was an even greater evil. He and his wife joined the Fellowship of Reconciliation and his two younger brothers were also conscientious objectors. As well as his ARP duties, Goldring worked on the land in Sussex. On one occasion while selling *Peace News*, he was attacked by a man with an umbrella outside Purley Oaks station. The genuineness of Goldring's pacifism was evident in the fact that his local vicar supported him at his military service appeal tribunal hearing even though he did not agree with his views, helping him to gain a conditional exemption from military service from Judge Hargreaves. Despite this, Goldring felt out of place when he went back to church after the war, feeling some subtle coldness from people who had lost sons in the conflict.

One of the 'Reconstructionists' was Wilfrid Green, an Anglican and, like Ernest Golding, a member of both the PPU and Fellowship of Reconciliation. He had written to Dick Sheppard immediately after having read his press appeal in 1934, expressing his renunciation of war. He began to hand out PPU pamphlets to work colleagues in his office and recalled that their reaction marked him as an idealist, and they treated him with 'amused toleration, not antagonism'. Green left the company he was working for before the war began because they were making weapons. He then joined an Anglican community in Sussex, St Hilda's Community based at Nuthurst, near Horsham. During the war, Green supported the community in the housing of evacuees from bombed cities.

In late 1939, leading PPU member Vera Brittain decided to put her literary talents to good use in the cause of peace. She had been receiving a daily quota of letters, which had increased rapidly since the outbreak of war. As she was unable to answer all her correspondents due to time pressures, she decided to publish a regular newsletter 'based on determined research behind the news'. Brittain sent out a letter to ask for subscribers 'to help in the important task of keeping alive decent values at a time when these are undergoing the maximum strain'. One early letter, published on 25 October 1939, commented on the futility of war in addressing the international situation:

> Even supposing that we do destroy Hitler, we shall not again be confronted by a Europe agreeably free from competitors for power. The disappearance of Herr Hitler will probably lead instead to a revolutionary situation in Germany, controlled by puppets who own allegiance to another Power. We, the democracies, will still be faced by totalitarianism, in a form less clumsy but no less aggressive, and even more sinister in its ruthless unexhausted might.

Donald Soper, writing in the Christmas 1944 edition of *Peace News*, argued that 'There is a false simplicity in the idea that we can concentrate upon the renunciation of war without at the same time concentrating on the abolition of capitalism and nationalism and power-politics.'

Despite being unified by the desire for peace, PPU members could hide widely diverging views on other matters. This led to the resignation, in 1943, of Dr Alfred Salter, a long-time campaigner for peace. (Plates, page 7) As a committed Christian, Salter believed that any physical relationship outside of wedlock was a sin. This was not a view shared by all PPU adherents, as some based their pacifism on libertarian ideas that rejected any external state interference when it came to war or personal relationships. However, Salter and his colleague James Hudson could not sanction what they considered immoral conduct, such as a man and woman living together outside wedlock. Therefore, a motion was put forward to the National Council of the PPU by Salter and Hudson that staff members 'should enter into no irregular sex relationship', otherwise they 'forthwith sever their official connection with the Union'. The motion was declined, and Salter and Hudson resigned as joint treasurers, writing a joint letter outlining their dismay:

> The moral code in these matters arises out of the need of the community for the sanctity and permanence of family life. Divinely sanctioned, as we think it is, the code cannot be disregarded without weakening a well-established and a necessary social institution, and at the same time imperilling the happiness and the rights of men and women and of their children and children to be. ... There can be no tolerance by either Christians or Pacifists for whatever tends to disintegrate a good and pure social life.

One practical measure taken by the PPU was an attempt to alleviate a growing humanitarian crisis on the European mainland. The Ministry of Economic Warfare had enforced a naval blockade of Germany and all German-occupied territories in 1939, and this was causing great distress for many people. In 1940, the PPU issued a pamphlet titled *Who Starves?* and in September 1941 the PPU Council organised a Food Relief Campaign, with Vera Brittain as the chairwoman. The campaign's launch took place at the Aeolian Hall, London on 24 January 1942. The objective was to persuade Allied governments to allow controlled food relief to be targeted at those in need, under the supervision of the Red Cross.

It was hoped that the usual PPU campaigning methods of leaflets, pamphlets and public meetings to influence public opinion would encourage people to put pressure on their MPs to support such a programme. Fifty-thousand copies of a special PPU bulletin, *Famine*, were sold and 4,000 people attended a rally in Trafalgar Square on 25 July 1942. In 1943, 700 people took part in a famine fast and six travelling shop displays toured the country. Despite this success, it was felt that leading PPU members did not have the necessary respect of key figures in the government to be able to directly influence policy, and so a Famine Relief Committee was established, with George Bell, Bishop of Chichester, as a leading member. Eventually some milk and foodstuffs were allowed into Greece, so the campaign did experience some success. One longer-term benefit of the initiative was that the local famine relief committee in Oxford continued as the Oxford Committee for Famine Relief (Oxfam).

The unfortunate Nazi sympathies that had been displayed by a minority of PPU members before the war continued into the 1940s. In 1943, the openly fascist Marquess of Tavistock was elected to the National Council, having written to *Peace News* on 30 October 1942 excusing Nazi aggression in Europe as being due to 'the very serious provocation which many Jews have given by their avarice and arrogance when exploiting Germany's financial difficulties, by their associations with commercialised vice, and by their monopolisation of certain professions'. Even as sincere a campaigner as Vera Brittain sought to dismiss the Allied governments highlighting the discovery of Nazi death camps as 'partly, at least, in order to divert attention from the havoc produced in German cities by allied obliteration bombing'.

The PPU continued to support the campaigns to end the mass bombings of Germany (see Chapter 10) and to press for a statement of government peace aims and an early negotiated peace. In the spring of 1945, the National Peace Council, supported by the PPU and a campaign in *Peace News*, collected 85,000 signatures on a Petition for a Constructive Peace. The petition argued that 'A world free from insecurity, injustice and war must be built, not on concepts of exclusive guilt, racial inferiority and preponderance of power, but on the principle of interdependence of all peoples and their common responsibility for the making of a peaceful order.' This petition was presented to Churchill and sent to the British delegates at the United Nations founding conference in San Francisco and to parliamentary candidates in the 1945 general election.

Although there was discord within the PPU, and some resignations from its ranks, a decline from 140,000 members in April 1940 to 98,000 by 1945 represented a resilience that would see the organisation emerge into the post-war world in a strong position to campaign against nuclear weapons and further wars throughout the world. Today the PPU maintains a strong campaigning profile, promoting sales of the white poppy each November. It continues to advocate peace and reconciliation throughout the world and promote the history of pacifism in the UK and the wider world.

Chapter 4

Pacifism and Politics

Whilst many mainstream politicians could at least give generalised support to the aims of the League of Nations Union, without necessarily ascribing to all its stated positions, the issue of pacifism was one that caused deep bitterness and splits within the Labour Party. Keir Hardie, Ramsay MacDonald and other Labour leaders had been outspoken critics of the First World War, and during the early 1930s, Labour swung towards pacifism in response to the increasingly jingoistic tone coming from the packed House of Commons benches of the National Government. The Labour Party had been reduced to fifty MPs at the 1931 general election, as Ramsay MacDonald threw his energies into supporting the National Government. This caused a split within the party, which had been, since 1906, an amalgamation of the Labour Representation Committee and the Independent Labour Party.

Labour's official position in the aftermath of the 1931 election was the same as before it, the policy pursued by Henderson and Dalton in the Foreign Office during the Labour administration of 1929–31. Officially, the Labour Party stood for multilateral disarmament by negotiated agreement, and security on the basis of the League of Nations Covenant. Nevertheless, large sections of Labour opinion were opposed to the use of force under any circumstances. Non-pacifists and pacifists could cautiously agree on an official formula, even though it held out the possibility of the use of force – so long as the danger that force might actually be used remained remote. With events in Europe and elsewhere, however, this fragile unity quickly collapsed. The threat of military sanctions by member nations against an aggressor, laid down in the League Charter, suddenly acquired a new importance, dividing those who supported it from those who did not. In response to the Japanese invasion of Manchuria in 1931, some in the Labour Party had urged an economic boycott of Japan. However, purist pacifists in the party believed that this would lead to war, with Japan bombing Chinese ports and the British colony of Hong Kong in retaliation. The proposal from Dr Alfred Salter MP, a committed Quaker and pacifist, was to offer opportunities for the surplus Japanese population to emigrate to other countries.

In 1932, the Independent Labour Party voted to disaffiliate itself, along with its five MPs, from the Labour Party. One of the surviving rump of the parliamentary party was Dr Alfred Salter, MP for Bermondsey, who, in 1935, tried to have military trappings removed from Armistice Day commemorations at the Cenotaph in Whitehall:

> Many of us would like to be able to share in a real service of remembrance of the men who died. We should be glad to take part in a civilian celebration which would proclaim and symbolise the ideals for which multitudes gave up their lives.

Salter's close friend and colleague George Lansbury had emerged as the leader of the rump Parliamentary Labour Party in 1931. During a speech while campaigning in the Fulham East by-election of June 1933, Lansbury made plain his continuing abhorrence of the military machine: 'I would close every recruiting station, disband the Army and disarm the Air Force. I would abolish the whole dreadful equipment of war and say to the world: "Do your worst."'

The 1933 party conference, under the leadership of Lansbury, whose pacifism was based on longstanding Christian and socialist principles, unanimously adopted a resolution that declared to 'pledge itself to take no part in war'. In addition, the National Executive Committee, the Parliamentary Party and the TUC were directed to take every possible step, including a general strike if necessary, to prevent the outbreak of war. However, this statement covered a multitude of attitudes, with some seeing it as a long-term aspiration of a world socialist commonwealth, whilst in the short term, some force might have to be used under the guise of the collective security of the League of Nations. Nevertheless, the same conference also unanimously approved a declaration by Arthur Henderson in support of collective security. There was a clear inconsistency between these two motions. Other leading figures, such as Stafford Cripps, also a committed Christian, opposed the official policy as being too centrist, as the League of Nations was 'nothing but the tool of the satiated imperialist powers'. In the long term, it would prove impossible for the party to reconcile the strong views of those in favour of collective security, and those who advocated absolute pacifism.

The attitude of the National Government's representatives at the Disarmament Conference probably angered Salter and his pacifist colleagues more than anything in his political experience. Although Stanley Baldwin acknowledged there was no defence against bombing, Britain opposed a German proposal to prohibit aerial warfare on the grounds that air forces were necessary to maintain order on the frontiers of the Empire. Mrs Corbett Ashley resigned from the delegation, complaining that:

> We have opposed in turn the proposals of France, Italy, the United States, Russia and the eight European powers led by Spain. We have opposed Mr Roosevelt's

new suggestions so contemptuously that I saw the USA delegation go white
with rage in the face of the insult. The attitude of our government during the
past two years in regard to peace has been sheer hypocrisy.

The failure of the Disarmament Conference was followed by a renewed
competition in arms. Salter campaigned ferociously against the prospect of
looming war: 'Whether it means loss of votes, loss of my seat in Parliament,
loss of worldly possessions, loss of liberty or loss of life, I shall continue to
oppose the mad race of death.' Salter, as a committed socialist, pointed out
the profits being made by companies connected with military provision.
The value of shares in De Havilland had risen from 15 shillings to 59 shillings
in the space of a year, and in Rolls-Royce from 44 shillings to 90 shillings
and 9 pence. In addition, in May 1934 the press reported that British firms
had just sold to Germany eighty powerful long-distance aeroplane engines.
Salter commented:

> This Bermondsey of ours will be bombed and laid waste and thousands of our
> people will be butchered by aeroplanes and munitions made in England and
> supplied by England to German and other countries for the purpose. That is
> just one example of how modern capitalism works. Profits! Profits!! Profits!!!.
> Nothing else matters.

However, Salter, and voices like his, were becoming more isolated within the
Labour Party as the 1930s went on. It was the Peace Ballot (see Chapter 2) that
really highlighted the inconsistencies between the two wings of the Labour
Party on the issue of peace. Whilst the party recommended a 'yes' vote to
questions 5(a) and 5(b):

> Should an aggressor nation be stopped by
> (a) Economic and non-military measures
> (b) If necessary by military measures

Salter advised for a 'no' vote. However, even in his own Bermondsey constituency,
despite his popular appeal, question (a) received endorsement by 23,403 votes to
4,189, whilst (b), although closer, was still affirmed by 13,038 to 11,228. This was
the highest 'no' vote in the country in favour of 5(b).

The Peace Ballot thus sharply defined the pro-sanctions policy of the Labour
Party from the ideals of the pacifists. Salter, although recognising that his views
were respected, began to feel increasingly out of step with the majority of his

parliamentary colleagues. He was no longer chosen as the party's spokesman in Commons debates, whilst leader of the Parliamentary Party, George Lansbury, found it increasingly impossible to reconcile his own pacifist views with having to articulate official party policy in the Commons.

The issue was brought to a head by Italy's invasion of Abyssinia in 1935. The Labour Party called for economic sanctions against the aggressor, but for the pacifist element in the party, this would lead to war, a war that would soon extend to Germany and the rest of Europe. Their somewhat idealistic preferred solution was to remove the reason for Italy's aggression by having the nations of the world agreeing to the pooling of economic resources. Thus, no nation would need to seek new territories for raw materials. It was becoming increasingly difficult for the deeply principled Lansbury to remain as leader of a party whose official policy was so at odds with his own. He was eventually forced from his position when the 1935 Labour Party conference rejected an absolute pacifist stance. Following the invasion of Abyssinia, Labour was forced into a position whereby it would support the National Government in countenancing a 'League war'. The TUC, at their Margate conference in September, had voted their support for sanctions against Italy, backed by the threat of force by the League of Nations. The organisation had pledged 'its firm support of any action consistent with the principles and statutes of the League to restrain the Italian government'.

On 17 September, Lord Ponsonby, Labour's leader in the Lords, resigned on the grounds that the Labour Party's position was incompatible with his pacifism. Not to be outdone, Sir Stafford Cripps resigned on the same day, in opposition to the 'capitalists' sanctions'. However, the biggest obstacle in the way of a coherent Labour policy on the issue was its leader, George Lansbury. The party's National Executive Committee convened a meeting on 19 September to work out how to accommodate the party's position with that of its leader. A resolution was agreed that stated that 'the question of leadership is a matter for the parliamentary party, but that in the opinion of the NEC there is no reason that he should tender his resignation.' Hugh Dalton noted in his diary, 'We don't want the onus of pushing him out.' The knives appeared to be out for Lansbury, with no one yet ready to strike the fatal blow to his leadership.

On 1 October 1935, at the annual party conference in Brighton, Hugh Dalton introduced a joint statement by the TUC and the National Council of Labour. It supported sanctions backed up by force against Mussolini if he were to invade Abyssinia. Dalton asked the movement to stand firm against Mussolini's 'barbarous and long premeditated assault on Abyssinia'. Then Cripps had his turn. He railed against the capitalists and imperialists as was his wont. Next, the floor passed to the Labour leader. George Lansbury gave a truly memorable speech, speaking passionately for pacifism and entreating the conference to heed his pleas. He was greeted with a standing ovation from the floor, excepting some of the trade union delegations, and two rousing choruses of *For he's a jolly good fellow*. *The Times* reported on his speech:

> He wished every one to understand that it was bitter and difficult for him to stand there and publicly to repudiate a big fundamental piece of policy. If he were in any doubt about that policy he would not take the line he was taking, but he had never been more convinced he was right and that the movement was making a terrible mistake than he was today. ...
>
> During the conference, scores of candidates had asked him to speak, and most of them profoundly disagreed with the position he took up. He had agreed to speak, but he was worried about what he was to say and how he was to say it. However, this disagreement, serious as it was, was not the overwhelmingly fundamental question that brought the party together. He knew that he was consistently inconsistent, and he had learned not to go through life looking over his shoulder at the ghost of what he had been. He had had an overwhelming conviction ever since he was a boy that force was no remedy. During the last six years he had been in the position of a Doctor Jekyll and Mr Hyde. He had had to speak for the party, and each time he had seen Sir Samuel Hoare he had tried honestly to state the party's position.
>
> Perhaps it was inconsistent of him to have joined the Labour Government, and equally inconsistent to have become leader. He believed that force never could bring permanent peace and permanent good will in the world. He had gone into districts where people were starving, and had told them that they must not riot, but must trust to the winning of Socialism through public opinion. He had no right to preach pacifism to starving people in this country and to preach something else in relation to people elsewhere.
>
> One whom he regarded as the greatest figure in human history had put it on record that they who took up the sword should perish by the sword. History had proved it. Yet there would very soon be much greater armaments in this country than before the war. Some of the schools were going to be moved inland from the South Coast. There was talk of removing Woolwich Arsenal to Wales, and children were being drilled against gas attacks. What was all that for? War became more beastly every day, and he could not see the difference between mass murder organised by the League of Nations and mass murder organised by individual nations.

If he had the power to go to Geneva backed by the people he would say there that Great Britain had finished with imperialism, and was willing that all people under her flag wherever government could be established should be free to establish their own government. He would also say that the resources under our control should be pooled for the service of all mankind under the control of an international commission. He would say further that we should be willing to disarm unilaterally, for he believed that the first nation with overseas possessions which would put into practice the rule of doing as one would be done unto would lead the world away from war and utterly defeat it.

In response to Cripps's left-wing analysis and Lansbury's moral agonising, Ernest Bevin, the General Secretary of the Transport and General Workers' Union, unleashed a torrent of invective that would alter the course of Labour Party policy on rearmament and war. First, he mocked Cripps, the wealthy lawyer:

People have been on this platform today talking about the destruction of capitalism. Lawyers and members of the professions have not done too badly ... the thing that is being wiped out is the trade union movement. It is we who are being wiped out and who will be wiped out if fascism comes here.

Then Bevin destroyed Lansbury, declaring, 'It is placing the Executive and the Movement in an absolutely wrong position to be hawking your conscience around from body to body asking to be told what to do with it.' The force of Bevin's rebuke was shocking. Boos and catcalls echoed through the hall as he spoke but the final vote was overwhelming. The anti-war cause was rejected by 2,168,000 votes to 102,000. Yet Bevin's speech was to have a far wider impact than the vote alone. Dalton wrote in his diary that Bevin had 'hammered Lansbury to death'. Eight days later, on 9 October, Lansbury resigned from the leadership of the party he had served for decades, for whose causes he had previously served time in prison. Clement Attlee was chosen as an interim leader, eventually becoming arguably Britain's greatest peacetime Prime Minister from 1945 to 1951. The pacifists within the Labour Party had been soundly defeated.

Events had meant that Labour could no longer paper over a fundamental difference of views through a compromise formula. In 1933, Labour was essentially a pacifist party, but by the end of 1937, influenced by the issues thrown up by the Spanish Civil War, it had become a party that believed in armed deterrence, a party that urged collective security through the League of Nations and a party that was bitterly opposed to Neville Chamberlain's policy of appeasement. Despite the Labour Party's support for rearmament and, from 1937, opposition to Chamberlain's appeasement policy, Lansbury's successor as leader, Clement Attlee, found the international situation a thorny issue for the party. The cracks were papered over by a position that opposed the government's proposals of financing the rearmament programme through borrowing, rather than the taxation of wealth. The Labour Party expressed concern that whilst huge rates of unemployment continued to cause poverty in the heavy industrial areas of northern England, Wales and Scotland, the government was unwilling to invest in public works to alleviate destitution in these regions. So, when in February 1937 Chamberlain proposed to raise £400 million for rearmament, Attlee was outraged, asking, 'Do you remember the scream against the Labour Party's unorthodox finance in 1931 when they borrowed £100,000,000 for life? ... Now we are going to have £400,000,000 for death.' Money spent on arms represents resources diverted from housing, schools, roads and other civil projects.

Whilst the parliamentary party under Attlee continued to tackle the government over the manner of the funding for rearmament, the pacifists within the party – Lansbury, Salter, Cecil H. Wilson and others – became increasingly isolated from their fellow MPs and turned their attentions to support for Dick Sheppard's Peace Pledge Union. In 1936, Lansbury and Salter undertook a month-long Peace Mission to the USA, addressing leading citizens in Washington DC and right across the states. (Plates, page 7)

Prior to leaving the UK, Lansbury issued a statement of aims through the Fellowship of Reconciliation, of which he was also a leading light:

> I hope to rouse public opinion in America against war and to enlist men and women of good will in a great campaign on behalf of a constructive peace. We who are pacifists are not idle dreamers. We are trying to be the true-hearted followers of the Prince of Peace, who was crucified on Calvary because He preached the only realist way of life. His message to the world has stood the test of time. Statesmen and others fear to accept His realism and continue to pin their faith on the worn-out policy of armaments, which can only end once again in universal destruction. My appeal to America is the first stage in a world-wide campaign that I hope to take part in.
>
> What is needed is that the organising genius, enthusiasm, and devotion given to the grim business of war shall be turned to the task, difficult and complex as it is, of discovering how we, who call ourselves civilised and Christian, can organise and share this wonderful world for the good of one another. I do not impugn the sincerity of leading statesmen, though I do question their judgement and their policy.

Salter estimated that they spoke directly to 200,000 people and reached tens of millions more through the wireless. Lansbury was granted a 45-minute interview by President Roosevelt, urging him to initiate the world conference that had been rejected by Parliament. Spurred on by the friendly reception they had received in the US, Salter continued the campaign for a world conference on disarmament in Britain, whilst Lansbury toured the capitals of Europe to put forward his case. He was granted personal interviews with both Hitler and Mussolini and received assurances from many statesmen that if a world conference were called, their nations would attend. Cordell Hull, the American Secretary of State, confirmed that Roosevelt would co-operate in arranging the conference if Britain would join in taking the initiative. However, Baldwin remained obstinate and refused to meet with Lansbury or Salter. This led to a situation where, according to Fenner Brockway, 'President Roosevelt and the most prominent figures on the political stage of Europe were ready to discuss with the unofficial ambassador of peace how war could be prevented; the Tory Prime Minister of Britain would not see him.'

Salter also took the lead in organising a Parliamentary Pacifist Group, numbering about twenty MPs and some peers. Large pacifist conventions were held in London, Manchester, Stoke-on-Trent, Bristol, Birmingham, Southampton, Norwich, Carlisle and Sheffield. But within British politics, Lansbury, Salter and other pacifists became increasingly isolated voices as Europe prepared for war. By the late 1930s the actions of Nazi Germany in supporting the fascist General Franco in the Spanish Civil War had convinced many on the left that Hitler needed to be opposed by force.

Fenner Brockway (Plates, page 7), who had left the party in 1932 to work within the Independent Labour Party, broke with absolute pacifism over Spain, and the anti-war Labour Politician Philip Noel-Baker, a leader of the International Peace Campaign from 1936 to 1939, advocated the bombing of Germany as the best way to bring the war to a swift conclusion. With the rise of fascism in Spain, Brockway began to believe that it might be necessary to fight to preserve the peace in the long run. Despite his previous pacifist commitment, he resigned from War Resisters International, explaining:

> If I were in Spain at this moment I should be fighting with the workers against the Fascist forces. I believe it to be the correct course to demand that the workers shall be provided with the arms which are being sent so freely by the Fascist powers to their enemies. I appreciate the attitude of the pacifists in Spain who, whilst wishing the workers success, feel that they must express their support in constructive social service alone. My difficulty about that attitude

is that if anyone wishes the workers to be triumphant he cannot, in my view, refrain from doing whatever is necessary to enable that triumph to take place.

Brockway assisted in the recruitment of British volunteers to fight Franco's fascist forces in Spain. He sailed to Calais in February 1937 and was believed to have been destined for Spain. Among those who went to Spain was Eric Blair (better known as George Orwell), supported by a letter of recommendation from Brockway to present to the ILP representatives in Barcelona. Following the Spanish Civil War, Brockway advocated public understanding of the conflict. He wrote a number of articles about the war and was influential in getting Orwell's *Homage to Catalonia* published.

But as far as the Second World War was concerned, Fenner Brockway found himself in a painful dilemma. Though 'instinctively a pacifist', who had served time in prison for his conscientious objection during the first war ('I could never see myself killing anyone and had never held a weapon in my hands'), Brockway could not now be wholly anti-war:

> The thought of mass killing was unbearable. But I also thought of the Nazi brutality I had seen. And I thought of brave German comrades who would now face concentration camps and the firing squad. I thought of what a Hitler victory could mean for Europe.

Brockway continued to speak out for the ILP's anti-war views, urging that the war should be ended by a people's revolution across Europe's frontiers, not by military victory. He also took part in the ILP's vigorous protest against British carpet-bombing of civilian areas in Germany. The 'brave German comrades' Fenner Brockway kept in mind were those who sent this message to the ILP office just four days before war was declared:

> In the moment before the cannons speak, before the world faces horror and manslaughter, we send our message to you. The German workers do not want this war. The German peasants do not want war. This war is not our war, this fight is not our fight. We ask you, in the midst of death and destruction: do not forget the ideas for which we died under torture, do not forget the ideals for which we have suffered in the concentration camps. ... Comrades, our common fatherland is our humanity.

However, Brockway's close friend and ally Philip Noel-Baker had come to a different conclusion on the matter of aerial bombing of Germany. Writing in 1940, he argued:

Compared to the concentration camp and the Himmler terror, air bombing is almost civilised. I am strongly of the belief that the thing for us to do now is to beat Hitler, and to put an end to his foul and brutal regime. We can then make a peace which will be real and lasting.

The British Union of Fascists and opposition to the war

Another political group that opposed the war, although for reasons that differed greatly from the Labour Party and the ILP, was the British Union of Fascists. They argued that a war with Germany was neither ideologically nor strategically necessary. Britain should, they argued, have sympathy with the Third Reich's anti-communist stance. On 16 July 1939, addressing a meeting of 20,000 followers at Earls Court, its leader Oswald Mosley warned, 'a million Britons shall never die in your Jews' quarrel.'

However, when war was declared, Mosley issued a message to BUF members, urging them to do what they thought was their duty to their country:

To our members my message is plain and clear. Our country is involved in war. Therefore I ask you to do nothing to injure our country, or help any other power. Our members should do what the law requires of them, and if they are members of any of the forces or services of the Crown, they should obey their orders, and, in particular, obey the rules of their service. ... We have said a hundred times that if the life of Britain were threatened we would fight again.

Mosley continued to campaign for a negotiated peace, opposing the war on the grounds that no British interest was served by intervening in Germany's quarrel with Poland. Mosley thought that the war was simply a pretext for having a war with the Nazis.

By 1940, the BUF had declined in influence, with a membership of around 9,000, and it was easily suppressed by the government, with around 800 fascists imprisoned under Defence Regulation 18B. Oswald Mosley was interned in Brixton in May 1940, with his wife, Diana, locked up in Holloway weeks later, 'in a dirty cell with the floor swimming with water ... and only a thin mattress on the dirty, wet floor'. One rank-and-file BUF member, John Charmley, argued that such treatment ran contrary to the British tradition of tolerating dissent against wars: 'this was the first time that opponents had been arrested and imprisoned.' Friends of the couple began a campaign for their freedom, lobbying Churchill. Along with various society figures, Lord Halifax, the former Foreign Secretary, sought their release. Churcihll took up the case with Herbert Morrison, Home Secretary in the wartime coalition government, and Mosley was transferred to Holloway, where he and Diana were allowed to live in a separate wing with female servants, receiving food parcels from their friends. Eventually, Mosley was released in 1943 'on medical grounds' and spent the rest of the war under house arrest at an Oxfordshire farm.

The issue of the locking up of BUF members was taken up in Parliament in November 1940 from a surprising quarter – by the ILP MP John McGovern. He asked Morrison:

> Is the Home Secretary aware that a considerable number of these people who may have been attracted by the attractive programme of this party are not really Fascists in intention; and cannot he speed up the consideration of their applications for a hearing, as some of them have pleaded for months for a hearing, and some young women especially who I do not believe had any evil intentions towards the State are lying in prison?

Morrison replied:

> I have always thought, and I have learned increasingly since I have been at the Home Office, that the members of this organisation are a very varied collection of people. I appreciate that point, and I assure the hon. Gentleman that no undue delay will be caused. I am looking into the matter very carefully to see that the cases of these people, in common with those of all other internees, are dealt with as soon as possible.

Many blackshirts, as members of the BUF had become known due to their distinctive uniform, remained in concentration camps, on the Isle of Man and elsewhere, until the end of the war as it was feared that public expression of pro-fascist sympathies would not be helpful to Britain's war effort.

Some cases were heard before a government advisory committee. One of those interviewed by the chairman, Mr Justice Birkett, was Mosley himself.

> **Mosley:** There appear to be two grounds for detaining us – a suggestion that we are traitors who would take up arms and fight with the Germans if they landed, and that our propaganda undermines the civilian morale.

> **Birkett:** Speaking for myself, you can entirely dismiss the first suggestion.

Mosley: Then I can only assume that we have been detained because of our campaign in favour of a negotiated peace.

Birkett: Yes, Sir Oswald, that is the case.

Although lacking in any significant appeal, and with an agenda that ran contrary to the essential British decency that ran through most sections of society, whether pro or anti-war, the BUF did form a small section of internal opposition to Britain's war aims and were thus subject to restrictions in order not to undermine the fight for Christian civilisation.

The Communist Party of Great Britain

At the other end of the political spectrum from the BUF, the Communist Party of Great Britain had around 18,000 members at the start of the war, and had, since the mid-1930s, been calling for a Peace Front with the Soviet Union and for the democracies to oppose the fascist states. However, the Molotov-Ribbentrop pact of August 1939, in which Nazi Germany and Soviet Russia signed a non-aggression pact, tore this policy to shreds.

On 2 September 1939, the CPGB issued a manifesto that argued for a fight on two fronts – a war against Nazi Germany and a home front against the reactionary and appeasing Chamberlain government. On 14 September, Harry Pollitt, the General Secretary of the CPGB (Plates, page 8), published a pamphlet titled *How to Win the War*, which declared:

> The Communist Party supports the war, believing it to be a just war. To stand aside from this conflict, to contribute only revolutionary sounding phrases while the fascist beasts ride roughshod over Europe, would be a betrayal of everything our forebears have fought to achieve in the course of long years of struggle against capitalism. ... The prosecution of this war necessitates a struggle on two fronts. First to secure the military victory over fascism, and second, to achieve this, the political victory over the enemies of democracy in Britain.

On the same date, a telegram arrived from the Soviet Union describing the war as 'a robber war kindled from all sides by the hands of two imperialist groups of powers'. R. Palme Dutt, a Stalin supporter who was eager to replace Pollitt, then raised the question in the CPGB's Political Bureau of changing the party's line.

A week later, the Central Committee decided to change the policy on the war, and issued a new manifesto in the *Daily Worker* on 7 October titled 'Peace or War?' It called for an immediate peace conference. Pollitt was removed from his post as General Secretary and replaced by Dutt, with John R. Campbell being replaced as editor of the *Daily Worker* by William Rust. Both Pollitt and Campbell were persuaded to submit declarations renouncing their previous position of supporting the war.

The new CPGB line was heavily influenced by Georgi Dimitrov, General Secretary of Comintern (the Communist International body based in Moscow), who, in a November pamphlet titled *Communism and War*, blamed the 'imperialists of Britain and France' who have 'hurled their people into war against Germany'. The *Daily Worker* echoed this line in April 1940, blaming Britain and France for the extension of the war into Scandinavia, after the German invasion of Norway and Denmark.

When Chamberlain's government fell, to be replaced by a coalition government in which the Labour Party played a full role, Dutt wrote, in *Labour Monthly*: 'In imperialist war there is no national defence, but only mutual extermination of the workers for the profit of the slaveholders.' As the Wehrmacht continued its advance through Western Europe during the spring of 1940, Dutt became concerned at 'the influence of a wave of national defensist feeling', which was allowing the government to appropriate greater powers. For Dutt, this ran the risk of 'the victory of fascism from within', disregarding the imminent threat of its imposition from without. In Dutt's mind, there was no distinction between bourgeois democracies and fascist states. The priority for Britain was not to defeat Nazi Germany, but to establish 'a new government based on the working masses of the people, a government in which there shall be no friend of fascism or representative of imperialism'.

Following the fall of France in June 1940, the line taken by the *Daily Worker* softened somewhat. Reference was made of the need for British workers to act as a free people organising their own defence against 'the danger of fascist invasion and tyranny'. Democratic institutions were once more deemed worth preserving against the threat of Nazism. However, this new line did not extend as far as supporting the government. For the CPGB, only a people's government could secure 'the unity and unbreakable will to victory that can guarantee the defeat both of the Nazi menace and of the danger which threatens from the British representatives of fascism'. The essential analysis of the party right up to the German attack on the Soviet Union was that the war should be opposed as a conflict between two rival power blocs, and to build an untied movement in order to bring about a new government of the working people in Britain.

But by 1941, the *Daily Worker* was becoming increasingly concerned about German actions in the Balkans, which directly threatened Soviet interests. The struggles of the Yugoslavian and Greek peoples were framed as just wars. On 22 June 1941, Hitler launched Operation Barbarossa, a full-scale attack on the Soviet Union. The Political Bureau of the CPGB met the same day and declared its solidarity with the Soviet Union and called for agreement between Britain and the USSR and 'a people's victory and a People's Peace'. This meant a revision of the party's line on the Churchill government and the new position was for 'the broadest united national front around the Churchill government'. Winning the war was now the top priority, not the establishment of a people's government. Harry Pollitt was restored to the position of General Secretary, with the approval of Comintern.

The CPGB's previous support for strikes in Britain ended and they called for a Second Front to be opened in Europe, in order to support the USSR. Despite this about-turn, the party peaked in membership in 1943, reaching around 60,000. The government shut down the *Daily Worker* as a result of some anti-war rhetoric. However, the CPGB did not instruct its members to claim conscientious objection due to the policy of trying to engage directly where the mass of people were gathered. Therefore, their contribution to the anti-war movement was, according to one historian, one of 'constant intellectual unease and evasiveness'.

Independent Labour Party

Another left-wing political party was the Independent Labour Party (ILP), which had split from the mainstream Labour Party in 1932 and had retained four MPs in the Glasgow area. Its two chairmen during the 1930s, James Maxton and Fenner Brockway, were both ardent pacifists. However, whilst condemning the thought of sanctions against Italy for its invasion of Abyssinia as 'imperialist', both men were critical of the British government's policy of non-intervention in the Spanish Civil War.

Initially, on the outbreak of war in Spain, Maxton had called for the government to support the policy of non-intervention but later he argued that the intervention of fascist Germany and Italy required a British response. Franco had had unrestricted aid from the two fascist powers, while Britain had done nothing to help the Republicans. This was because, for Maxton, the British government's 'class prejudices were with Franco'. Had Spain been ruled by a right-wing government, it would have been granted all the rights normally accorded to foreign powers. Nevertheless, as a pacifist, Maxton opposed rearmament in the 1930s and supported the appeasement policies of Neville Chamberlain. After the outbreak of the Second World War, Maxton continued to oppose Britain's role in it.

Some of the ILP's former absolutist conscientious objectors, such as Fenner Brockway, had supported the armed struggle against Franco during the Spanish Civil War, but stated that a war against Germany would be an imperialist one unless Britain were to become a socialist country. Brockway stated: 'If I were in Spain at the moment, I should be fighting with the workers against the Fascist forces.' He became a supporter of the International Brigades who went to Spain to fight for the Republican cause and visited Barcelona in the summer of 1937, writing a letter of introduction for George Orwell, which smoothed the author's path to fight in the war. Brockway became convinced that the Spanish Communist Party was undermining the Spanish Republic, seeing its prime task as destroying its political opponents on the left.

The Spanish Civil War had the effect of altering Brockway's previously unswerving pacifist views:

> There is no doubt that the society resulting from an anarchist victory would have far greater liberty and equality than the society resulting from a fascist victory. Thus, I came to see that it is not the amount of violence used which determines good or evil results, but the ideas, the sense of human values, and above all the social forces behind its use. With this realisation, although my nature revolted against the killing of human beings just as did the nature of those Catalonian peasants, the fundamental basis of my old philosophy disappeared.

This led Brockway to supporting Britain's involvement in the Second World War. He later wrote:

> It was in all my nature opposed to war. I could never see myself killing anyone and had never held a weapon in my hands. But I saw that Hitler and Nazism had been mainly responsible for bringing the war and I could not contemplate their victory. In a sense, the Spanish Civil War settled this dilemma for me; I could no longer justify pacifism when there was a fascist threat.

Some ILP members did take the conscience clause on the outbreak of war, and the party retained an anti-war stance through to 1945, although other leading members, such as C.A. Smith, demurred from this position at various points in the war. By the end of the war, membership had fallen to a tiny 2,500, with many, including Brockway, rejoining the Labour Party.

Opposition in Parliament

Another leading political figure whose anti-war stance was, in many ways, surprising was the former wartime Prime Minister David Lloyd George. Lloyd George had been one of the main architects of the Treaty of Versailles, ensuring heavy punishment for Germany, but by August 1934 he was insisting that Germany could not wage war, therefore there was no risk to European security for the next ten years. In September 1936, he went to Germany to meet Hitler, who said that he was pleased to have met 'the man who won the war'. In response, Lloyd George called Hitler 'the greatest living German'. On his return, Lloyd George wrote in the *Daily Express* that 'The Germans have definitely made up their minds never to quarrel with us again' and that Hitler, 'the George Washington of Germany', was only rearming Germany for defence, not offence. Although he spoke in the Norway debate in the Commons in May 1940 undermining Chamberlain as Prime Minister, he still advocated a negotiated peace with Germany following the Battle of Britain. He remained critical of the government's organisation of the war effort throughout.

During the course of the war, a handful of maverick MPs continued to espouse the cause of pacifism, and to campaign against certain aspects of the conduct of the war. Some of these MPs formed a Parliamentary Peace Aims Group, under the chairmanship of Rhys J. Davies and with Dick Stokes as secretary, with the idea of forcing the government to state some clear objectives to be achieved in fighting the war. (Plates, page 8) In 1940, they issued a pamphlet titled *Peace Aims: The Case for Stating them Now*, which declared:

> The necessity for stating our Peace Aims has become more imperative and British Labour should bring immediate and strong pressure upon HM Government for such a statement NOW. While it has been argued that the time is inopportune; that the Government should be allowed the choose the moment for such declaration, etc. etc., it is clear from statements made by certain Conservative leaders that they wish for no statement of aims during the war. 'Win the war first, then we can deal with peace.' That is their slogan. But we are convinced that this involves grave dangers and will bring profound disillusionment to the middle and working classes and involves risk of the history of the post-1918 period being repeated – with even greater suffering.
>
> A statement has become more than ever necessary since the formation of the present Coalition Government. How far does the Coalition Government accept the stated Aims of Labour in this war? It has been suggested that, having put our representatives in the Government, we should trust them.

We should, as well, stimulate and help them in this matter. We need to create a public opinion which will enable Labour's aims to prevail inside the Government.

A statement of Peace Aims must not be confined to the British attitude towards European problems; Imperial and home issues are also involved. India cannot be left out; neither can our future policies towards the colonial world be ignored. It is essential that the aims that we can put into practice during the war should not be the subject of a mere statement. They should be put into practice immediately; example is better than precept.

The pamphlet went on to call for equality of sacrifice during the war, and for progressive social policies to be enacted following it, unlike the misery of unemployment that followed the end of the first war. A list of reasons why it would be advantageous for the government to issue broad peace aims was given:

(a) It would shorten the war; it might even stop it.
(b) It would prove to Christian and other elements in Germany that we do not seek their destruction, and they may then rally against Hitler. They never will so long as our leading speakers threaten their destruction.
(c) It would give encouragement and hope to the peoples of all the invaded countries.
(d) It would convince the people of this country and of the Empire that they will not once again be cheated by the forces of reaction.
(e) It would greatly assist in the rallying of American public opinion.
(f) The moral leadership of the world cannot be won on a negative policy.
(g) The civilised way of life is settlement of dispute by discussion without loss of principle. If the stated Peace Aims of HM Government are just, the moral forces of the World will rally to support them and in so doing eliminate the unchristian despotic elements in their own countries.
(h) If a statement is not forthcoming our friends abroad may conclude that the British have naught to proclaim, whereas in face we can offer something much better than 'Hitler's New Order'.

In 1942, members of the Peace Aims Group met with David Lloyd George. Indications had been received by Salter that, should Stalingrad fall to the Germans, then Russia might sue for a separate peace with Hitler. The group hoped that the former wartime Prime Minister would table a motion in the House of Commons calling for a general armistice in such an eventuality. However, as the Russian resistance at Stalingrad succeeded, such plans never came to fruition.

One MP who sought to hold the government to account for its wartime actions was John McGovern, the ILP MP for Glasgow Shettleston. During a Commons debate on conscientious objection held on 8 February 1940, he challenged the Minister of Labour, Ernest Brown, on the figures of the outcomes for the Glasgow tribunal (see Chapter 6). At the time, of 465 cases heard, 167 had been refused any kind of recognition of their objection, 91 had been ordered into non-combatant roles in the armed forces and 109 had been registered conditionally on undertaking civilian work. McGovern queried Brown:

> Is the Right Hon. Gentleman aware that a large number of genuine conscientious objectors, many of whom are known to me, are being refused exemption by this tribunal, and can he explain why no representative has been sent to the tribunal who has any understanding of conscientious objectors, and why no representative sympathetic to their point of view is on the tribunal?

Brown rejected McGovern's assumptions, pointing out that ninety-eight cases had been granted absolute exemption. McGovern replied that this was a small percentage, and many had not been given a fair hearing. He then asked Brown about figures for the appellate tribunal in Edinburgh, claiming that many genuine objectors had been turned down and not been able to have a friend to support their evidence. For McGovern, the actions of the tribunals were political: 'Does the Right Hon. Gentleman know of the growing discontent at the action of these Tory die-hards who sit on the tribunal?' He went on to raise the case of Mr James Jones, aged 67, of Auchinraith Avenue, Hamilton, who appeared before the local tribunal at Glasgow on 24 January 1940, claiming exemption on moral and religious grounds. He was refused exemption on the basis that he had not consulted his local priest and taken his advice as to whether or not he should appeal on conscientious grounds. McGovern asked Brown to set aside this decision and to order a retrial.

Brown pointed out that it was not within his powers to set aside the decisions of local tribunals, but that the case could go to the appellate tribunal if necessary. McGovern argued that it was unfair that ministers of religion, including one Rabbi, were being brought before the tribunal to verify the positions of their denominations, when the conscience was a matter for the individual. The following week, on 15 February, McGovern submitted a written question on the fees paid to tribunal members. Brown responded that whilst those who were county court judges received no extra remuneration, other chairmen received three guineas for a half day sitting, subject to a maximum of twenty-four guineas per week. In addition, there were subsistence allowances of up to twenty-five shillings per night. Other members received three guineas per day.

McGovern remained a constant thorn in the side of the government throughout the war, challenging ministers on many issues, such as the batman system, which he argued should be abolished as Britain was fighting for democratic principles. He also spoke on the treatment of conscientious objectors in prison, repeatedly pressed for a clear statement on Britain's war aims, asking on 4 February 1941, 'Do the Government really know what the war is about?'

On 12 March 1941, he challenged the Minister of Information, Duff Cooper, on the exclusion of pacifist voices from the BBC:

> Is the Right Hon. Gentleman aware of the growing anxiety among a large number of people in this country at the exclusion of people from the microphone—that on account of their pacifist views they are not allowed to broadcast music and literature? Is he aware that there is this growing anxiety among people, many of whom support this war and think it is a great contradiction that we should be pretending to fight for liberty and at the same time adopting Nazi methods at the BBC?

On 1 April 1941 he complained to Herbert Morrison, the Home Secretary, about the under-reporting of the death count following an air raid on Clydeside, and the inadequacy of public canteens for the survivors. However, it was not just those opposed to the war and civilians that McGovern spoke up for. In January 1945 he asked the Foreign Secretary, Anthony Eden, about provisions made by the Japanese authorities for prisoners of war to be able to send letters to relatives, as some had not been heard from since September 1943.

Richard Stokes, Labour MP for Ipswich, was another frequent critic of the government, most notably on the inefficiency of tank design and the bombing of Germany. Soon after the outbreak of war, Stokes published an article titled *What is Happening in Europe?* (January 1940). He argued that Hitler had been forced into his actions by the behaviour of others, and called for the revision of the Versailles Treaty and a redistribution of borders to be imposed on Poland and Czechoslovakia in Germany's favour. Stokes argued that Germany should be allowed domination of the continent in return for acting as a bulwark against the Soviet Union. Furthermore, he tried to persuade former Prime Minister David Lloyd George to lead the campaign in favour of a negotiated peace with Germany.

Dr Alfred Salter MP spent the duration of the war calling for an end to the hostilities. His first wartime message was issued through the *Labour Magazine* and addressed to his Bermondsey constituents:

For years past I have done everything that one man could to prevent war and preserve peace. If the course advocated by the group with whom I act in Parliament had been followed, there would have been no war today. Now that war is here with all its ghastly slaughter and suffering, I am giving and shall continue to give the remaining strength and effort of which I am capable to bringing about an armistice and the restoration of peace at the earliest possible moment.

Salter called for a truce based on the fact that Russia had invaded Poland, exactly the same reason for which Britain had declared war on Germany. 'Do we propose to declare war on Russia? Not a bit of it. Well then, what are we fighting about?' He wrote to the Labour Party's NEC and the PLP urging for pressure for peace negotiations at the earliest moment. During the Phoney War of the winter of 1939–40, Salter urged the British government to accept the offer of Queen Wilhelmina of the Netherlands and King Leopold of Belgium to negotiate a truce.

Although in early September 1939 only six Labour MPs, including Salter and Lansbury, had declared themselves against the war, in November, twenty-two of them signed a manifesto calling for a world conference and an armistice:

We urge the Government to offer here and now to enter into conference at any time with enemy, allied and neutral nations which are prepared to co-operate with us in such a conference to see how far these things (proposals for an enduring peace) – without which the danger of war will be always and imminently with us – may be achieved. We exclude no country and no government. So soon as such a conference is agreed upon and the date of the meeting is fixed, we are prepared to agree to an immediate armistice.

The twenty-two MPs advocated a new European system in which every country would be prepared to sacrifice some measure on national sovereignty in the interests of general security internationally guaranteed. Salter was dismayed at the way in which the Labour Party under Attlee was sacrificing its principles of liberty in order to fully support the war by, for example, imposing conscription. This, for Salter, was a victory for the fascism that Britain was supposed to be fighting against. In the Clackmannan by-election of October 1939, Andrew Stewart, a PPU member and socialist, stood against the Labour candidate under a Stop the War ticket. For the first time in his thirty-three years in the party, Salter opposed the Labour Party:

Religious belief and political instinct alike urge me, whatever the consequence to myself from a party point of view, to support the Peace candidate at

Clackmannan. For the love of Christ and for the sake of humanity, for the salvation of the threatened new generation, I implore the electors in the division to vote for Andrew Stewart.

Stewart lost his deposit but the Labour Party, generally tolerant of a broad range of views within its members, did not take any action against Salter and Cecil Wilson MP, who had also supported the Peace candidate.

Salter was instrumental in gaining a concession for conscientious objectors from the government. Those who had served with the military and then expressed an objection were, after three months' imprisonment to demonstrate the genuineness of their belief, able to have the right to appear before a tribunal. This meant that many were saved from long periods of imprisonment. Salter suffered from a breakdown in health early in the war, and then had to endure the bombing of his house when he and his wife were inside. Knowing that his health was in decline, he decided to make one final appeal to the House of Commons for peace. His close friend and later biographer Fenner Brockway described the occasion, which took place on 25 November 1941:

The attendance was not large when Salter rose in the House, but for those who were present the occasion was unforgettable. The members were hushed in silence even before he uttered a word. He stood straight and erect, but his body swayed momentarily, and it was evident that only his spirit and will sustained him. … The impression he made was profound. Except for the little group of pacifist members who sat near to encourage him, every member of his audience regarded a plea for peace as a betrayal of the nation. But the courage of the speech, the courage of its unpopular view, the courage of this sick man whose spirit conquered physical weakness, compelled respect.

Salter's words encapsulated the anguish and passion held by many who opposed the war but felt themselves powerless to alter its course:

As this is probably almost the last occasion on which I shall have the opportunity of addressing this House, I can no longer refrain from rising to oppose the present war and everything connected with it. There are only seven or eight of us in the House who are resolutely opposed to all war for any purpose whatsoever, and our opposition is based primarily on religious grounds. But there is evidence that outside this House there are at least 2,000,000 people who share these views, or roughly about one in 20 of the population are equally strongly opposed. For centuries the Churches have sought to harmonise the Christian command 'Love one another' with the nationalist slogan, 'Kill one another'. If you fully accept Christ and his Gospel, the two positions are wholly incompatible. No one dare assert that Jesus Christ would have accepted the latter suggestion. His whole message was that any creed, however brutal and bestial, could only be overcome and finally eradicated by spiritual weapons and never by destroying men, women and children indiscriminately. His teaching was to meet evil with good and hatred by love and sympathy.

Salter then positioned his interpretation of the Christian faith as being wholly at odds with the leaders of the mainstream British churches:

I believe that it is my duty to proclaim my testimony against all war, whatever the bishops, the archbishops and the Free Church leaders may say to the contrary. I am thankful that my own religious body, the Society of Friends, of which I am a humble member, has spoken officially and with no uncertain voice about the wholesale slaughter which is now going on. I can take no notice of the Church leaders, who declare in one voice that all war is opposed to the spirit and teaching of Jesus Christ, and in another, talk war, preach war and pray for victory in the war. They are doubtless perfectly sincere and honest, but I am convinced that they are mistaken. There will be no spiritual revival in this country, no forward movement in religion, until the leaders have abandoned this betrayal of Christ and until they have repented of their apostasy.

Salter then returned to the idea of a negotiated peace that could prevent further bloodshed:

I am thankful that the Cardinal Archbishop of Ireland uttered these words a few weeks ago. He said: 'After two years of war, and although passions have been inflamed and anger, hatred and revenge aroused, I say that there is incomparably a better chance of attaining a just peace now than if the war is fought till it ends in victory for one side or another or in stalemate. The statesmen on both sides must know this much better than you or I. I am not saying this rashly. I have considered it, and I think it is somebody's duty to say it. I think it is time for somebody to speak out openly and say this.' He went on: 'The poor plain people of the world to whom victory on either side will not mean very much are suffering every day the loss of their dear ones— husband, brother, father or son—and day after day they know that untold incalculable wealth is being poured out in this war and they also know it will leave a heritage of suffering and want of misery for them.' He added: 'I think that the statesmen of the world should now come together and see whether it is not possible to arrive at a just peace. I am convinced that it is my duty to say that. In view of the sufferings of the world, there is a grave obligation upon the statesmen to make more of an effort than they seem to be doing to bring about a just and lasting peace.' The people of Europe are undergoing hell at the present moment. The appalling, the fearful, slaughter on the Russian front, the wholesale starvation of Europe, and the massacre of men, women and children cry aloud for pity, but there is no suggestion of stopping the war. Is there no one who, for humanity's sake, will call a halt? I say, with the Cardinal Archbishop of Ireland, that I do not believe—whatever may be said of the untrustworthiness of Hitler and the difficulty of negotiating with him— that it is really impossible for the statesmen of Europe to arrange an armistice and make peace. A suffering and defenceless Christ went out to Calvary though he could have called down legions of angels to defend him. Christ went unresistingly to Calvary, and it may be that we may have to undergo martyrdom first. But I have the faith that in the end the Kingdom of God will come, but it will be not as a consequence of this war. God will triumph, but not in the way the Allied Governments imagine.

Salter then identified how the war had already led to a decline of the moral basis on which it was being fought, and that any victory based on such tactics would be a hollow one:

Note the steady moral deterioration that has accompanied the struggle so far. Open retaliation and revenge are now being advocated in the highest quarters, and the position is growing worse and worse. No apologies are now being offered for the indiscriminate bombing of women and children. At first people hesitated to preach blatant revenge, and in the early days of the war only strictly military targets were said to be the objectives of our Air Force. Now we have photographs showing whole streets of working-class houses being blown sky-high by our bombs. Hatred is being engendered between nations by the Press and by the BBC, and it will only intensify and aggravate the international problem, so that every day the war continues it will become harder, not only materially but spiritually, to build a new and better world. The present war will leave behind it a pandemonium of hatred which is terrifying to the imagination. All this is founded on the great and terrible fallacy that ends justify means. They never do—never, never. That is an eternal truth which no casuistry can get around or can overthrow.

We cannot believe that any new or righteous order of society will be achieved by evil means, by overcoming evil with greater, more potent and more effective evil. We offer, only an indefinite prolongation of the agony of Europe. Is there to be no end to this torture of millions of human beings? Is there no pity in the whole world? Are all our hearts hardened and coarsened by events? There is apparently little or no hope of moving the Government, but all the same I beg them, I implore them, to seize the first opportunity of making peace. Britain and all Europe are rushing down the steep slopes to collective suicide and damnation. Will not somebody, for the love of God, for the sake of Christ, demand sanity and peace? Must the war continue by its own inherent momentum until the final crash ends in prolonged anarchy and social confusion? I pray God it may not so end, but that some statesman may step in and secure the control of events that the leaders of the peoples in all the lands have apparently lost.

Although MPs opposed to the idea of conducting a war were in a small minority in the House of Commons, many of them showed energy and resilience in holding the government to account across a range of war-related issues. Despite not being able to shorten the war, they performed a valuable role in a democratic country: that of challenging the government and therefore keeping alive the very ideals of a free society that the war was being fought for. They were able to effect changes in the way that some conscientious objectors were treated in detention, and the government had to act in the knowledge that their decisions would be scrutinised in the House of Commons. Despite renouncing war, or some aspects of it, these parliamentarians were able to contribute to the fair execution of the war, in so far as was possible, and where it was not, to vociferously articulate the counterview.

Chapter 5
Pacifism and Religion

Christian organisations were major voices in the British inter-war pacifist movement. Most organised churches had their own pacifist group, for example the Methodist Peace Fellowship, the Anglican Pacifist Fellowship, the Baptist Peace Fellowship, the Unitarian and Free Church Peace Fellowship and the Congregationalist Pacifist Crusade, whilst the Fellowship of Reconciliation drew pacifists from across the denominations. Many leading members of the Peace Pledge Union, including Professor Charles Raven, Donald Soper and Canon Dick Sheppard, were Christians. Many Christian pacifists were also socialists, and therefore committed to working with other socialist non-pacifists to change the social ordering of society, whilst others were individualists whose consciences trumped any other consideration.

Although some Christians had campaigned for pacifism in the immediate aftermath of the First World War, it was from the late 1920s onwards that Christian Pacifism really gained momentum in the British churches. Christian Pacifism was a multi-faceted phenomenon, with some Christians approving of the use of force by police or an international army whilst disapproving of one state attacking another. Some saw their absolute pacifism as a fundamental expression of their faith, therefore whatever the reality of the international situation, nothing could shift them from that position. Others thought that pacifism was a perfectly reasonable approach to preventing war, as aggressive nations would be shamed by world opinion into laying down their arms if confronted by a pacifist population.

The British churches had been largely supportive of the work of the League of Nations. Each year, Christian newspapers would print long extracts from the sermon preached in Geneva at the opening of the Assembly. Domestically, every Armistice Day sermons implored worshippers to pray for the success of the League, emphasising the dual-faceted meaning of the day for many: as a remembrance of the dead, and as an annual rededication to peace. One letter writer in the Anglican weekly newspaper, the *Guardian*, asked on 26 October 1934 if it was right to sing *I Vow to Thee my Country* at Armistice Day services, as it referenced 'the love that asks no questions'.

In 1935, the Roman Catholic sculptor Eric Gill was approached by the Foreign Office to design a panel for the front of the Assembly Hall at the League of Nations building in Geneva. His work represented the recreation of mankind, which the

League of Nations was assisting in achieving, and was adorned with religious texts. Included were the words *'Quid est homo, quod memo res ejus?'* (What is man that thou art mindful of him?), from Psalm 8:4, and *'Ad imaginem Dei creavit illum'* (God created man in his own image), from Genesis 1:26. (Plates, page 9)

Lord Robert Cecil, Britain's representative to the League of Nations under both Conservative and Labour Prime Ministers, had been inspired to devote his life to the League by a sermon given by his brother, the Bishop of Exeter, in 1921, about British responsibility for moral leadership in the world. He wrote to his wife, 'I have had a great feeling that I have been "called" to preach the League spirit on public affairs and there seems to be so much in the Bible about that kind of thing.' In 1933, both archbishops, and other leading churchmen, appealed to Christians to join the LNU and in 1934 the Archbishop of Canterbury, Cosmo Lang, appealed to people to stand by the 'one existing public barrier against fear and the lawless forces'. Arthur Henderson, a devout Methodist who served as Labour Foreign Secretary from 1929 to 1931, and who was president of the World Disarmament Conference from 1932 to 1934, optimistically welcomed the Kellogg-Briand Pact of 1928 with the words, 'wars of conquest or aggression to gain national ends are things of the past, and force is eliminated as a means of settling international disputes.'

The contrast between the attitude of most mainstream Christian leaders and the more overt absolute pacifists towards the League's policies of sanctions and collective security was encapsulated in a leader column in the Anglican *Guardian* of 10 August 1934:

> Those who believe in the necessity of sanctions belong to the Church type, while the pacifist conforms to what he describes as the sect type. The Church type means those who recognise that it is the business of Christians to consecrate as much of worldly practice as possible, to Chrisitanise the structure of human society, recognising the necessity for order and the element of good in the natural world. The sect type, on the other hand, is apocalyptic. What must be maintained, even if the heavens fall or the world goes up in flames, is the purity of faith, and of the individual conscience. It is significant that the earnest pacifist, when pressed, generally admits that he does not expect that in the world as it is his pacifism will prevent war. The supporter of the League is on the other hand confident that his plan could be successful.

Despite this distinction, most prominent church leaders were critical of the Treaty of Versailles. In 1932, William Temple, Archbishop of York, attacked the War Guilt clause in a sermon at the Geneva Disarmament Conference and in

1933 he wrote: 'In the Treaty of Versailles the victorious nations imposed upon the chief vanquished nation an assertion that this nation was the only real culprit. … It was disastrous because it was bound to create in Germany a festering sore of resentment – as has in fact occurred.'

Fellowship of Reconciliation

Whilst most mainstream churchmen were broadly supportive of the ideals of the League of Nations, there were those who took up a more overt pacifist position. The Fellowship of Reconciliation had been founded in Cambridge in 1914 by a group of pacifist Christians following an ecumenical conference that had been held in Switzerland. However, war broke out before the end of the conference and, at Cologne station, Henry Hodgkin, an English Quaker, and Friedrich Siegmund-Schultze, a German Lutheran, pledged themselves to a continued search for peace with the words 'We are at one in Christ and can never be at war.' Inspired by that pledge, about 130 Christians of all denominations gathered in Cambridge at the end of 1914 and set up the FoR, recording their general agreement in a statement that became 'The Basis' of the Fellowship, namely:

1. That love as revealed and interpreted in the life and death of Jesus Christ involves more than we have yet seen, that is the only power by which evil can be overcome and the only sufficient basis of human society.
2. That, in order to establish a world-order based on Love, it is incumbent upon those who believe in this principle to accept it fully, both for themselves and in relation to others and to take the risks involved in doing so in a world which does not yet accept it.
3. That therefore, as Christians, we are forbidden to wage war, and that our loyalty to our country, to humanity, to the Church Universal, and to Jesus Christ our Lord and Master, calls us instead to a life-service for the enthronement of Love in personal, commercial and national life.
4. That the Power, Wisdom and Love of God stretch far beyond the limits of our present experience, and that He is ever waiting to break forth into human life in new and larger ways.
5. That since God manifests Himself in the world through men and women, we offer ourselves to His redemptive purpose to be used by Him in whatever way He may reveal to us.

In 1929, The FoR launched a 'Christ and Peace' campaign, directed at the churches in order to convince them that Christ and peace were inextricably bound together. This marked the beginning of a decade in which the organisation's main focus was opposition to war based on Christian principles. There were thirty-five meetings attended by about 25,000 people, as well as letter-writing to MPs and education of church members on disarmament.

The Oxford Conference of the Christ and Peace campaign in April 1931 revived the idea of a 'Peace Army', a group of volunteers who would stand in no-man's-land to prevent armies fighting. Harry Brinton, a LNU staff member, wrote a book titled *The Peace Army* in 1932, in which he outlined the concept. According to Brinton, the Peace Army was of purely psychological value. It was assumed that soldiers would not wish to destroy defenceless people. Therefore, the Peace Army was an appeal to human goodness in an environment of evil. Maude Royden, Dick Sheppard and Herbert Gray, a Presbyterian minister and former army chaplain, put out an appeal for volunteers and 800 people responded to the call.

Other FoR members, although sympathetic to the idea, thought it impractical as it would require an immediate change of heart on the part of the soldiers, rather than a long period of education about the evils of war, which is what most members thought was necessary. An FoR leaflet in July 1931 averred that:

> The Christian will be unable to change the heart of the aggressor, the conqueror, the man of coercion, until he has discovered a way of leaving behind the protection of the State and of civilisation and of walking straight out into No Man's Land – defenceless.

A letter appeared in the London Press in February 1932 stating that a Peace Army was destined for the Far East, but could be deployed elsewhere if the League of Nations saw fit. However, Sir Eric Drummond, the secretary general, replied that such matters could only be brought before the League by member nations. Despite some sympathy from Sir John Simon, Britain's chief delegate at Geneva, the idea was dropped.

G. Norman Robbins, who had been an FoR member since 1915, published a book called *Security by Disarmament* in 1932, in which he tried to explain the reasons for people's insecurity, citing physical and spiritual deterioration, natural catastrophes, oppression and poor economic conditions. For Robbins, if a person knew the reasons for their fear, they would be able to overcome it and therefore would not need the protection of arms. He argued that war created psychological and moral wreckage, which gave rise to further insecurity. The only solution to this was total disarmament.

Like many works by FoR members, *Security by Disarmament* did not offer any detailed programme about how to achieve the desired transformations. That is not to say that the FoR was blind to the dangers being presented by the Nazis. Their magazine, *Reconciliation*, carried an editorial in November 1933, commenting on recent events in Germany:

> It may be that the mentality that can fire the Reichstag to provide an excuse and an occasion for seizing power would not hesitate to set Europe alight if power seemed ever so slightly to be slipping from its grasp and if any such device could even temporarily rally to its popular support. And people of that sort are certainly dangerous to the peace and well-being of Europe. Moreover, they are not, at first sight, of a kind to respond to peaceful persuasion.

However, this indictment did not mean that the course of disarmament had to be abandoned:

> Let us ignore the noise and get on with the work. Let us go about to make better and still more genuine use of the League of Nations, even if the German representatives are absent.

Following the withdrawal of Germany from the World Disarmament Conference in October 1933, with multilateral disarmament for all countries now an impossibility, the remaining members wished to engage in collective wars of defence against aggression. This posed a dilemma for FoR members. This was summed up by Lewis Maclachlan: 'Is it better to promise to make war if necessary, knowing that it will then not likely be necessary, than in the name of pacifism make a repudiation of war which is very likely to make war inevitable?' For Maclachlan, any peace founded upon the threat of war, even if the threat were unlikely to be carried out, was only war in disguise.

As well as the Fellowship of Reconciliation, most mainstream Christian denominations had their own pacifist organisations, the most high profile of which was the Anglican Pacifist Fellowship. The fact that two of the most prominent Christian pacifists, Charles Raven and Dick Sheppard, were ordained Anglican ministers gave the movement an enhanced status that it would have struggled to achieve had it just been associated with Quakerism and other Nonconformist groups.

Charles Raven had served as an army chaplain during the First World War, an experience that radically changed his view of himself and his ministry. He had felt the nearness of Christ and the spirit of companionship and self-sacrifice among the men he served, in the 22nd Royal Fusiliers and the 1st Royal Berkshire

Regiment. In 1932, he was elected Regius Professor of Divinity at the University of Cambridge, a post he held until 1950. Raven had become a pacifist in 1930, and joined the Fellowship of Reconciliation, becoming its chairman in 1932. He was one of the sponsors of the Peace Pledge Union and became known as the first major figure in the Anglican Church to give a comprehensive theological justification of pacifism.

In 1935, Raven published *Is War Obsolete?* in which he argued that whilst wars had been a necessary part of the evolutionary process in previous societies and generations, they had now become anachronistic. Slaves had been emancipated, the emancipation of women should open the way for their ordination, the ecumenical movement was bringing together churches that had been divided, and pacifism ought to bring previously warring states together.

A further aspect of Raven's pacifism was that it was not based on revulsion of the pain that war brought, but rather an embracing of pain as the ultimate Christian endeavour. 'Martyrdom is the Christian's ultimate endeavour,' he wrote, citing Christ's crucifixion as the ultimate act of pacifist non–resistance. His 1938 book, *War and the Christian*, acknowledged that the Japanese invasion of Manchuria, Italy's attack on Abyssinia, and the Spanish Civil War posed serious questions for pacifists, but those events showed that war was growing more ghastly by the year, being 'organised hate'. Raven accepted the need for an international police force, collective security and sanctions given the current conditions, on the basis that parts of the world had not yet evolved sufficiently to embrace pacifism.

However, the way to truly disarm aggressors should be through active pacifism:

> Assuming the worst that can be said of Mussolini or Hitler, it remains true that
> an intelligent psychology will approach them fearlessly and without the parade
> of arms, will strive to understand and discuss their grievances and ambitions
> and will meet their advances with generosity and 'sweet reasonableness'.

Raven's next work, published in 1940, was *The Cross and the Crisis*, in which he argued passionately in favour of the power of love to overcome aggression. However, the work did not offer any practical advice to pacifists on how to approach the current situation.

Another member of the APF was the writer Evelyn Underhill. In 1940, she published *The Church and War*, in which she made out a strong case for Christians to renounce war. Underhill argued that the Church had to come to a defined position on war in order to preserve its integrity and spiritual influence. The Christian church, she claimed, was the Body of Christ, with a mission to spread the Spirit of Christ, which is based on wisdom and love. Therefore, the church should never support an individual human or collective action that is hostile to wisdom or love.

War, she continued, is the inflicting of destruction and death on one group by another in pursuit of worldly aims. Those aims are always based on either mortal sin – pride, anger, envy and greed – or a spirit of self-regarding fear, 'which is a worse infidelity to God than any mortal sin'. Christians should look towards Christ's actions in the Garden of Gethsemane, where Peter was rebuked for raising his sword to defend Christ from arrest. If the direct defence of Christ with violence was not justified, then neither could any cause be noble enough to bear arms for. The world was not to be saved by resort to arms, but by the 'suffering, patience and sacrificial love of the Cross'.

Evil should be defeated by love, to 'open a channel for the inflow of the creative grace of God'. Underhill asserted that this was the only struggle in which a true Christian could take part. There was no place for retaliation, revenge, or even a defensive war, which she likened to 'destroying our brother to prevent him from destroying us'. Armament factories were designed to produce weapons to kill, from a notion based on fear, whilst the gospel of Matthew had stated, 'Fear not them which kill the body.'

The Christian Church, she went on, should not consider questions of expediency, practicality, national prestige or national safety, as these derive from human egotism and human fear. The business that the Church should concern itself with is the law of charity, thus bringing the will of man into harmony with the will of God. Loving and selfless co-operation between man and God would lead to selfless co-operation between men. Energies now wasted on conflict will be turned to the purposes of life.

The Church will only have an effective message, argued Underhill, when it devotes its message to the will of God: 'She cannot minister with one hand the Chalice of Salvation, whilst with the other she blesses the instruments of death.' Individual Christians needed to find the boundary between keeping order between humans, without using destructive force. The right ordering of society is part of a creative task, but war cannot be compromised on. The Church cannot stand aside and take a neutral stance on war. War, at its worst, is 'devilry', and the church falls from grace if it condones it.

The Church was, for Underhill, being granted a great opportunity to work for the Spirit of God, through the stirring in minds of a desire for peace. Only Christianity can say why the effects of war are evil and offer a method to address the evil at source, in the hearts of men. 'Christianity alone holds to solution of humanity's most terrible and pressing problem.'

However, the church was still too concerned with pleasing men, and not in renouncing the world's methods. Therefore, its influence is weak, and only when it accepts its true purpose, will it become 'the organ of earth of the Divine transforming power'.

Canon Stuart Morris was another architect of the APF, an organisation he created as well as serving as chairman and secretary of the PPU. Morris resigned from Holy Orders shortly after the outbreak of war and was arrested in 1942 for having breached the Official Secrets Act by receiving documents on how an Indian uprising led by Gandhi would be dealt with. He received a nine-month prison sentence and was forced to resign from his position within the PPU.

One young Anglican curate who was a convinced pre-war pacifist was Rupert Godfrey. (Plates, page 10) A graduate of Oxford University, he had been a student at the time of the anti-war motion of 1933 and had subsequently joined the PPU. By 1938, he was serving as a curate at St George's Church in Edgbaston, Birmingham, and on 18 September he preached a sermon based on the text of 1 Chronicles, 28:3: 'But God said unto me, "Thou shalt not build a house for my name because thou hast been a man of war and hast shed blood."' His sermon notes recorded:

> While we kneel here this morning there are people just like us in Germany shuddering inwardly. They know that modern war means bombing of civilian populations, incendiary bombs and machine-gunning from the air. They know that Britain's long-range bombers will be used for that end against them. ... How can we as Christians remain on our knees a moment longer without saying, 'No, under no circumstances whatever will we lift a finger to set those infernal machines to work.'
>
> The question is no longer – are we prepared to die for our country or are we prepared to defend our dearest? The question is now – are we prepared to let our menfolk rain destruction and torture on innocent women and children? Can we imagine Christ doing such a thing under any circumstances whatsoever? We cannot. Therefore we ought not to ourselves.

Godfrey went on to point out the cost of 40 million lives of the previous war, with no worthwhile outcomes. Therefore, there was, for him, no other course for a Christian minister but to preach war renunciation, and to lead his congregation to pray for peace. By March 1940, during the period known as the Phoney War, before Germany's blitzkrieg through much of northern Europe, he preached on the text from Matthew 5:25: 'Agree with thine adversary quickly whiles thou art in the way with him.' He recognised that the Christian pacifist faced a dilemma in wartime; between publicly expressing his views that might undermine the national war effort, and refraining from the public expression of views, thus not being true to himself.

For Godfrey, the implications of the words in his chosen text were that the current lull in hostilities presented a chance for a negotiated peace with Germany. He cited Jesus's forty days in the wilderness and his rejection of the temptation of the kingdoms of the world, as an example to Christians that force should not be used to bring in Christ's kingdom. Christian pacifists were therefore under a moral obligation to declare their view, like the Old Testament prophets, 'whether they will hear or whether they will forbear'.

However, Godfrey, like many pre-war Christian pacifists, found that the events of 1940 challenged and profoundly altered his view. In September of that year he preached on the text from 1 Maccabees 2:40: 'And one of them said to another, If we all do as our brethren have done and fight not for our lives and laws against the heathen they will now quickly root us out of the earth.' He likened the situation of the Maccabees in the Bible to that of Britain, of a small and peace-loving nation at war with a cruel and unscrupulous alien power. Some of the Jews of the time had offered no resistance when the enemy attacked, 'and were unfortunately mown down to a man'. Their fellows were thus stirred into taking up arms. The unwelcome truth had dawned that pacifism would lead to Britain and its libertarian traditions being rooted out of the earth.

Godfrey commented on the 'seven solid years' he had spent giving voice to pacifist opinions, 'in season and out of season, by printed word and word of mouth, from pulpits, platforms and soapboxes'. These were weighty arguments backed by scripture, and some of profoundest thinkers of the age, and ones that in time, 'the whole of mankind must come'. However, the pacifist position for Godfrey was no longer tenable. Britain's national heritage, democratic institutions, and traditions of liberty were under threat from the 'clutching claws of the German werewolf. ... The Pax Germanica bears no resemblance to the Kingdom of God.'

Therefore, it was the current world situation, not the principles of pacifism, that were at fault: 'in a world of sinful mortals its counsels of perfection are no longer applicable. We have tried to lead humanity too far forward on the path of progress and it has got left behind.' Godfrey then made the brave statement: 'I would therefore wish to repudiate and take back all such statements of mine as have in the past suggested that the Christian's duty today lies elsewhere than in supporting the war.' There was no acceptable middle ground for him. Allowing for Britain's part in allowing the war to begin, 'surely even the God who looks down from heaven, a God who we know through Jesus Christ, a God who is a moral God, must differentiate between those of his children who, however imperfectly, try to follow what is right and those others of his children who in their own interests deliberately flaunt it.'

The upcoming National Day of Prayer was therefore 'in full accordance with the will of God'. The prayers would, in a dark time, ensure that 'God in our hour of trial will not desert us, but having heard our prayer will secure the ultimate triumph of light over darkness, of freedom over slavery, of humanity over ruthlessness.'

Following this sermon, Godfrey joined the Royal Army Chaplains' Department and was attached to the 48th Light Anti-Aircraft Regiment of the Royal Artillery. In December 1941 he set sail for the Far East theatre of war and was captured by the Japanese. He was imprisoned in Java and Japan and kept meticulous records of the men he served with, and the sermons he preached while in camp.

The Roman Catholic equivalent of the APF was the PAX, a peace organisation established by Eric Gill, E.I. Watkin and Donal Attwater. Gill's grandfather and great-uncle had been Congregational missionaries, and his father had moved between Congregationalism and Anglicanism. Gill had created controversial war memorials, notably the one at the University of Leeds, unveiled in 1923, depicting Christ expelling well-to-do Leeds citizens from the Temple with the inscription, 'Go to now, ye rich men, weep and howl.' In 1939, Gill pointed out that British, Irish and American Roman Catholics had taken opposing moral views about the war, and that, 'In any case, it is Catholic teaching that the individual conscience is the final judge.'

The Quaker churches had been committed to non-resistance since 1661, with many of their number exercising the conscience clause during the First World War. Of the tiny number of 350 total exemptions given to the 16,500 applicants for conscientious objection during the first war, the majority had gone to Quakers. The sect was always known for its practical actions, and the Second World War would prove no exception, with large-scale civilian relief operations organised (see Chapter 7). However, the Quakers did not wait until the outbreak of war to organise to alleviate suffering. In 1933, the Germany Emergency Committee of the Religious Society of Friends (GEC) was set up. This committee, alongside other groups, was responsible for helping Jewish children escape Nazi persecution in Germany, Czechoslovakia, Austria and Poland. For those children fortunate enough to be liberated by the GEC, support was then given to settle into life in their receiving countries. This was part of a wider effort organised by the Friends Service Council to report and act on conditions in Germany for those persecuted for racial, religious and political reasons. The GEC, whose secretary was Bertha Bracey, also assisted in the evacuation of refugees from Italian fascist oppression through the free port of Shanghai, the only city in the world where refugees could enter without a visa.

The most well known of these relief operations with a significant Quaker involvement was the Kindertransport. (Plates, page 9) Following Kristallnacht, the night of broken glass, on 9 November 1938, it became clear even to most Nazi apologists that there was a systematic persecution of Jews being enacted in Germany. Jewish shops, buildings and synagogues were destroyed throughout Nazi-controlled territories, with homes, schools and hospitals also targeted. Ninety-one Jews were killed and 30,000 arrested. Thus, it was apparent that Jewish people were in immediate and severe danger. Therefore, a consortium of British Jews arranged for six Quaker volunteers, including Bertha Bracey, to travel to Berlin to report on the situation there.

Bracey met with Wilfred Israel, who had been using his department store in Berlin to engineer the release of many Jews from concentration camps by allowing Nazi leaders great leniency in settling their accounts. He introduced her to the heads of Jewish women's organisations from across Germany. These meetings were crucial to the success of the Kindertransport, as it persuaded mothers to allow their children to leave Germany unaccompanied by any members of their family.

Bracey reported back that unaccompanied children should be granted entry into Britain. This information was passed to Prime Minister Neville Chamberlain, who refused the request. In response to Chamberlain, a joint Quaker and Jewish delegation met with the Home Secretary, Samuel Hoare. The government's response was to 'give the necessary visas and facilitate entry into this country'. The lobbying had proved successful, and the government announced it would permit an unspecified number of children to enter the UK.

The children were labelled 'transmigrants' and a £50 bond was required for each child. On 8 December 1938, former Prime Minister Stanley Baldwin launched the Lord Baldwin Fund for Refugees in a special 15-minute national radio appeal broadcast by the BBC. This fund contributed a considerable amount to the financing of the Kindertransport.

By the summer of 1939, the Lord Baldwin Fund had raised over £500,000. Next, a network of Quaker and refugee organisations issued statements in many Jewish communities in central Europe. Parents were able to register their children for the transportation in offices that issued travel papers allowing the children to pass to Britain through the Netherlands.

Quakers and the Refugee Children's Movement sent notices to cities from Stuttgart to Prague. Jewish community centres were also crucial to getting the news of the transports to parents and communities. The large Jewish communities in Prague and Vienna were key in co-ordinating the evacuation of children from these areas. Within days of the announcement, thousands of children had signed up to leave in the first wave.

On 1 December 1938, trains packed with children left European cities bound for the Hook of Holland. Quaker volunteers chaperoned each stage of the journey to ensure the safety of the children. The British government assured the safety of the transports, but not the children. Travelling on the Kindertransport was far from pleasant. Apart from the agony of separation from family, the Nazis made sure the journey was humiliating and terrifying. Trains were grimly sealed. Parents were sometimes not permitted to say goodbye in public. The children had to take trains to Holland so that they would not 'sully' German ports. Their luggage was torn apart by guards searching for valuables.

The first train brought 200 children from a Jewish orphanage in Berlin that had been destroyed during Kristallnacht. When the trains began to arrive in London they were met by Quakers at Liverpool Street station. Here the children were given food and accommodation was arranged for them. They were found homes with Quaker families and communities throughout the country. There were anywhere from 120–250 children on each transport and in total, 10,000 refugee children made the journey.

Once Kindertransport children had reached the safety of Britain, they needed to be supported, assessed and allocated appropriate places. The Quakers formed the Movement for the Care of Children from Germany and this group purchased the Palace Hotel in Bloomsbury, London, which became known as Bloomsbury House. This was a vast, decaying building but it was large enough to provide accommodation for the refugees and administration areas. There was a huge reception hall where refugees would sit to wait to have their case discussed. The Kindertransport, now renamed the Movement for the Care of Children from Germany, was under the day-by-day supervision of Sir Charles Stead, a Home Office civil servant, and the chairwoman, Lady Reading, widow of a former viceroy of India, would visit nearly every day. Anna Freud, daughter of Sigmund, was the consultant psychologist for Bloomsbury House. She put an end to the hostel's rule that children must line up, plate in hand, for their food to be doled out to them. Freud said they must all sit round a big table and be served by the House Mother.

Arrangements then had to be made for the children's long-term education and training. Once again, Quakers were to the fore. Throughout the 1930s, Ayton Quaker School in North Yorkshire, one of twelve such establishments in England, accepted refugees from Germany and occupied territories. In 1935, the school was a refuge for forty children from Germany, Austria and Czechoslovakia. By 1938, this number had increased substantially. Ayton became known as an established destination for scholars fleeing persecution. Scholarships were arranged through refugee aid organisations including the GEC. Hans Reichenfeld, one of the children to arrive in 1938, was one such refugee helped by this process. He would later become a pioneer of geriatric psychiatry in Canada.

The Butlin's Dovercourt Holiday Camp near Harwich was also taken on by Quaker and Jewish groups as lodging for newly arrived children. The organisations paid for all provisions at Dovercourt, agreeing that Butlin's would provide the food. Lady Marion Phillips of the Women's Voluntary Services, who visited Dovercourt in January 1939, reported that the children seemed 'wonderfully happy, considering all they had been through'. Other visitors remarked that 'the heating, clothing, sanitation and health were good'.

Another centre that housed Kindertransport children was Bunce Court in Kent. Anna Essinger, the headmistress of Landschulheim Herrlingen school in Baden-Wurttemberg, had raised funds from British Quakers to purchase the property. Essinger was placed under Nazi investigation in April 1933 when she was denounced for refusing to fly the Nazi flag and swastika at the school. She informed the parents of her desire to move the school to England and received permission to evacuate sixty-five children with her. The old school was seized by the Nazis and used to house Jewish seniors who had been forcibly relocated from Wurttemberg. When the Kindertransports began, Bunce Court and Kent Quakers took in as many of the refugees as possible. When the transports stopped in 1939, Bunce Court continued to take in refugees on scholarships. After the war, orphaned children who had survived the concentration camps and Buchenwald and Theresienstadt, and the ghetto at Częstochowa, were brought to Bunce Court in 1946. Over 900 children passed through the school before its closure in 1948.

The Cheadle Local Meeting in Lancashire opened the first refugee hostels for Kindertransport children and later hostels for refugee children spread across the north-west of England in Liverpool, Manchester, Blackpool, and Southport. Despite the strict enforcement of 'alien' restrictions many children were able to study, and young adults found work. Hilde Rujder, who had travelled to Britain in 1938, remembered her time in Liverpool: 'The Quakers had no conversionist intent in this relaxed hostel, [when] in the evening the residents would gather in the lounge to solve the problems of the world.' Hilde later enrolled at Liverpool School of Art and regularly attend Cheadle Quaker meetings.

Although the Kindertransport scheme ended out of necessity on 30 August 1939, British Quakers had been instrumental in the salvation of 60,000 children from German-controlled Europe.

Stanley Baldwin.

Benito Mussolini, Adolf Hitler and Neville Chamberlain meet in Munich in 1938.

Above: *Canon Dick Sheppard.*

Left: *Robert Cecil.*

Pablo Picasso's anti-war painting Guernica, *1937.*

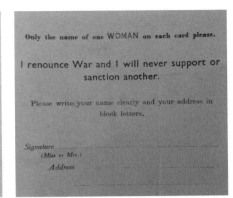

Peace Pledge Union cards for men and women.

League of Nations Union badge.

An appeal for funds from the Peace Pledge Union for the Basque Children's Centre at Langham in Suffolk.

Peace Service Handbook issued by the Peace Pledge Union in May 1939.

Selling Peace News, *the pacifist magazine first published in June 1936.*

Cyril Joad.

Max Plowman.

Above: *Dr Alfred Salter (left) and George Lansbury.*

Right: *Fenner Brockway.*

Harry Pollitt.

Richard Stokes MP.

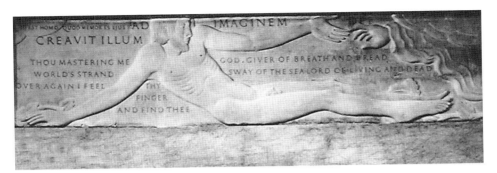

Eric Gill's panel for the Assembly Hall in the League of Nations building in Geneva.

Frank Meisler's bronze sculpture Kindertransport – The Arrival, *which stands at Liverpool Street station, London.* (Courtesy of Bryn Reynolds)

Rupert Godfrey. (Courtesy of the Godfrey family)

Leslie Weatherhead.

Judge Edwin Cooper Burgis, Chairman of the North West conscientious objection tribunal.

Norman Proctor, human guinea pig.

Hans Krebs.

Vera Brittain.

NATURE NOTES
Birds in Scrubland

Cartoons from The Flowery, *the magazine produced by inmates of Wormwood Scrubs from 1942–44.* (Courtesy of the University of Sheffield Special Collections)

(*October*, 1942)

A UTUMNAL days bring out in Scrubland the pale beauty of the Lesser Wryneck (*Wormwoodia Scrubicus*). Owing to the peculiar crest or visor with which a misguided Providence equipped the species, the baleful eyes are seldom seen. (There are those who aver that this idiosyncratic baleful eye is what attracts the female in the mating season. There is however no verification of this.) Its mournful tones pervade the scrubs at all hours, but it is well to remember that as a Protected (Jail) Bird there is no shooting season.

O CTOBER! The time of year when all Nature lovers are regaled by the bright crimson throat plumage of the Scrubby Bullfinch (*Stevii Prisonicus*). A shy bird, and it is with intense pride that we reproduce this unique telescopic infra-red ray close-up. In its natural element it can be seen only by the most patient of watchers. Its gentle call, on the other hand, is known to all—"Git-abucket, Git-abucket."

13

Oliver Postgate. (Courtesy of the Postgate family)

Conscientious objector Harold Hitchcock (second from right, in spectacles), who worked as a wartime bomb disposal officer. (Courtesy of Leonard Hitchcock)

18 Oakholme Road, Broomhill in Sheffield, where conscientious objectors were subjected to medical experiments.

Dresden in ruins after the Allied bombing campaign of February 1945.

Hiroshima laid to waste after the atomic bomb of 6 August 1945.

Debates about peace and war had consumed much of Methodist thinking throughout the 1930s. In November 1929, a meeting had been held at Kingsway Hall in London titled 'Methodism and World Peace'. In the weeks preceding the meeting there had been discussions in the pages of the *Methodist Recorder* on the subject. One October editorial had declared that a resort to war was justified on some occasions and that pacifism was a 'counsel of despair' and that its adherents would be more at home in a debating society than the real world. One young Wesleyan who objected to the tone of this piece was Reverend Leslie Weatherhead. He was given the right of reply in the 7 November edition, in which he bemoaned the fact that the younger generation knew little of the 'wickedness and waste of war', and that war itself was unchristian. The medals that had been awarded in previous wars were rewards for 'murder and mutilation, tears and treachery, lust and lies'.

Weatherhead's piece caused outrage amongst many Methodists, some of whom accused him of 'slander' and of causing hurt to the families of those who had died in the first war. Weatherhead responded with the declaration:

> No nation has yet been Christian enough to try Christ's way. If it did and even the worst happened – which I do not think possible – then a crucified nation would do for the world what a crucified Christ did and is doing. If a whole nation is determined to take Christ's way it may have to give up its life for its beliefs.

Following his outspoken response in the *Methodist Recorder*, Weatherhead emerged as another leading pacifist voice within the Church. He spoke regularly on the wireless and was appointed as minister of the Congregational City Temple in London in 1936. He argued, in 1935, that the possession of many overseas territories meant that Britain was in no position to criticise Mussolini's attack on Abyssinia and his desire for an Italian Empire. Weatherhead had been vocal in his denunciation of political attempts to solve the international tensions throughout the 1930s, but began to alter his position following the invasion of Czechoslovakia in 1938. In 1939, he published *Thinking Aloud in Wartime*, in which he stated that it was 'retrogressive at this stage to abandon the final appeal to force' and that 'it would be wrong not to resist' the challenge of Nazi Germany. He concluded, 'I used to think that it might be better to be invaded than to fight, but a realisation of the doctrines which those hold who now threaten us makes me feel that it would be wrong not to resist that for which they stand.' Weatherhead accepted that international affairs required a sober analysis of specific situations, as well as consideration of abstract principles.

Four years after the Weatherhead debate, following the Oxford Union 'King and Country' motion, Reverend Henry Carter wrote on similar lines in the *Methodist Recorder* that 'the abolition of war ... is dependent upon the absolute renunciation of war and the war-spirit by the Christian because he is a Christian.' Carter stated that he would 'reason, preach and write against it', and advised the use of any lawful means to dissuade others from recourse to fighting. However, A.W. Harrison argued for a more diplomatic approach. Whilst a distaste for war was shared by most Christians, there should be no attempt to undermine attempts to address the complex international situation, including supporting the League of Nations and providing it with sufficient resources to ensure the success of collective security. The case made by Harrison, and many others within the Methodist Church, was that pacifism was a position based on emotion rather than reason.

The Methodist Conference of July 1933 came to an agreement on its attitude to war, issuing a declaration that war was a 'crime against humanity' and arguing for a worldwide reduction in armaments. On the question of the individual's participation in war, both pacifists and believers in collective security were acknowledged in that there were those 'whose inward conviction and loyalty to Christ compel them to oppose war in all cases' whilst others 'with equal sincerity [accept] obligations, commitments and loyalties of a national or international character which they deem binding on the body politic and themselves within it'.

In the same year, a Methodist Peace Fellowship (MPF) had been set up by, among others, Henry Carter and Donald Soper. Its covenant proclaimed that war was 'contrary to the spirit, teaching and purpose of Jesus Christ our Lord' as modern warfare in particular involved 'the destruction of human life without mercy or limits'. The MPF gained 500 ministers shortly after its inception, a figure that rose to over 750 by 1939. There were also 3,000 lay members. Reverend Henry Carter also accompanied George Lansbury on some of his Embassies of Reconciliation to Europe, hoping to foster personal ties that would break down barriers of distrust and fear. He also visited Spain in 1937, during the civil war, an experience that led him to attack Franco as responsible for the conflict.

Both Carter and Donald Soper, whose 1935 book *Question Time on Tower Hill* set out his belief that war was contrary to the spirit and teaching of Jesus Christ, hoped that a renunciation of violence could transform social and political force, hence Soper's claim that 'pacifism contains a spiritual force strong enough to repel any invader.' They both hoped to persuade the British government into a policy of unilateral disarmament, which would alter the dynamics of world politics. Thus Methodist voices formed a significant part of Christian pacifist thought and action during the 1930s.

Although following a generally pacifistic line throughout most of the 1930s, the Methodist press was also broadly tolerant of Hitler's tearing up of the terms of the Treaty of Versailles. In the week following the remilitarisation of the Rhineland in 1936, the *Methodist Recorder* noted, 'sometimes the only method of procuring an amendment of an unjust law is simple and with forethought determination to break the law.' However, the newspaper was condemnatory of the Nazi's domestic policies. In August 1938 it carried an editorial on 'Christian Civilisation', which argued that Christians should not ignore persecutions and suffering across Europe.

However, letters to the paper revealed the continuing split in Methodist ranks about the best way of securing peace. One letter claimed that rearmament was a 'purely pagan policy', whilst others argued that aggression could only be stopped if Britain were better armed. One correspondent termed the pacifist movement 'mistaken and mischievous'. A 'Liberty of Conscience' agreement at the 1936 Methodist Conference helped to prevent a split in the Church but did not bring the two sides closer together.

One of the most outspoken Methodist critics of the government's appeasement policy from 1937 onwards was Isaac Foot, a Liberal politician and the father of future Labour leader Michael Foot. He argued that, following the Munich Agreement of 1938, relief over the avoidance of war should be tempered by a 'sense of shame'. Speaking to the *Methodist Recorder*, questioning the morality of a peace based on the surrender of central Europe's only democracy to an arbitrary power, he argued that Chamberlain was reacting to events rather than trying to shape them. Methodists, Foot claimed, had 'higher standards to observe than any Cabinet or Parliament', and should find ways to resist the forces of militarism and destruction.

For most in the Methodist Church, the grotesque character of the Nazi regime served to clarify the ethical questions that had been debated during the 1930s. The idea of any moral equivalence between the Allied and Axis powers was a difficult case to make, and those pacifists who continued to oppose Britain's part in the war could only do so on the grounds that the ethical imperative to eschew the taking up of arms under any circumstance outweighed any moral obligation to bring to an end the Nazi terror. However, there was further debate to be had between those Christians who argued that victory should be gained at any cost, and those who thought that the conflict should be fought along the just war principles outlined by St Augustine many centuries beforehand.

The first dilemma facing the Methodist Church was its response to the introduction of conscription for men aged 20 and 21 in 1939. Membership of the MPF grew after this policy was adopted, and the organisation committed itself to supporting young men who raised a conscientious objection to military service at tribunal hearings. The MPF gained further recruits in the period leading up to the fall of France in May 1940, and whilst letters critical of the group continued to be published in the *Methodist Recorder*, they did not contain the same degree of animosity as had been directed against the conscientious objectors of 1916. However, there were references to 'pacifists, peace-cranks and conscientious objectors' and calls for those holding pacifist views to be refused entry into the ministry.

The 1941 Annual Conference passed a statement referring to the 'sacred cause' of the war, bringing objections from Henry Carter and others. However, staunch pacifists like Donald Soper were forced to re-evaluate their views on pacifism as a viable means of preventing conflict. Soper noted, towards the end of the war, that 'The utilitarian argument for non-violence breaks down under the overwhelming pressure of brute fact. ... I am alone sustained by the Christian faith which assures me that what is morally right comes with the ultimate resources of the universe.'

By the 1943 conference, some pacifists were beginning to question whether a Christian life could be led in the secular world, or if a retreat into Christian communities separated from contemporary culture was needed. However, leading Methodist pacifists such as Henry Carter thought that this would be giving up on the cause of peace, and, alongside the Anglican Charles Raven, formed a Pacifist Council of the Christian Church, in order to try to influence public opinion. By this stage of the war there was overwhelming popular support for the war against the axis powers, and improved morale following the victories in North Africa and Italy.

Therefore, Christian pacifist groups such as the Fellowship of Reconciliation had to accept the reality of the situation, although an order of service produced for use at Christmas in wartime showed that their core principles had remained:

> Although the nations see Him not at work; though brutal minds discern no design in the unfolding picture of events; while science can construe the face of skies and penetrate the secrets of the earth, but cannot read the signs of these our times though the house of heaven be invisible and the world's ears untuned to hear the angels' song, we sing
>
> Glory to God in the highest and on earth peace
>
> Not by confederate violence or nice adjustment of opposing might; but reconciling each to each by bringing all the God, thus following the way by which a little child shall lead, we give
>
> Glory to God in the highest and on earth peace

By the meekness and the gentleness of Christ; by refusal to coerce and willingness to serve; shunning to exercise authority and owning no man anything but love, we render
Glory to God in the highest and on earth peace.

As the effects of the Blitz worsened, some members of the FoR renounced their absolute pacifism, and joined the armed services. One person had worked for a mobile hospital unit in London during the air raids, but, 'I did not feel it was right for me to enjoy home comforts and a relatively good wage when these were denied to most people of my age, so I volunteered for the RAF Medical Service.' The issue of pacifists either renouncing their absolutist stance or finding an accommodation of their pacifism within the military machine will be examined in forthcoming chapters.

During the 1930s and 1940s, Britain was, by many measurements, a Christian country. Most people had, at some point, been exposed to the Christian message at Sunday school or church, and the overwhelming majority ascribed to a belief in God, largely one of a Christian conception. It was no surprise, therefore, that a substantial philosophical thrust of the peace movement was based on one interpretation of Christian principles, that of Christ as peacemaker and eschewer of violence. This interpretation was shared by Christians across all major denominations and those leaders who represented these views were able to generate a great deal of publicity for their cause. Their views were sincerely held and steadfastly clung on to during wartime. However, the fact remained that the vast majority of Christians in Britain who were liable for military service agreed to serve in the armed forces, or industries directly related to the war effort. Christian pacifism remained, therefore, a voluble but minority strand of thought within the British churches.

Chapter 6

Refusing to Serve –
Conscientious Objection

On 26 April 1939, Prime Minister Neville Chamberlain announced to the House of Commons that His Majesty's Government intended to introduce a limited form of conscription for men aged 20 and 21. He had correctly judged that public opinion was ready for such a decision, although both Clement Attlee, the leader of the Labour Party, and John McGovern, the Independent Labour Party leader, accused the Prime Minister of breaking previous promises. Chamberlain attempted an emollient tone:

> We all recognise that there are people who have genuine and very deep-seated scruples on the subject of military service, and even if we do not agree with those scruples we can respect them if they are honestly held. I think we found it was both a useless and exasperating waste of time to force these people to act in a manner contrary to their convictions.

However, this was nowhere near enough to appease some pacifists. In a letter published in *The Times* on 1 May 1939, Henry Carter, Charles Raven and others claimed that 'the compulsory training of men to slaughter their fellow-men is to us intolerable … socially too, conscription is a retrograde step, a move away from democracy towards the enthronement of militarism and totalitarianism.'

A demonstration took place in London's West End involving 5,000 men and women, but there was little widespread protest throughout the country.

Provisions made for conscientious objection enjoyed wider public support than they had in 1916. All men had to register for military service at a local employment exchange, and at that point they had the option to be officially registered as a conscientious objector. All registrations took place on a Saturday, and men (and later, women) were allocated a date to attend based on their date of birth. If they did register as objectors, they would be called before a local tribunal to state their case. There were four possible outcomes the tribunal could decide: firstly to give the objector complete exemption from any compulsion to serve in any capacity; secondly to grant an exemption from military service, but to order work of national importance on the land or elsewhere; thirdly to grant exemption from combatant duties within the military, through service in a non-fighting service such as the Royal Army Medical Corps (RAMC) or the Non-Combatant Corps; and lastly, the objection could be overruled, and the individual left liable for any military service against his or her will.

The local tribunals were chaired by a judge, rather than a military officer, to ensure adherence to the law, and 2.2 per cent of the first wartime batch of conscripts availed themselves of the conscience clause. This number fell over the course of the war to 1.2 per cent of those called up. In 1941, conscription was extended to single women aged from 19 to 31, with the option for them to choose industrial or civil work if they so desired. Around 1,000 women became conscientious objectors. The range of reasons given for a conscientious objection fell into three main areas, although often they overlapped each other. There were religious convictions, political beliefs and outlook, and moral and humanitarian reasoning.

Sixteen regional tribunals were set up across the United Kingdom, based in county courts in major cities under the auspices of the Ministry of Labour. Initially a tribunal panel consisted of a chairman and four other people. The chairman was always a county court judge, or a sheriff in Scotland. The four other members had to include a trade unionist and a woman if a female objection case was being heard. The average age for a panel member was 65, far removed from the 20-somethings who made up the bulk of objectors. If an objector's case was rejected, he or she had recourse to an appellate tribunal.

Denis Hayes, chairman of the Central Board for Conscientious Objectors (CBCO), claimed that the tribunals were 'quite nice to folk on the whole'. *Peace News* of 3 November 1939 was forced to concede that, in early cases at least, there was an 'almost complete absence ... of the scorn and hatred for COs' evident in the first war. The CBCO helped some objectors to prepare for their hearing by holding mock tribunals, and local groups produced pamphlets with advice on how to tackle questions. One, published by the London Friends' Local Conscription Committee with the assistance of the Fellowship of Reconciliation, was *The London Tribunal Questions the CO*. In it were questions such as:

> Are you sure that your objection is one of conscience and not of reasoning or mere dislike?
>
> Why would you not be willing to defend other people's happiness and freedom?
>
> Do you not think the soldiers are standing up for what they think is right?

If you love your fellow men do you not want to protect them?

If you object to taking life, are you a vegetarian?

What would you do if other people, or children, were attacked in your presence?

Why is it wrong to defend your country in time of danger?

The objective was not to provide model answers to the questions, but to help the objector clarify his thinking before appearing before the tribunal.

There were fewer absolutist objectors than in the first war as the issue of assisting the war effort during the Second World War posed a more nuanced challenge than it had in 1916 for the committed pacifist. Whilst direct military service could be objected to under a conscience clause, it was harder to justify a refusal to take part in Air Raid Precaution work. On the one hand, state-directed preparation for war could be seen as part of a wider agenda of militarising the population, but a refusal to take part in ARP work could be seen to be putting fellow citizens at risk. J.D. Bernal had written in *Peace* magazine, 'It is in the day-to-day local struggle against Air Raid Precaution that the question of war or peace can most closely touch the citizens of this country.'

Once air raids became a regular occurrence during the war, the Peace Pledge Union's stance on pacifists assisting the ARP work was ambiguous, deciding that the degree of involvement was a matter for individual consciences. However, it was when men were called up for military service that a direct objection to war had to be acted upon and argued through to a logical conclusion. From November 1939, tribunals were empowered to grant a conditional registration to a man as a conscientious objector as long as he undertook civil defence work or agricultural labour.

By January 1941, just 2,239 out of 34,793 conscientious objectors who had appeared before a tribunal had received an unconditional registration, not required to work for the war effort, and 12,907 were conditionally registered, on the understanding that service on the home front would be undertaken. Therefore, the majority either volunteered for, or were directed into, non-combatant military service or enrolled into the armed services. Behind these figures were significant regional variations, with the tribunals covering the most heavily bombed areas; London and the industrial areas of Lancashire and Glasgow were less likely to grant objectors a conditional or unconditional registration.

Just because a tribunal had directed men towards a particular area of work, it did not mean that services were comfortable absorbing them into their ranks. In June 1940, the London Fire Brigade objected to the number of objectors applying for employment on the grounds that many firemen were ex-servicemen, and there could be some friction between the two groups. The London County Council ordered the London Ambulance Service not to enrol conscientious objectors in their ranks. A march of army Northern Command late in 1940 saw the Royal Army Medical Corps contingent booed as they passed through the city of Leeds, due to the impression that had been formed that the corps had become a receptacle for objectors within the armed services.

Central Board for Conscientious Objectors

In 1939, around 100 groups across Britain came together to form the CBCO. Many of them were led by veteran conscientious objectors from the first war and worked to advise and inform COs of their rights under the Military Service Act, to act as a government-recognised organisation that should be consulted an all matters relating to conscientious objection, and to keep records of objectors and tribunal hearings. In the CBCO's early stages it agreed to represent all COs, whether they be absolutist pacifists or people who only objected to certain tasks within the war effort.

The CBCO scrutinised often complex legislation, issuing monthly bulletins and broadsheets. The CBCO endeavoured to attend all tribunal hearings and filed a report to the board's headquarters. The material needs of the families of COs were catered for while periods of imprisonment were served. An employment agency was established, under licence from the London County Council, for COs who found it difficult to obtain work on their release from prison, or who wished to do work of benefit to the community.

Fenner Brockway, the veteran pacifist, socialist and founder member of the CBCO, reflected at the end of the war that 'Conscientious Objectors are often regarded as fanatics, and fanatics are difficult people to get on with. Yet, without any qualifications, I can say that in forty years' experience of innumerable councils and committees I have never known such a harmonious body as the Central Board for Conscientious Objectors.' The group harmonised the approach of pacifists and non-pacifists, of every religious denomination from Catholics to Quakers, of absolutists and members of the Non-Combatant Corps (NCC), socialists and individualists. That was due, for Brockway, to the basic principle of tolerance and respect for the convictions of others.

One aspect of the CBCO's work was to arrange mock tribunals. John Bishop, a young Methodist conscientious objector from Luton recalled:

> Yes. I think my brother first had become aware of a group that met once a
> week in the Quaker, in the Friends Meeting House in Luton and I began to

go to that fairly regularly and made one or two friends there. ... So yes, we did talk about it and one or two embattled old Conscientious Objectors from the First World War gave us mock tribunals and sort of gave us a roughish time in order that we had some understanding of what we were likely to face when we went to, as I understood it, five county court judges [who] made up the tribunal.

Concerns were raised in Parliament about such coaching. On 6 June 1940, Sir Henry Morris-Jones, the Liberal National MP for Denbigh, asked the Home Secretary, Sir John Anderson, whether his attention had been drawn to PPU meetings recently held in Wales, particularly at a college in Bangor on 25 May. Morris-Jones was concerned that PPU members from London were infiltrating the rural areas of Wales, 'endeavouring to thwart and divert our war effort'. Anderson replied that this was, according to his sources, a meeting of local PPU members at Bangor Baptist College. Morris-Jones claimed that the PPU was holding classes to coach conscientious objectors before they appeared before the tribunals and wished that the chief constables of the Welsh counties have their attention drawn to this practice.

However, the government maintained good relations with the CBCO and the organisation continued to publish literature to guide COs through laws relating to conscription. This tolerant attitude of the state ensured that, on the whole, objectors were fairly dealt with. Nevertheless, there were some notable exceptions to this overall picture.

The work of the tribunals

The chairman on the South-East tribunal drew up some guidance notes for its members in autumn 1941, which displayed some degree of sympathy for the arguments he anticipated being brought before them:

> It must be borne in mind that a belief that war is horrible or futile or unnecessary may lead to a conviction that it is wrong ... the fact that an applicant balances the evils of war against the evils of submission to Hitler is not necessarily inconsistent with his being convinced that military service would violate his conscience.

However, not all tribunal chairmen were as sympathetic to the views of COs. The CBCO kept meticulous records of the outcomes at different tribunals, with the north-west tribunal being particularly criticised for its harshness. Tribunals heard cases from objectors who expressed their renunciation of war based on a variety of premises, including political objection to fighting a capitalist war. One example of the treatment that political objectors faced, and the response that could be provoked by those of a left-wing outlook, was seen in Scotland in early 1940.

The decisions of the Glasgow and South-West Scotland tribunal had given concern to John McGovern, an Independent Labour MP, and led to a fiery exchange of words, which was reported in *The Scotsman* of 19 January 1940. McGovern, while representing an applicant, announced, 'I have been watching the operations of this tribunal and I consider that all the time we are getting biased opinions – so much so that we have decided to raise the whole behaviour of this tribunal in the proper quarter.' McGovern was joined in his protest by members of the Glasgow Town Council. In response, the tribunal's chairman, Sir Archibald Campbell Black, ordered the courtroom to be cleared, with the applicants being heard in the presence of the tribunal members, two officials, the court officer and members of the press. No other members of the public were permitted.

The applicant who was being examined at the time of the disturbance was P.H. Cuthbert, a grocer with the Co-operative Society. He had declared that he had been brought up in a pacifist home and would rather die than kill a man. Mr R. Bryce Walker, a tribunal member, challenged him by asking what the German Reich would do under such circumstances. It was a rhetorical question, as Walker also supplied the answer that German leaders considered 'might is right', and were strong enough to take any action and had the entitlement to do so.

Councillor T.A. Kerr, a socialist member of Glasgow Town Council, then rose from his place on the public benches to declare, 'As a former Senior Magistrate of the City of Glasgow, I feel constrained to protest against members of the Bench delivering political speeches.' His remark was greeted with loud applause from the public, leading the chairman to have the court cleared. Joe Taylor, an ILP member of the town council, shouted, 'What about this British freedom you talk about – this freedom you talk about – this freedom we are fighting for? It is an absolute farce!'

Before his removal, Councillor Kerr explained that he was due to appear on behalf of another applicant, and was told by Black, 'You may wait outside and come in with the applicant.' Kerr replied, 'I bow to your verdict, but under protest.' Once the court was cleared, Mr Bryce Walker asked John McGovern, who was supporting the applicant, if he thought there was anything unfair in the questions he had asked. McGovern replied:

> I consider the whole line of questioning unfair. I am not clear whether you
> are sitting in a judicial capacity or not. You are continually asking a number

of hypothetical questions, which I consider trick questions. It is outrageous the way young men have been bullied and tricked. The Sheriff has been asking whether people are prepared to defend themselves as distinct from the question of being armed, equipped, drilled, and taken to foreign countries to fight and kill. There is a tremendous difference. A man may be a conscientious objector to this war – not war in general.

I put it to the Sheriff that if this young man was unemployed, could not pay his rent, came before you and you gave an eviction order, the Sheriff's Officer would come to evict him. I suggest I am as much entitled to ask whether that young man would be entitled to kill the Sheriff's Officer to defend his wife and children, as some of the other hypothetical questions which have been put.

If a young man has a genuine conscientious objection you are entitled to give him the benefit of the Act, but you are not entitled to ask him trick questions about what young men may do under certain circumstances which can hardly be envisaged.

I am talking about the whole line of questioning from the Bench. There is supposed to be a working-class representative on this Bench. He is supposed to defend the interests of the working-class young men. He is not here, the voice of these young men is not heard and the mass of the people think the tribunal is not representative.

The chairman replied that the line of questioning was designed to help the applicant, and that McGovern was labouring under a misapprehension.

Another type of objection related to the inferior way in which people of different racial background were treated in society. The *Manchester Guardian* of 3 April 1940 reported on the case of Frederick O'Cora, a riveter, described as a '20-year-old coloured man'. O'Cora told the tribunal:

[H]e had had a hard struggle to gain the job he was now in owing to the colour bar. He did not wish to take any part in military service. He was not allowed to join in times of peace.

Mr A. Roberts: 'There are some of us in this country who believe all equal, irrespective of colour. If you felt, as the result of this war, that you would be treated as an equal would it alter your opinion?'

Applicant: 'There is no freedom for the coloured man, whatever you say. We do not get treated as equals.'

In reply to Judge E.C. Burgis, he said that, had he been treated as an equal, he would have fought. Judge Burgis said O'Cora had favourably impressed the tribunal by his frankness and honesty. He said that as in times of peace he was the victim of prejudice and had not an equal chance with the white man. The tribunal was satisfied that conscience did not prevent the applicant from joining the army, and his name would be removed from the register without qualification.

Judge Burgis, chairman of the North-West tribunal based in Manchester, had the reputation of being particularly combative, and disquiet was expressed about the workings of his tribunal. (Plates, page 11) In its early months, 23 per cent of applicants received an unconditional registration and 37 per cent a conditional registration. During the first weeks of 1940, these fell to 12 per cent and 34 per cent respectively; 53 per cent of people were struck off the conscientious objectors register entirely. This was not down to, according to an anonymous correspondent to the *Manchester Guardian* who signed themselves 'Fair Play', any reduction in the quality of the applications. Rather, 'the tribunal has become much more severe, and applicants are more often dismissed as unconscientious should they stumble on any nice point of logic or hypothetical question.' 'Fair Play' contrasted the words of the tribunal chairman from 2 November, that 'we realise that matters of conscience are sacred; they are something to be respected and revered' through to various phrases uttered by in him in January referring to despising applicants' views, of one applicant with a 'warped and twisted' conscience, and another as 'warped and perverted'.

A letter from James Riley, the clerk of the Quaker Marsden Monthly Meeting, was published in the *Manchester Guardian* of 15 March 1940. Riley commented on what appeared to be a 'growing unsympathetic attitude on the part of the tribunals towards conscientious objectors'. There had been many complaints made by Quakers who had attended the tribunal sessions. Riley continued:

> Even when unconditional exemption has been awarded this has in many cases been accompanied by references to 'strange' types of conscience. In one case recently heard in Manchester the applicant said that both of his parents had suffered imprisonment on account of their pacifist beliefs, and was told that he had been unfortunate in his home surroundings.

When the bill dealing with conscientious objection had been introduced by the previous Minister for War, Lesile Hore-Belisha, he had said that conscience would be its own tribunal. However, Quaker members had detected a change. Crucially, Riley put forward the view that all objectors deserved a fair hearing:

> Our objection as members of a religious society to conscription springs from our religious convictions, but we feel that those who are claiming exemption on political ground are not receiving the fair treatment which they were promised. We further object to the charge that we, along with other pacifist bodies, are making conscientious objectors. The Society of Friends welcomes those young men who have a conscientious objection to taking part in war and are glad to offer fellowship to those who are the victims of ostracism in industry and, worse still, in the Churches in which they have been brought up.

One particular individual took it upon himself to deal with Judge Burgis directly and violently. Henry Ballantine Best (24), a clerk of Blair Road, Alexandra Park, Manchester, had appeared before the tribunal on 4 April 1940 and had had his case dismissed. After a night to ponder on the decision, Best stabbed the judge seven times as he boarded a train at London Road Station en route to his home in Macclesfield on 5 April 1940. The *Lancashire Evening Post* of 6 April 1940 reported that Burgis 'was violently attacked from the rear and stabbed in the neck and various parts of the body'. Best later handed himself in to a police station and was charged with wounding with intent to murder, to which he replied, 'I did not intend to murder.'

Mrs Burgis spoke to the press, stating:

> He is almost unable to move, and says he feels he is in a plaster cast, but the nurses say he is a model patient, and feel he is helping them in their efforts to get him better again. He is very philosophical about the whole matter, and regards it as having been all in a day's work.

Later that month, Best was sentenced to five years' penal servitude for the attack. Before being sent down, his statement was read to the court:

> The Chairman of the tribunal, Mr Burgis, appeared to my mind to assume from the start an antagonistic attitude towards me. Before I read my statement he asked me a number of irrelevant questions. After the adjournment the chairman announced my case would be dismissed.
>
> I felt that this was a grossly unfair decision and that fact, coupled with his general demeanour, filled me at the time with intense dislike for the man. My mind played on this constantly.

On Friday, April 5, I went to town intending to listen to some of the cases in the afternoon of the tribunal. I felt exceedingly depressed and went into a public house and started drinking. I went to a store in Newton Street and bought the instrument with which I committed the felony. Subsequently I went to the Tribunal Court, arriving late. I saw Mr Burgis emerge and followed him from the Town Hall to the London Road Station.

Just as he was about to enter the carriage I was filled momentarily with savage rage and struck at him with the knife. I cannot remember clearly what transpired exactly during the next few moments. I can only recollect that he swung round with his attaché case and caught me on the side of the head. I struck blindly several times. Not knowing exactly was I was doing I ran wildly away from the scene.

It transpired that had the wound in Burgis's neck been an inch to the left or right, it would probably have been fatal. Detective Inspector Pierpoint said that Best was connected with several political and youth organisations, and had served ten months in the Territorial Army before being discharged on medical grounds. He was secretary of the Manchester branch of the British Socialist Party.

Best's father was a retired police officer, who had served twenty-seven years with the Manchester City Police Force. He said his son had never shown violent tendencies:

> He is very highly strung, but as to his committing violence I cannot imagine it. He is a very good boy and very studious. His view and mine are not similar, but there have never been any disturbances between us. He is very young for his years and sometimes I think of him as a boy of 16 or 17. The day he came back from the tribunal he never mentioned his case at all and made no remark about Judge Burgis. I was astounded when the police called at my house for my son had never shown any hatred towards the judge.

The case of Burgis and Best was not typical of the way objectors reacted to the tribunals. At the other end of the spectrum, one pacifist, James Byrom, recalled that he felt 'full of appreciation of the fairness [of the tribunal, and] could not help reflecting that a country so tolerant towards the liberty of the individual conscience was a country that richly deserved to be fought for. The wave of patriotism nearly carried me into the nearest recruitment office.'

Judge Wethered, chairman of the South-West tribunal, noted in 1942 that of the 4,056 cases he had heard, some 3,000 had based their objection on religious grounds, with 662 of them being Methodists. Wethered was dismissive of many of these cases, noting that for many, 'their position is the result of simple Bible teaching operating on a mental background of almost complete ignorance of the external world, outside a very small circle of home, friends, work and Chapel.'

Some people who initially registered as conscientious objectors subsequently renounced that position. Clifford Simmons, who had originally undertaken relief work during the blitz on London in 1940–41, came to feel that 'The inactivity of my pacifist role became increasingly irksome. I still believed that the position of the pacifist was ultimately right but I was beginning to realise that, at the same time, I could not stand aside from the struggle which was engulfing my contemporaries.' Simmons therefore enlisted in 1942. A change of heart based on less altruistic outcomes was reported in the *Manchester Guardian* on 10 February 1940:

> The chairman, Sir Artemus Jones, at the North Wales conscientious objectors' tribunal at Caernarvon yesterday, read a letter from W.J. Hughes, of Newborough, Anglesey, quarry labourer, stating that he wished his name to be struck off the list of conscientious objectors and asking the tribunal to send him a military certificate.
>
> The letter added: 'You must not regard the statement I made as false, but I want you to understand that my wife has been doing nothing but nagging since I received my first objector's certificate. When I received the letter to appear before the tribunal she has been unbearable.' He asked the tribunal to make it possible for him to hear no more about this objectors' business and arrange for him to be medically examined and called to the colours with the men of the 20–22 class in his district.
>
> He concluded his letter: 'I am awfully sorry to cause this unnecessary trouble, but I would rather be in the armed forces for the rest of my life than stay at home with my wife for another month.' His name was withdrawn from the register.

One man who was a determined objector from a young age was Maurice Beresford. Born in Sutton Coldfield in 1920, he had attended Bishop Vesey's Grammar School in the town before leaving in 1938 to go up to Cambridge University. His parents had expressed loathing of the First World War, and he recalled his paternal grandfather, who 'rather liked human beings and disliked seeing them killed' and disliked young Maurice playing with soldiers. Growing up as an intelligent young man in the 1930s, he took part in many discussions in sixth form about the international situation. He also wore a white poppy each Armistice Day. At the same time, he was attending a Congregational chapel, the minister of which was an active pacifist. This helped to confirm his 'instinctive' belief that it was 'so totally wrong for anyone to want to kill anybody else under any circumstances', and that 'there was only one stance for a principled chap to take'. Beresford then joined the PPU soon after its foundation, and, after a year attending Jesus College, Cambridge, he went to the labour exchange in the city to register as an objector. In that particular academic milieu, Beresford experienced no hostility towards his stance. Appearing at his tribunal, Beresford's statement read:

> I am registering as a CO because I am convinced that for me no other way is compatible with those Christian teachings which I have accepted and whose truth is unalterable. I am sure that not only is it contrary to God's will and Christ's teaching to kill and inflict suffering, but also that to be confident of material force is fatal to that love expressed in Christ's life and death. I realise that this places a responsibility on me to show that I have not lost a sense of the service due to my neighbour by taking up my attitude, and it would be hard to equal the physical sacrifice of those who fight. The same sense of responsibility tells me that to compromise by accepting what does not conform with the standards I have accepted will not only tarnish that cause for me today and in the future but for others to whom the attitude of Christian conscientious objection may be an example. I have held these views for at least five years, and on my sixteenth birthday I felt I was resolved to join the PPU, of which I am still a member. I have since joined The Fellowship of Reconciliation and International Voluntary Service for Peace, and I can submit evidence to this if the court wishes, and I have statements from some who have known me.

Beresford appeared in a courtroom in Cambridge, where he had been studying – a circumstance Beresford reflected was fortuitous. Had he registered in his native Birmingham, he felt he would have been in for a rougher time, as the chairman of that tribunal was 'a notorious Conscientious Objector baiter'. He recalled the hearing being very short in duration. Beresford's statement was supported by a testimonial from Bernard Manning, a leading Congregationalist historian and a senior tutor at Beresford's college. In a future twist of fate, the chairman of the tribunal was J.H. Clapham, who had served as the first Professor of Economics at the University of Leeds, and in later life, Beresford was to become the first Professor of Economic History at the same institution. The outcome was that his registration was to be deferred until he had completed his history degree.

John Bishop, a young Methodist from Luton, had realised at a young age that he did not believe in war:

> I know that by the time I was about ten or eleven I had, within myself privately, objected very strongly to some remarks that were made at a remembrance service when ... the headmistress was telling us about the brave sacrifices of the men in the First World War and how they had gone out and fought and lost their lives. 'And of course, you boys will do the same if you're ever called upon', and I remember thinking no, I jolly won't. I don't believe that that's a good idea at all.

Bishop's tribunal hearing took place in Great Portland Street, London in the spring of 1940. He was accompanied by his brother for support, who was already a registered objector doing farm work. In a prepared statement, Bishop said, 'Believing as I did in Jesus Christ, he'd taught me to love my neighbours and love my enemies, I couldn't believe that I had the right to take for any reason whatsoever the life of anyone else.'

Bishop was challenged by the tribunal members. 'They said to me "what do you really mean with your religious background that we should have gone back on our promise to Poland made in a treaty?"' To which he responded, 'I don't think we should ever make a promise offering military help in any case.'

> They, they directly asked me about whether I would take part in Air Raid Precautions and I said I regarded that as part of the preparation for war. They ignored that. They said was I prepared to do agricultural work and I said 'yes'. So they then said 'go and sit down'. And I sat down in some trepidation and they had a little conference between themselves.

Bishop was then registered as a conscientious objector, on the condition that he undertook work in connection with agriculture and ARP. Later in the war, Bishop was compelled to undertake some fire-watching. He thought, 'Well, that's after the event; I don't see that as doing much,' so agreed to do so.

Discrimination against conscientious objectors

By the middle of 1940, many public bodies, including councils, education authorities and ARP organisations, had prohibited the employment of objectors.

However, after an intervention by Labour MP Herbert Morrison, who had been a conscientious objector during the First World War and was now serving as Home Secretary, a new National Service Bill was passed in April 1941 that explicitly allowed for the employment of conscientious objectors in civil defence work.

Arthur Smailes, a Methodist lay preacher, was dismissed by Portsmouth Council from a teaching job in a college on declaring himself an objector, whilst Walter Bartley, a laboratory technician from Brighton, was also dismissed on account of his pacifism. However, for Bartley, this led to a series of events that had a hugely positive effect on his future career and marital happiness, meeting his future wife during the course of wartime experiments conducted on human volunteers. (See Chapter 8)

One authority that was particularly draconian in its treatment of objectors was Bermondsey Borough Council. It decided to dismiss all known conscientious objectors from its service. A form was presented to all employees asking them if they held views that were against the war. Thus, all employees, whether of military age or not, were affected, and one man, aged 60, was sacked, losing not only his livelihood but his pension. Some workers refused to sign the form, and were summoned before an Establishment Committee for interrogation, including those with distinguished army records from the first war. The National Union of Public Employees sent a deputation to the council to express regret at the decision, which had only been passed by one vote in the absence of two members who would have voted against it, including Ada Salter, wife of Alfred Salter MP. After the war the decision was reversed and the sacked workers were reinstated.

By July 1940, the CBCO had evidence that eighty-six local authorities had decided to dismiss conscientious objectors from their employ, thirty-three to suspend them for the duration, and thirteen to put them on a private soldier's pay. Birmingham Corporation had 140 COs on its staff and suspended them without pay. Manchester dismissed them when legally possible, whilst Stockport decided to dismiss them despite the town clerk's advice that this could incur a £50 fine. Such actions did not receive support from the Archbishop of York, and even Winston Churchill made it clear that 'anything in the nature of persecution, victimisation, or man-hunting is odious to the British people.'

The Corporation of Lytham St Annes passed a resolution stating 'that in the opinion of this council Conscientious Objectors should be compelled to carry out work of national importance on rates of pay no higher than, and under condition no better than, those of HM Forces.' This was opposed by the Trades Union Congress due to a range of complications, including the fact that soldiers also received board and food, and that many employers were making up the shortfall between army pay and wartime pay.

Amongst the first wave of objectors was Cecil Davies, a Methodist from Cornwall. Davies had been a member of the PPU since his teenage years, and when it was discovered that he was likely to register as an objector, the *Daily Express* ran a piece on him on 2 May 1939 under the headline 'Conchie No. 1', picturing him standing in front of an ornate fireplace nonchalantly smoking a cigarette. *The Cornishman* newspaper helpfully followed up on the story two days later by giving his parents' address: 'Although it is not mentioned in the report, Cecil (as the "Daily Express" refers to him) is a Penzance resident. His parents reside at Green Bank.' Davies then received a good deal of hate mail, including one letter containing the *Daily Express* photograph, on which the correspondent had wiped his or her bottom.

A full-page feature by the novelist Lesley Storm appeared in the *Sunday Pictorial* in the form of an open letter on 7 May under the headline:

> He says he 'Won't Fight', but Lesley Storm, who is a wife and a mother, has a great deal to say TO THIS YOUNG MAN!

Whilst Storm acknowledged that she did not wish to see a return to the days of 'Death or Glory' militarism, she did state, in bold capitals, that the time for abstract intellectual positions was over:

> WHAT I DO ADVOCATE FOR THE SAKE OF MOST OF US IS THE WEANING OF OURSELVES FROM THE INTROSPECTIVE INDULGENCE OF THE PAST DECADE. UNLESS WE WANT OUR PERSONAL PROBLEMS SOLVED FOR EVER BY FASCISTS OR NAZIS WE SHALL HAVE TO BEGIN BY TOUGHENING THE TEXTURE OF OUR MINDS.

She concluded by implying that a sincere conscience would lead a man such as Davies to heed the call to arms:

> Do you imagine there are no conscientious objections in the hearts of thousands under arms today? Has a man no conscience except when he strikes an attitude about it and shouts it from the roof tops?
>
> Think again, young man.
>
> You have a lot to say. Too much, I think. For one has come to suspect the jugglers with words.

The aesthetic intellectuals in the past decades have destroyed more than they have created. We have no reason to thank them or to listen to them now. What we are listening to is the voice of the common man, and what we are thankful for is the spark that exists in the humblest soldier.

Davies recalled that his statement to his tribunal was 'very intellectual, though it was meant to be passionate, saying that the individual human being was the only holder of values such as beauty, truth, goodness, and to destroy human beings was to destroy those ultimate values too.' One of the tribunal members suggested alternative service. 'No,' said the chairman. 'If we give him that he'll refuse,' and granted unconditional exemption. Davies spent the war working with evacuated children in Devon and acting in plays to entertain the crowds in London bomb shelters.

Discrimination against conscientious objectors could even extend to their religious lives. The Vicar of St James' Church, Selby, Reverend J.G. Bynell, was quoted as saying, 'I would sooner put a handle on the organ than have a Conscientious Objector on the staff of my church.' This was in response to five out of eight applicants for the post of organist being registered conscientious objectors. One CO had 'conchie coward' chalked on his gate.

John Bishop faced opposition from fellow members of his Methodist church. 'I was deliberately cut by an old school friend and by a couple from the church, the Methodist church that I went to, who regarded me with great diffidence and would speak only if absolutely necessary.'

Sometimes this ostracism had the effect of helping to persuade others against the conscientious objection route. Bishop recalled:

> One lad who was becoming a Methodist local preacher had agreed with us and was going to be a Conscientious Objector and I said, 'did you register as a Conscientious Objector?' He said, 'no, I don't need to because I knew that I was medically unfit, and they wouldn't take me anyway.' So, he was already at that time I think easing his stance, and a little while afterwards during what was thought to be an air raid, it turned out to be a false alarm, his mother had fallen downstairs and hit her head. They thought nothing was the matter she just had a bad headache but sadly she had cracked her skull and because they did nothing about it till the following morning she died. Immediately he said, 'this is terrible' and began arguing that we ought to get out there and fight the Germans regardless of the fact that this had been a false alarm. The logic of his position didn't sort of really grab me but there it is.

John Bishop did not recall any cat-calling due to his stance but did experience some very warm pre-war friendships becoming cold and distant, but that others were 'interested and sympathetic'. Interestingly, Bishop felt that he received fair treatment.

> It did seem to me to this country's credit in a way that first in the First World War when there was conscription they had given Conscientious Objectors a hard time but actually allowed the thing to go through with prison sentences and so on, and in the Second World War when there was conscription whilst it was not an easy thing it was legal and it was permissible.

Although conscientious objectors within the armed forces were not subject to the same degrees of brutality as they had been during the first war, and most COs felt that, on the whole, they were treated reasonably by the authorities, there were well-documented instances of physical abuse. One of the most notorious venues for this treatment was Dingle Vale training camp in Liverpool. Letters were smuggled out of the camp and brought to the attention of the CBCO, alleging that COs who were refusing to obey orders were being beaten up, starved and having their heads shaved as punishments. Sustained abuse was meted out to five COs on a firing range on 26 September 1940, and on 9 October the same year, eleven COs were badly beaten for having refused to parade. The men were beaten into submission and then threatened with the charge of mutiny, which could carry the death penalty.

As news of the beating leaked out, the twenty-six COs who had been abused were transferred to a camp in South Wales. However, the matter was far from over. On 5 November 1940, James Milner, MP for Leeds South East, asked the Under Secretary of State for War, Sir Edward Grigg, what the results of a confidential inquiry into the Dingle Vale case were. Grigg replied that he was waiting for a report to be written, but that 'the Army desires to treat conscientious objectors with scrupulous fairness, in whatever unit they may be serving.' Milner repeated his request for information on 19 November, with Grigg responding that he still had not received a report. By the end of February 1941, the report had not been published, leading James Maxton, the pacifist and Independent Labour MP for Glasgow Bridgeton, to ask the Minister of State for War, David Margesson, whether there was any intention of revealing its contents to the public. Margesson responded that the matter would be subject to a court martial.

On 5 March 1941, Lord Faringdon, speaking in the upper chamber, made the Lords aware of some of the details of the allegations emanating from Dingle Vale:

1. Forcible dressing.
2. Charged by the commanding officer with 'not complying with orders' instead of 'disobeying orders', given fourteen days' detention and assured that in no circumstances would they be court-martialled.
3. Bread-and-water diet with one slice of bread for breakfast, one for dinner and two for tea.
4. Solitary confinement in cells less than 4 feet wide, 10 feet high and 10 feet long. No light or ventilation and one blanket covering.
5. During the week beginning September 3 prisoners were aroused at 12, 2 am and 4 am and paraded round playground in shirt sleeves. It is not certain how many nights this occurred. On at least one occasion a regimental policeman refused to get the men up and asked them to report that he had done so.
6. Heads completely shaved.
7. Severely and brutally beaten by Provost Sergeant Cullins for refusing to work. Knocked about by other soldiers on exercise.
8. Very hard physical exercise on bread-and-water diet. Made to run round drill shed and jump sand bags for an hour. Fainting from exhaustion, were treated by buckets of water and the men kicked to their feet. Told to move a pile of coal in handfuls and not in sacks, and a little later to fill sacks and run round the square. Awakened at 10.30 pm and made to scrub a block floor and jabbed when they stopped.

Farringdon provided a case study of one of the objectors who had received some of the above treatment. Leslie Worth, from Leeds, had submitted a Christian basis for his conscientious objection, and had been registered for non-combatant service by the North-East tribunal. The *Leeds Mercury* of 1 November 1939 had briefly reported his case. Worth, then 20 years of age and a library assistant of Lewis Avenue, Leeds, had told the tribunal, 'I regard war as the complete negation of all that Christianity means to me,' and that he was not prepared to do anything to further the war.

As an absolutist, Worth found the direction into non-combatant service unacceptable and went to appeal. This was rejected on 21 December 1939, and on 10 June 1940 he was fined £5 for failure to attend a military medical examination. His case again made the press, the *Yorkshire Evening Post* of the same day reporting that, the prosecution having set out the case of how Worth had ignored all demands to submit to medical examination, he attempted to reply. He stated, 'I have little to say except that what you might think is my defiance or truculence ...' but was not allowed to finish the sentence. The magistrate accused him of being 'obstinate'.

He received call-up papers on 27 June instructing him to attend a Non-Combatant Corps unit in Glasgow. Upon ignoring this he was arrested on 31 July and taken to Crookston Camp. Worth was court-martialled in Glasgow on 17 August and sentenced to twenty-eight days' detention. He was then removed to Barlinnie Detention Barracks, and upon the completion of his sentence was sent to Dingle Vale School under escort and in uniform. On 14 September he had dressed in civilian clothes and was ordered by the regimental police to put on his uniform. On refusal, Worth was threatened with forcible dressing and asked to see the orderly officer to enquire by what regulation he could be forcibly dressed. He received no reply to this, and a colonel then appeared and, as reported by Worth, 'The interview grew more and more stormy, ending with a crescendo of abuse and an order to put me on bread and water.' On Sunday, 22 September, having refused to work, he was 'dragged about a bit', and on the 23rd he was beaten up in a guard room, marched to a butcher's shop and told to clean it out. He refused and was given a further beating. Water was then thrown over him and he was repeatedly struck around the head.

Worth was then taken out to drill with a party of men with rifles, and received blows back and front from the butts, was kicked on the legs and struck in the face. He was then placed in solitary confinement. Over the following days he was roused repeatedly during the night, made to walk round a freezing parade ground in shirtsleeves, and had his head shaved. On 9 October, he was one of a number of men dragged and kicked round the parade ground.

Worth's testament, as relayed by Farringdon continued:

> There Captain Wright (second in command) ordered us to come to attention and right turn; we refused each time. The Captain then ordered us to be taken into a long shed, where we were ordered to double round. We stood still. We were then kicked and struck by the NCOs until we would move. The NCOs (about ten of them) were spaced out and we were thrown from one to another, being struck with sticks and fists and kicked as we passed. The Captain all the time was giving encouragement. We could not stick this longer than half an hour, when we gave in. By that time there was a pool of blood from Foster's nose, Jordan had two black eyes, and all of us were very sore all over. We were all made to promise to be soldiers and the Captain then said he bore us no malice, and as far as he was concerned, now that we had been punished, nothing further would be done.

Worth's letter continued:

> The rest of the day we went about our normal duties. In the evening we were taken before the Major and the evidence about refusing to obey orders

given. No mention of the beating up. We were told that we should be charged in the morning with mutiny and insubordination. We were taken to the guardroom. The next morning we were taken before the Major again, formally charged and remanded for the CO (Colonel Greenwood). We were told that the penalty for mutiny was death. We all went before the CO together. He was polite this time and gave us a chance to speak. Some of them repeated their promise to be soldiers – some did not. Nothing was said about the beating up, nor was there any mention of trial or of punishment. We were further remanded and taken back to the college guard room. Late last night we were taken to have our equipment checked, and we were got up early this morning and escorted (with sixteen others from the college including Cook) to the station.

A series of prosecutions took place in March 1941 of officers and NCOs charged with assaulting the conscientious objectors. First to appear was Captain Frank Kenneth Wright, attached to the Pioneer Corps, at a court martial in Liverpool. He appeared on five charges: ordering NCOs to assault privates, permitting NCOs to assault privates, assaulting Private L. Worth, assaulting Private R.W. Bailey, and finally of not reporting the assaults to a commanding officer. The alleged assaults, which had taken place in October 1940, were outlined as per Worth's letter, which had been read out in the House of Lords.

The *Liverpool Daily Post* of 29 March 1941 reported on the case. The court martial convened to hear charges of assault against members of the Auxiliary Military Pioneer Corps by one officer and five NCOs. Sergeant Francis Richard Norris pleaded not guilty to four charges of assaults on Privates E.A. Walker, L. Worth, R.W. Bailey and A. Foster. The case for the prosecution was that assaults took place on the miniature rifle range during detention drill. It was alleged that Private Walker was kicked and pushed by Sergeant Norris; Private Worth was struck with the open hand; Private Bailey was struck by Sergeant Norris behind the ear and Foster was struck on the body. Sergeant Norris denied striking any conscientious objector, or seeing anyone else do so. His testimony was corroborated by his fellow NCOs Cooper, McPhail and Weatherall. Although the prosecuting officer, Captain Thesiger, submitted that the case against Norris was clearly proved, the court immediately found him not guilty on three of the charges, although found him guilty of assaulting Private Bailey.

Speaking of Sergeant Norris's character, his commanding officer, Colonel H. Greenwood, told the court that he was one of the best NCOs in the unit. This was affirmed by Major Flateau and Lieutenant Fargher, who stated, 'it was a pity that eleven conscientious objectors, determined to get out of the Army, should be the cause of a man like the accused being in that position.' Fargher asked the court to take into account Norris's good service, and the fact that he was a soldier, while the people who accused him were conscientious objectors: 'possibly one of the most dangerous Fifth Columnists that we had to deal with today. I have tried to show their multifarious activities. We know they work underground, and that they are determined by their actions possible to sacrifice the liberty of us ourselves and the liberty of the nation to Hitlerism.' Therefore, Norris should receive no more than a reprimand.

Another NCO, Sergeant Donald McPhail, was also charged with nine charges of assault on Privates A.B. Campling, E.A. Walker, A. Gregory, L. Worth, A. Foster, J.F. Harvey, J.F. London and J. Taylor. The alleged assaults took place on the stairs leading to the guardroom and in the miniature rifle range. The allegations were that one man was kicked and dragged and had water thrown over him, another was hit by McPhail in the stomach and another man was struck twice on the jaw. One of the alleged victims, Private Walker, admitted going to the house of a Unitarian minister to take a message about the case but denied manufacturing evidence to get men into trouble as 'Jesus Christ never taught me to lie.' It was probably this visit through which news of the brutality was leaked out.

Two of the sergeants eventually received a severe reprimand, and McPhail, a former boxer, was found guilty of two assaults and reduced to the rank of corporal. Captain Wright received a reprimand. In an ironic twist, one of the objectors called upon to give evidence to the court, Frank Chadwick, handed a note to the president of the court stating, 'Sir, I regret I must refuse to give evidence against Ex-Provost Sergeant Cullen. ... I have already forgiven him and cannot reconcile the giving of evidence, which might appear vindictive, against him.' The president ordered Chadwick to give evidence. Twice he refused, and was marched away and later court-martialled on this and two other charges. He was sentenced to a total of two years' imprisonment, shortened to twelve months. He was then re-registered as a conscientious objector, subject to him undertaking land work. Another objector, Albert Foster, had tried to help Cullen's wife, whom he had heard was in financial difficulties. This was twisted by the defence to give the impression of a corruption of justice, and Foster received a week's solitary confinement.

The ten-day trial was witnessed by Joseph Brayshaw, a caseworker for the CBCO, who made 142 pages of notes in close typescript. Having witnessed the lenient sentences carried out on those found guilty of gross brutality, and the unwillingness of two of the objectors to testify against their tormentors, it is appropriate for the final word on this appalling case to be left to him:

I do not know that I should have the forgiving Christianity to do it, but if ever men turned the other cheek it was these two young men, who sought to help their persecutor, and who were so shamefully used for doing so. I never expect to see greater moral courage than that of Frank Chadwick, sitting silent before a deeply hostile and suspicious Court, and bearing punishment because he would not bear malice.

No one who sat through those ten days of trials could possibly doubt that there had been systematic brutality to coerce Conscientious Objectors from their stand, though it was true that the evidence as presented did not sustain most of the detailed charges against the individuals accused. Still, the convictions showed the world that at any rate something irregular had been happening, and the slight penalties imposed relieved the anxiety of many COs who had reluctantly given evidence. Above all, the Inquiry and courts martial were sufficient to ensure that throughout four further years of war no planned coercion was attempted in the Army.

Another case of military brutality towards a conscientious objector was that of Robert Foster, a Methodist. Foster was already a member of the armed forces when war broke out, and was serving in Singapore. However, he had developed doubts about the compatibility of his religious views and military career but, due to the fact he was already in the army, was ineligible to have his case heard by a tribunal. Eventually Foster found himself forced to resist, and was sentenced to one year in prison for refusing an order to type a letter, was transferred to Britain and sent to Aldershot Military Prison and detention barracks. Whilst many conscientious objectors had little trouble in detention barracks, Foster, possibly because he was seen by NCOs as a 'turncoat', received particularly harsh treatment. In evidence presented to the Oliver Committee's Enquiry into Detention Barracks in 1943, Foster made a statement that laid bare the attitude and treatment he received.

Having been issued with a rifle, he refused to either sign for it, or obey an order to pick it up. The sergeant dealing with him told him, 'I've been sent here to cure conscientious objectors and I've never failed.' At a reception room Foster was forced to stand against a wall so his nose touched it. The sergeant entered the room:

> 'So you won't take a rifle and equipment – I'll show you,' and he gave me a blow on the back of my head with his closed fist and caused my face to be crushed against the brick wall. He had occasion to pass me five times and each time he repeated this – both the saying and the punching. I remember falling

backward and crashing the back of my head on the floor. I think I could not have lost consciousness any length of time. I made an effort to rise and an NCO fetched a bucket of cold water which he threw over me – and another NCO did likewise.

The NCOs present began to bully me in an attempt to get my obedience – bullying was followed by punches to my face and head, also my body, and particularly by attempts to wind me. The NCOs were joined by other NCOs until finally ten took part. ... Wrist, leg and arm-twisting and kicking of my body were means adopted in attempts to coerce me into consenting to take the rifle and equipment. I received one kick on the bone below the left eye. ... In view of the condition of my eye the NCOs must have seen the red light, or probably their time on duty was nearing an end, and, after again refusing to take the rifle and equipment, I was doubled by two NCOs each holding an arm, to the Detention Hall and placed in a cell on the third floor.

In some respects, worse than the brutal treatment he had received were the lies that those in command used to try to cover up the mistreatment. The next day Foster made an application to see the commandant to complain about the illegal treatment, and was taken for a medical inspection by a lieutenant in the RAMC, who requested to be left alone with Foster. The lieutenant was aware of Foster's history and expressed his disagreement with his continued conscientious objection. He therefore agreed with the previous day's actions by the NCOs, and that they would cover themselves by charging Foster with attempting to use violence against them. Foster asked for his support in proving that the physical damage was worse than would have been received had it been a mere case of restraint, but the medical man refused.

Foster was then taken to the assistant commandant, a Major Davidson, who read out a charge of attempted violence against an NCO. Three NCOs testified against him, but Foster maintained he had been respectful throughout. Davidson stated that he had to accept the evidence of the NCOs and Foster was sentenced to sixteen days' detention, a term he reflected was 'absurdly lenient for an offence which was considered to be clearly proved'.

Other COs who had been removed from the register for their stance found themselves in civilian prison. Roger Page, who had served time in prison during the first war for his objection, wrote a pamphlet titled *Citizens in Jail*, which was published by Peace News Ltd at the beginning of the war. Page covered how he thought conscientious objectors could make good use of their time in prison.

He advised objectors to prepare a detailed, dispassionate and accurate testimony of their experiences. From these testimonies, the wider issue of prison reform, not just for pacifists, but for the whole prison population, could be addressed. He wrote:

> This body of testimony from the CO prisoners will inform the pacifist movement as a whole which can then press for reform, for abolition. It must sweep away the mediaeval bread-and-water punishments and solitary confinement; the sadism of the 'deprivation of mattress'. There must be revision of the whole system of work in prison so that prisoners do not spend weary hours on deadening tasks which machines could do in minutes or seconds. The full routine must be scrapped as out of date and the long fourteen-hour stretch of confinement after 'supper' abolished. Prison diets should be overhauled and brought into line with modern standards; the 15-hour gap between 'supper' and breakfast be closed up. Prisons should be made self-supporting in the matter of garden produce. This would give the prisoners more outdoor work and more fresh vegetables.

Page also identified a need for the overhaul of prison staffing, with better pay, training and working conditions producing a better quality of staff, thus impacting on the reforming potential of prisons.

One way in which conscientious objection sought to make the experience of prison more palatable was by the surreptitious production of written material. In Wormwood Scrubs, the inmates produced a magazine dubbed *The Flowery*. The name was derived from the Cockney rhyming slang of 'flowery dells', meaning cells. It ran to seventeen issues from August 1942 to March 1944, with written contributions from different inmates. They were forced to write in secret, in a corner of their cell out of sight from the spy hole, and the magazine was sewn under the cover of a mail bag.

Editions were handwritten on sheets of ruled prison paper, and bound together with stout waxed thread. In June 1945, a compilation booklet was published, *The Flowery, 1942–4: The Scrubs 'Conchie' Review*. Fenner Brockway, in an introduction, wrote:

> This is a unique book. Among all the hundreds of thousands of publications which have been issued from the press since Caxton carved his first type there has been nothing like it. It gives to the public the contents of an underground journal published during the war in a British prison, Wormwood Scrubs.

The cover designs featured barred windows, blackout curtains, towers and roofs of prison buildings. Readers were exhorted to hide the copy down a sock or under a shirt when it was their turn to read it. Only one copy was ever discovered by a warder. It was destroyed, but no action was taken against the person who had it at the time.

The Flowery was described as being:

> a small unofficial contribution towards the unity and fellowship of COs who are 'NOHMS' and therefore temporarily detained in Wormwood Scrubs. But its value is more than that. This reproduction reveals the quality of the men who have gone to prison as conscientious objectors; the absence of bitterness and of spiritual pride, the simple humanity, the great sense of fun, the generosity of spirit, the devotion to principle and ideals. Whilst these remain the characteristics of COs they will not only witness peace; they will be among the instruments of its coming.

There were amusing contributions, such as caricatures of some of the prison warders. (Plates, page 13) The August 1942 edition featured a story that was full of sadness:

> 'You will be shocked to hear that Jack was killed on active service last week.' So ran the first paragraph of my letter from home last week. Jack had been a great friend of mine. Many time he had driven me in his car on PPU work; to Hyde Park in the snow to hear Dick Sheppard and others protest from coal-carts, against Rearmament; and again in the summer to the same part with gay yellow and green flags, for that procession; to meetings in the open air where he sold *Peace News*, and the speaker used the back seat of the car for a platform and stood up through the sunshine roof.
>
> Far-off days, but his youth is fresh in my memory. I can see him now, one night in March, driving his car from Victoria with an elderly Jewish refugee from a concentration camp outside Berlin whom he had helped to safety in this country.
>
> Jack thrived in the group and we watched with interest his appearance before the Tribunal, our first and also our youngest. 'Land work' was the decision and he left us. At first he kept contact and then he no longer had time to call. I pinned him down to a dinner with the family one day and he came. But despite the friendship we only talked superficialities and after he had gone we felt sad.
>
> A year later he was in the RAF – having refused his father's offer to buy him a 500-acre farm. He got married and went to the States, and come back with his 'wings' – to pilot bombers.

Five weeks ago during a chance meeting with one of the group he revealed this: 'I couldn't make it,' he said. 'The loneliness of the land – no groups, no time for reading – the physical exhaustion combined with the crude remarks of those I worked with – the animosity of the village – I felt friendly and was rebuffed – so I joined up.'

And he finished by saying as he stood there in his smart uniform: 'I suppose the group don't think much of me now.' The member he was speaking to had just finished six months in Maidstone, and he knew only too well what it meant 'to hand on'. So he only said: 'Jack, they only want to see you back to fulfil all that promise of the past.'

Jack, however, went to Scotland and of the crew of the crashed bomber he was the only one killed. No details are available, but the local papers speak of 'those that died for their country'. But a group of his friends could see beyond the empty phrases and through the Union Jack that draped his coffin, to their unfulfilled hopes that were being lowered there.

But they still believe that one day men will die for their ideals in the same spirit as they are now trying to live for them. It may be the same death, the same suffering, the same bereavement as for war, but it will yield a harvest of peace and not futility.

For a generation who experienced childhood in the 1960s and 1970s, the name Oliver Postgate is associated with the creation of such well-loved television programmes as *Bagpuss*, *The Clangers* and *Ivor the Engine*. However, Postgate, a grandson of George Lansbury, had been a conscientious objector during the war. (Plates, page 13) Having originally served in the Home Guard before the age of 18 and undergone a medical examination for this, he was initially barred from registering as an objector. Postgate described the inner arguments that he experienced once he had publicly declared to a friend his intention to see through his conscientious objection via military channels. He accused himself of being prone to muddled thinking, and that he would be called a coward. Part of him thought this would be justified. Although his father, Ray, had been a conscientious objector during the First World War, he was not keen on his son becoming one during this war, due to the different international situation.

Postgate received his call-up papers in November 1942, instructing him to report to the Household Cavalry at Combermere Barracks in Windsor on 9 December. He had collected a PPU leaflet outlining the procedure for someone in his situation, which was to join the unit but refuse to put on a uniform. He would then be court-martialled and sent to a civil prison, and then on to a tribunal. Postgate wrote to the commanding officer in advance to advise him of his intended course of action, in order to minimise any inconvenience on both sides. However, on arrival it appeared that no one had any knowledge of the letter. Postgate recalled what happened next in his entertaining autobiography, *Seeing Things* (2000):

> I tapped on the window. [The guard] looked up and waved to me to come in through the door, which was open.
>
> 'Hallo,' I said, 'I've arrived.'
>
> 'Yes?'
>
> 'I've come to give myself up.'
>
> He looked up. 'To give yourself what?' he asked.
>
> 'Up.'
>
> 'Up what?'
>
> 'No, not exactly.'
>
> 'You've come to join up?'
>
> 'No, not really.'
>
> 'Got any papers?'
>
> 'Papers?'
>
> 'Look, you can't join the army if you haven't got the proper papers.'
>
> 'No, I'm not here to join the army.'
>
> 'What then?'
>
> 'I'm here *not* to join the army.'
>
> The soldier thought about this for a moment. Then he said, 'You know, I'd have thought you would have been better off doing that somewhere else.'
>
> 'Oh dear,' I said. 'May I sit down?'
>
> 'Help yourself.'

There followed a farcical few days of sleep, meals, ablutions and discussions, while the army decided what to do with him. A situation was eventually contrived whereby Postgate could repeatedly refuse to put on a uniform. He was then court-martialled and sentenced to serve a three-month prison sentence at Feltham Juvenile Prison, where he shared a room with twelve other 'conchies', two each from the Quakers, Seventh-Day Adventists and Plymouth Brethren, one Anglican, three Jehovah's Witnesses and three non-religious persons. Each religious sect received a weekly visit by a minister who conducted a short service. The highlight of Postgate's stay was when he was ordered to prepare the stage for a visit by a local amateur dramatic company who were to perform a version of R.C. Sherriff's *Badger's Green*.

From Feltham, he was taken to Wandsworth Prison for a short stay before his conscientious objector tribunal. Eventually it was decided that Postgate be dismissed from His Majesty's Forces and set to work in coal mining. He was then taken from the tribunal, back to Wandsworth Prison and Combermere barracks, where he had originally reported to in December. The staff were nonplussed at what they were meant to do with him. They could not put him in the guardroom as he was no longer under arrest; he could not go into the dormitories because he was no longer a member of the military; he could not go back to prison as he had served his sentence; but he could not be discharged as his papers had not yet come through.

Eventually a camp bed was set up for him in the storeroom. The following day the exasperated colonel sent him on his way with a rail warrant and a ten-shilling note. Fifty years later, Postgate admitted to a sneaking admiration for his younger self. Although he later considered his stance misguided, it was principled and took moral fibre to see it through. Like his grandfather, George Lansbury, he ascribed the cause of the war to the consequence of the anger emanating from Germany following the poverty caused by the Treaty of Versailles. War would not be the end of the cycle of oppression, retribution, aggression and devastation.

Postgate accepted that Hitler and fascism were evils that needed destroying, and wholeheartedly respected society's right to do so, eschewing the choice to campaign against the war. Part of his logic was based on numbers. If he had had the chance to kill Hitler personally, he would have done so as it would have saved the lives of many millions of people. However, had he joined the armed services and taken his part in the military machine, then even more people would have died. As a young man of 18 he was given a choice of doing as he was told and going somewhere to kill people with whom he had no quarrel, or refuse to do so and accept the consequences. 'As an immediate decision was required, I chose the option that did not involve killing people.'

Significantly, Postgate considered the treatment he received to be very fair and considerate, even though he had underlying misgivings that he had become something of a stranger in his own country by setting himself apart from the majority of his generation. He concluded his reflections on the experience:

> By virtue of its inherent goodwill and kindness my county had allowed me to continue to live and eat. It had not only allowed me to stand by my convictions, it had respected them. After that I knew I could not, in good conscience, refuse to reciprocate that generosity; that I would always have to respect the convictions of others even though I might disagree with them.

For the remainder of the war, Postgate undertook land work, before going to occupied Germany to work for the International Red Cross in social relief work, as an ambulance driver employed by the Save the Children Fund, until 1948.

Conscientious objectors could experience a hugely varied treatment from civil and military authorities during the war. Many felt that their concerns had been heeded, and that efforts had been made to find ways in which they could fit in with a society geared for war. For some this meant appropriate work that was not directly military. However, for others, their objection extended to having their lives directed by the government. Some of these individuals found themselves in direct opposition to the authorities, with the sometimes violent and unpleasant consequences that brought.

Conscientious objectors were able to take ownership of much of the process of objecting through the work of the CBCO and other organisations. Generally, relations between these groups and the authorities were productive. The following chapters will examine the spaces in which men and women were able to operate in the war, in line with their objection to taking part in armed combat.

Chapter 7

Humanitarian Work

Social work

In anticipation of the Blitz, in the summer of 1940, Pacifist Service Units (PSUs) were established for young men and women of a pacifist background. They committed to undertaking welfare and civil defence work, providing emergency relief to the civilian population. By September 1940 they were busy helping evacuees and organising rest homes for workers whose houses had been rendered uninhabitable by the German aerial bombardment. Recruits to the PSUs were recruited on the basis of their character and physique and wore army style combat jackets and initialled armbands, giving a quasi-military appearance to their members. They were trained in first aid, construction work, child care and crowd psychology.

By 1942, there were fourteen PSUs with eighty-two volunteers in total. They undertook social work among bombed-out populations, including on an estate in South East London that housed 5,000 people from Bermondsey and Deptford. PSU workers moved into a house on the estate and established youth clubs, welfare services and community centres. Similar work was undertaken by a PSU in Newport, South Wales. PSUs worked with families to improve hygiene conditions and were eventually renamed Family Service Units, continuing in that form until the 1980s. Two PSUs were located in Liverpool and Manchester, undertaking casework from February 1942 to October 1943. A third unit that opened in Stepney, East London, in March 1943, had to close after eighteen months due to the shortage of staff and the disruption of bombing. Other units were located in London and Cardiff.

Each PSU was given the use of a large house in the area in which it worked, where the volunteers lived. The house also acted as an office. The PSU members lived communally, sharing domestic work. They received board and lodging, clothing, and personal expenses in order to carry out their work, and pocket money of ten shillings per week. The funds to provide this, which amounted to approximately £2,000 per annum for each PSU, were raised through small subscriptions from the pacifist community and locals who supported the aims of their work. Many PSU members had previously been engaged in church social work or youth club work. While serving with the Units, nine members were prosecuted by the Ministry of Labour for refusing to be directed to other work, and five of them served prison sentences.

Each unit was led by a Fieldwork Leader, under whom served a secretary and a team of caseworkers. Each caseworker had fifteen cases at any one time, as that was felt to be the limit of what could be done effectively. There was a relatively small turnover of cases, so an individual worker would typically get through twenty to twenty-five per year.

Denis Hayes described one of the families that a PSU worked with in order to give a flavour of the social problems being addressed:

> [a] mother, a daughter and a son of eight who used to sleep on a mattress on the parlour floor, which was soiled with excreta. The only furniture in the four-roomed house was in the kitchen and there wasn't much of that (one chair and that had no seat). It was the height of winter and they had no coal. All were filthily dirty and in rags. The father and a son of nineteen were in gaol, the mother had a broken arm, which was in plaster, the boy of eight had never been to school and the girl of fourteen was pregnant by an Indian seaman.
>
> Members of the Unit cleaned the house and were able to get some domestic equipment for them. The mother soon started to help as well as she could and the family began to use the front door, which they had hitherto been ashamed to do. Next they were able to get the girl to a home, where her baby was born: she proved to be mentally backward and both she and the baby were found to be suffering from VD. They later went into homes to get proper treatment.
>
> As the mother's arm improved she made a great effort to build up a home and, when PSU got the little boy to school, she took a job, so as to be financially independent. The aim was to help her build up a decent and stable home for the father and the son to return on their release from gaol and good progress was made in that direction.

Another PSU worked at the Honor Oak Park Estate in Deptford, which, as a development of twenty-seven blocks of flats that had been built on an island site from 1933 to 1937, was bounded on three sides by railway embankments. The estate housed 5,000 people, rehoused slum dwellers from dock and riverside areas. However, no provision had been made for the social needs of the community. There was no community centre, church, cinema or post office, and only six shops. In such conditions, neglect and apathy grew amongst the inhabitants. One of the PSU workers, L.E. White, described their work there in detail in his book *Tenement Town* (1946). The PSU formed a club for the hundreds of children who otherwise would have been left to run wild around the estate. However, the workers had made the mistake of appearing to be 'outsiders' attempting to do good and the club was not an initial success. Therefore, they followed the example of the Liverpool and Manchester groups and rented a flat on the estate and lived simple lives, and the children they were trying to reach became more receptive.

A library and youth club were established. White described:

> This library, well stocked with good modern children's books, is greatly patronised, and is proving a useful antidote to the inevitable 'comic'. Even a backward eleven-year-old problem child is struggling hard to learn to read. On the whole the children take great care of their books. This is in marked contrast with previous library experiments in Tenement Town, which have all ended abruptly with the disappearance of the books.

Children who had never seen the countryside were taken on Youth Hostelling holidays and White recalled two children who had previously been in trouble with the law becoming 'model' Youth Club members.

Having a religious focus, the PSU in Tenement Town found the attitude of the parents frustrating:

> Whilst most parents are only too glad for their children to belong to the Club, it is almost impossible to get them to come along even to social gatherings or Club shows. It was hoped that from the parents we might have formed the nucleus of the Church congregation, but, except when a play or film has been incorporated, few have ever attended.

The PSU then attempted to undertake social work with the parents of the children enrolled in the Youth Club:

> This has formed an invaluable background to most of our social work as it has provided us with an intimate knowledge of the children in their homes. Much of this seems very humdrum and routine – calling to enquire why Jimmy failed to keep his dental appointment, to take Mary to the psychologist or perhaps the rheumatism clinic. But it does provide a live and vital contact with parents, and enables our work to be done with families instead of isolated children. Of course, 'problem families' are always with us, continually in and out of trouble, but whilst we keep a friendly eye on them, pressure of other work never allows time for the intensive family casework without which their real rehabilitation is impossible.

White summed up the philosophy of the members of the PSU who worked in Tenement Town:

> Behind all this goes on our personal experiment in trying to live as a group of friends and neighbours, believing implicitly that there is 'that of God in all men' and that the way of friendship which we seek to follow is the only one that can work in such a situation. So, in Tenement Town, where, because of the mistakes of the past, community is at the lowest ebb, we seek to build even now the 'New Community'.

Social work was also undertaken by the Anglican Pacifist Fellowship. During the blitz on London in 1940, many of London's rough sleepers were so filthy and ridden with lice that they could not be allowed to share close quarters in public air raid shelters. Westminster Council converted a railway arch under Hungerford Bridge, located between the Strand and the Embankment, for their use, and in early 1942, an Anglican Pacifist Service Unit took over responsibility for its functioning. The team was led by Bernard Nicholls, a conscientious objector who was granted a rare unconditional exemption due to the fact that he had actively decided to undertake this humanitarian work before being summoned to a tribunal.

Many of those helped by the PSU suffered with mental health issues and alcoholism, and others who were not made welcome in the main shelters. The arches under Charing Cross station were converted into a shelter with a capacity of 200, three-tiered bunks, a canteen, a medical first aid post, baths and lavatories. It was one of the most 'exclusive' clubs in London, with access being subject to a special pass from the City of Westminster's shelter service.

One of the workers, Sidney Greaves, described the work of what became known as the Hungerford Club in the pages of *The Flowery*, the unofficial prison magazine for those conscientious objectors incarcerated in Wormwood Scrubs:

> We began with a membership roll of about 40 men and 20 women, but during the first six or eight months it increased to about 90 at which it remained fairly constant. We have bunks and nearly twice this number, and could quite easily fill them every night with those to whom a free bed means more than beer, but we endeavour to sort the sheep from the goats, and to take in those who, for perhaps only a few days, really are without money for a bed, or those real down-and-outs who are unable to look after themselves through physical or mental weakness. About two-thirds of our flock would come under this latter head – they are the 'regulars' – and many have been with us right from the

start. They scrape a meagre living in odd ways such as selling newspapers, carrying 'boards' (surely the most degrading of all jobs), entertaining theatre queues and various forms of begging.

When a newcomer arrived at the Hungerford Club, they were first interviewed by one of the APF workers, in order to ascertain his or her story. Sometimes, they were not admitted, if the worker thought that they were perfectly capable of paying for a room and were just looking for free lodging for the night. Those cases were referred to Bruce House or the Salvation Army hostel. If, however, a man was considered to be genuinely in need, they would be permitted to stay, and perhaps be given money for breakfast and supper in the canteen.

The canteen was staffed by Fellowship of Reconciliation volunteers, and a hearty meal of a pint of tea, a large sandwich, a plate of porridge and a plate of hot soup could be purchased for a penny. There was also a Medical Aid Post, where a member of the PSU was assisted by a sister from Charing Cross Hospital. This gave access to treatment at the hospital, as well as outpatient care. A chiropodist visited the post once a fortnight, and members could be de-loused, but only if they volunteered to have this treatment. PSU workers also encouraged men to visit the Labour Exchange in order to make some effort to find a job.

Alongside all this practical support, members of the 'club' were also given human friendship and sympathy, so the PSU workers spent much time talking with men and women, or playing chess or darts with them, leading to what Greaves claimed were 'signs of a re-awakening social consciousness', with some of the members offering to assist with the running of the service. Ernest Brown, the Minister for Health, commented in the House of Commons that 'a number of voluntary workers are doing excellent work. ... So far as I know there are no counterparts elsewhere.'

Pacifists also undertook social work under the auspices of the International Voluntary Service for Peace (IVSP). The Ministry of Labour permitted the IVSP to be registered to provide alternative service for conscientious objectors. Some were put to work on afforestation programmes in remote areas like Hawkshead and the Kielder Forest, as this timber would be used after the cessation of the war rather than to support the war effort. Other objectors had the opportunity to work abroad, and in February 1944, the first unit of twelve volunteers left for Egypt. Another unit served in Italy and was able to assist 25,000 refugees with registration, clothing and reconstruction. A third unit served in Crete, whilst a fourth worked in Holland and Germany through to the end of the war and beyond, assisting with the organisation of displaced persons and welfare work in Berlin.

Another Quaker-based organisation was the Friends' Relief Service (FRS), which had originally been formed as far back as 1870 as the Friends War Victims Relief Committee to relieve civilian suffering in the Franco-Prussian War. After work during the First World War, it was reformed in November 1940 and renamed the FRS in 1941, and an old mansion house at Spiceland in Devon was transformed into a training centre for young objectors, some of them Quakers but many of other faiths and none. At its zenith, in 1942–43, the FRS boasted a full-time staff of nearly 500, nearly half of them being Quakers and almost all of them being conscientious objectors. The FRS had outgoings of £5,500 per month, much of this funded by donations from Quakers in America.

Work included assisting with evacuees who found it difficult to get accommodation in private homes due to their age, family size or other disadvantage, and organising hostels for those who had found billets but who were merely existing, rather than living as evacuees. They also assisted in air raid shelters and spent any spare time by undertaking odd jobs such as making toys and equipment for the Nursery Schools Association.

Although anyone was welcome to join the organisation, their work had an underlying spiritual aspect, with the aim being not just to address the symptoms of the problems that had been exacerbated by warfare, but to look for solutions that could remove the causes. A leaflet was issued that explained this:

> In some ways Quaker Relief in this war is living rather than giving. Many of the sufferers can pay for their material wants, but need the help of others to adapt themselves to emergency conditions. In bombed areas, personal standards, frail enough before bombs fell, have too often collapsed altogether during 'lull'. This deterioration among citizens, old and young, threatens the ruin of much fine effort of 'reconstruction'. Only by living right in among the people can they be helped, and, what is more important, led to help themselves.

Members of the FRS were able, towards the end of the war, to work in Europe under the auspices of Secours Quaker, an international Friends group. Assistance was given to prisoners of war and refugees, including 200,000 stateless Spaniards, driven out by Franco's dictatorship into southern France. Following the end of the war, FRS members were also able to work in areas of Germany and Austria that were under British military occupation. Some pacifists saw the relationship between FRS members working in relief work and military commanders as an uneasy one, as it was easy to imagine that the former were still in the country working with an occupying force. It was therefore a case of balancing the opportunities for doing positive work against the dangers of being too closely associated with the military. To this end, FRS workers wore 'Quaker grey' uniforms instead of khaki. FRS members were among the first civilians to enter the concentration camp at Belsen.

Friends' Ambulance Unit

The Friends' Ambulance Unit (FAU) was a Quaker organisation that had been established in the early months of the First World War, and whose members had undertaken medical relief work among the civilian populations of Belgium and France. When war began on 3 September 1939, the FAU was immediately re-formed to provide opportunities for active service for conscientious objectors, particularly those of the Quaker denomination. It was led by Paul Cadbury, of the famous Birmingham Quaker confectionery family. A training camp was established at Manor Farm in Northfield, near Birmingham.

The original trainees in the 1939 training camp issued a statement expressing their intention:

> We purpose to train ourselves as an efficient Unit to undertake ambulance and relief work in areas under both civilian and military control, and so, by working as a pacifist and civilian body where the need is greatest, to demonstrate the efficacy of co-operating to build up a new world rather than fighting to destroy the old. While respecting the views of those pacifists who feel they cannot join an organization such as our own, we feel concerned among the bitterness and conflicting ideologies of the present situation to build up a record of goodwill and positive service, hoping that this will help to keep uppermost in men's minds those values which are so often forgotten in war and immediately afterwards.

Despite its name, the Friends' Ambulance Unit in the Second World War was not an official body of the Religious Society of Friends. Thus, it was able to extend its membership beyond the Quakers to any pacifist who wished to be involved with humanitarian relief work. With Quakers making up approximately half the FAU's wartime membership of 1,300, the balance consisted of Methodists, Presbyterians and Baptists, as well as those of no defined religious faith.

The FAU offered an opportunity to alleviate the suffering of civilians in war zones where needs were likely to be most acute. For some, whose moral objection to taking another life was reinforced by an objection to society forcing them to undertake a role within a military structure, the FAU seemed a more acceptable alternative to the service in the Royal Army Medical Corps or the Army Pay Corps.

The FAU drew from people of all social backgrounds, who sought a vocation rather than an alternative employment. Food, clothing and pocket money of 25 shillings a month were provided, as in contrast to the army private's 75 shillings and the miner's 280 shillings. Sixteen men and one woman lost their lives while in the Unit, a death rate proportionately higher than in the army up until June 1944.

Volunteers joining the FAU had the opportunity to take part in five main different areas of work:

1. Air raid relief in Britain. Having completed a six-week training camp, FAU members found work as medical orderlies or porters in understaffed hospitals, with eighty hospitals using COs in this manner. When the Blitz began in September 1940, members were deployed in air raid relief in rest centres, shelters, transport and a work squad which carried out maintenance and repairs. Later, as more work abroad became available, so did further training in lorry driving and maintenance, tropical medicine, mass catering and foreign languages.

2. Working alongside armies in the war zones. Members served as ambulance drivers, medical orderlies and blood transfusion technicians with Casualty Clearing Stations and Mobile Hospitals with the 8th Army in North Africa from El Alamein to Tripoli and Sousse, and then on into Italy, while others served with a Free French Army Mobile Hospital in Syria and North Africa.

3. In civilian clinics overseas. In Syria, up to 24 men served in clinics in the capital and villages near it, and in villages some distance from the larger towns, with one clinic in the Lebanon. In Ethiopia, after the Italians withdrew in 1941, forty men assisted with medical work and the development of medical and social services.

4. In Asia, 200 members served in the China Convoy over five years, in a variety of medical and civilian support activities. In India, the FAU assisted with the organisation of large-scale air raid precautions and post-raid information services in Calcutta, followed by flood and famine relief on a large scale.

5. Civilian relief in mainland Europe. Two members started in 1943 visiting hospitals in Sicily, and by 1944/5, sixty were engaged in transport, health and welfare work in refugee camps in Italy. More members travelled to Greece in October 1944, where a Medical Supply and Transport Unit (MSTU) covered 250,000 miles and distributed 30,000 cases of medical supplies throughout Attica and the Dodecanese; in addition, a Field Bacteriological Unit (FBU) conducted an extensive inspection of water supplies in Athens, Macedonia and two of the Greek islands.

In October 1940, FAU units were organised to provide relief on the home front. Five rest and food centres were set up in the East End of London. By November 1940, there were eighty FAU workers, and this number continued to increase. FAU members worked with the Ministry of Food Messenger Convoy; two female members joined the staff of Bethnal Green Hospital.

The demands of civil defence and the need for emergency assistance provided a space for pacifists to engage in work that saw them stand alongside their fellow citizens during a time of crisis. They could exercise their social consciences in ameliorating the worst effects of German bombing raids, thus demonstrating their service to their fellow humans whilst highlighting the need for additional social service and welfare work in damaged communities.

One particular area of FAU work, the China Convoy, was a remarkable piece of humanitarian relief organisation. The Sino–Japanese War of 1937–45 had led to deteriorating social conditions in China, with part of the country under the control of the Japanese, other areas being held by the Communists, with a landlocked area known as Free China. In 1941, agreement was reached for the FAU to deploy forty volunteers to deliver medical aid to suffering Chinese civilians. They were affiliated to the International Red Cross and took on the transportation of aid. This aid effort became known as the China Convoy.

Transporting aid to stricken areas was far from straightforward. One driver recalled a long and difficult drive:

> We are now in the grip of the worst road in the world, with windscreens and doors rattling loud enough over such a surface to drown all other noises and make conversation impossible. We keep an average speed of some 15 miles per hour, with a 150 to 200 yards' interval separating the trucks.

At first, supplies were delivered along the Burma Road, to Kunming in Free China, but when that country fell to the Japanese in May 1942, the FAU volunteers had to escape to India. Their job then became to secure the delivery of supplies via the Burma Road, the sole remaining route. When Burma fell to the Japanese in May 1942, the FAU volunteers escaped to India and China. They regrouped and took on the distribution of medical supplies delivered by 'The Hump', the air transport route to Kunming. It is estimated that 80 per cent of medical supplies to China were distributed by the FAU. The FAU's role expanded and they provided a range of medical treatments, preventative measures and training of Chinese medical personnel. This expanded further into the reconstruction of medical facilities, notably the hospital at Tengchong in 1944, and into agricultural improvements and training.

The FAU's activities in China were international, employing personnel from Britain, China, the United States, Canada, New Zealand and elsewhere. Around 200 foreigners took part; eight died and others had their health permanently damaged. About half of the recruits were Quakers but all had a commitment to pacifism and wished to deliver practical help.

Like the FAU as a whole, the Convoy was at first exclusively male, but eventually around one in ten of its members were women. The Convoy also absorbed an exotic handful of individuals who had found themselves in wartime China. They included: a White Russian, Valentine Beltchenko; Sabapathy Pillai Arasaratnum from Sri Lanka; Edmundo 'Squint' Marques, a Hong Kong Portuguese; and John Peter, a Tamil Zulu from South Africa who had fled Burma on the motorbike he had used as a daredevil wall-of-death rider in a circus in Rangoon. This multinational membership worked alongside upwards of 300 Chinese paid employees, together with Chinese military and civilian medical and transport staff. Thus the China Convoy was a strange mix of religious affiliations, nationalities and cultural backgrounds, all united in the desire to help those in need due to the war.

The average age of FAU members arriving in China was about 23. Peter Tennant, the first commander, was, at the age of 29, regarded as being something of a veteran. Members shared many youthful characteristics – boldness, idealism and hope, and the questioning of authority through registration as conscientious objectors, standing outside of the mainstream opinion of their generation in wartime.

However, FAU members in the China Convoy were not there to proselytise or to convert others to their point of view. One of them, Peter Leyland, recorded in his diary the unease of his travelling companions en route to China when one of their number saw fit to engage in an argument on the morality of participation in warfare with some soldiers they had come across. Another member, Duncan Wood, concluded that his military shipmates were equally conscientious in their military stance against fascism as he was in his objection to bearing arms. He was subsequently invited to provide a lecture on the work of the FAU to soldiers heading to Singapore.

The FAU was engaged in civilian relief work throughout mainland Europe. On 6 September 1944, two twelve-man sections with eight vehicles, named the FAU Relief Sections No.s 1 and 2, landed at Arromanches in Normandy. They were attached to the British Army's Civilian Affairs branch, with the job of providing relief to civilians in Normandy, a region that had been left devastated by the fierce fighting that had taken place since the D-Day landings of June the same year. From there, No. 2 FAU Relief Section was posted to a newly liberated refugee camp at Leopoldsburg in Belgium, and its members were given the tasks of managing the reception, registration and departure of the refugees, and ensuring that the dormitories and other areas were disinfected, and that catering was provided.

The value of the work done by the FAU Relief Section was recognised when the 21st Army Group, led by General Montgomery, requested five more sections, which were established and arrived in Europe at the end of 1944. Two future MPs were involved in this work: Gerald Gardiner, who served as Lord Chancellor in the Wilson government from 1964–70; and Richard Wainwright, the Liberal MP for Colne Valley from 1966–70 and 1974–87. Wainwright had joined the Methodist Peace Fellowship in 1937 and faced continued challenge about his beliefs, but adhered to his principles, working first in a hospital in England before transferring to work in Europe from 1944 onwards.

After a period in Nijmegen, assisting local civilian medical organisations during Operation Market Garden, No. 2 FAU cared for a group of mentally ill patients near Cleves in Germany, a demand that grew to a population of 25,000. By April 1945, the main work had become the accommodation and care of the millions of displaced persons on the continent until such time as they could return home. No. 2 FAU was also heavily involved with the care and support of inmates at the newly liberated Stalag X–B prisoner of war camp near Sandbostel, between Bremen and Hamburg in northern Germany in May 1945.

In Holland, the FAU transported sick civilians from vulnerable towns, while in Belgium three sections operated an ambulance service for the victims of German flying bombs, the other two sections concentrating on refugees. When the British Army entered Germany on 23 March 1945, four FAU teams accompanied them to care for refugees, providing registration, delousing, catering and camp management.

Further FAU action was seen in southern Europe. In March 1944, a second MSTU landed in Yugoslavia and distributed canned food, milk, potatoes, drugs and supplies for the Partisan hospitals in Split and Dubrovnik. Elsewhere, soap, veterinary supplies, clothing and even the complete equipment for a 200-bed hospital were dispensed. Water supplies were surveyed, which helped to combat outbreaks of typhus and dysentery.

Another theatre of operations in which FAU members worked was Greece. A CBCO bulletin of early 1945 referred to the country as a:

> Political Storm centre … In Greece today is being played one of the great dramas of humanity and co-operation, a drama that will be remembered in retrospect when the ephemeral politics of the Balkans are clouded in the past. In this drama British COs are playing their part.

Five conscientious objectors in the FAU under the command of Harold
Dromard had formed part of the first detachment of Voluntary Service
Workers to enter Athens in October 1944 with the United Nations Relief and
Rehabilitation Administration (UNRRA) mission. This group had since been
joined by eighteen other members. Some of them had been into territory held by
ELAS, the Greek People's Liberation Army, the military wing of the National
Liberation Front, during the civil war that was raging in Greece. The volunteers
had brought back ELAS hostages to Athens, the condition of the freed people
being described as 'piteous in the extreme'. Eleven FAU members had been
despatched to Corfu, where they were providing relief for 20,000 refugees from
mainland Greece.

The CBCO bulletin provided an excerpt from Dromard's diary, which showed
the danger in which FAU members were placing themselves in Greece:

> Dec 8th. Decided to collect the other two at once, and run gauntlet of stray
> bullets, as there was plenty of work for them to do at the depot. Was obliged
> to make two runs without Red Cross flag, as none available. Lively experience
> on second run. Collected them under the noise of much firing. They had just
> had a bullet through the window, which had just missed Bill Blick, who was
> standing there. Bill, Don Nichol and an 'other rank' (returning from a visit to
> the dentist!) were loaded, and we went. Just short of the University we were
> stopped by Greek Red Cross man and five frantic nurses who wanted us to
> help a wounded British soldier.
>
> Proceeded up long side-road to find ourselves in the thick of ELAS. There
> was no going back. Overshot the turning where the wounded were: decided to
> go no further, but leave the others with the truck and proceed to the spot; went
> on, with Red Cross man waving his flag violently amidst crackle of firearms.
> Thank God, most of it stopped as we began a seemingly endless trek up a bad
> road at the foot of Monastery Hill.
>
> Towards the top could see one or two British very close to Mother Earth,
> and shouted that I was coming for the wounded. Reached café on small
> crossroads strongly reminiscent of Hellfire Pass. Located one injured man, not
> seriously hurt, and then found ELAS had stipulated surrender of rifle as price
> of pass through their lines. British OC on other side of the road refused to let
> either of us leave; said they were in a tight corner, but tanks and armoured cars
> coming. After many and varied suggestions (shouted from a prone position)
> he agreed we could leave and chance it – without the wounded man, however,
> because of the stipulation.

My long absence had me worried about the truck and the others, so I left, retracing my steps through a deathly silence. The majority of ELAS men there were well disposed towards us and seemed bewildered at events; but it's too complicated for me.

John Hick, who recorded his experiences in an interview for the Second World War Experience Centre in Wetherby in 2002, was another who saw action in southern Europe having been with the FAU for over two years. Hick had joined an FAU camp in Birmingham in the summer of 1942, which was under the command of Michael Cadbury from the confectionery family. During a month's training there he undertook first aid training and more extended paramedic–style skills including delivering a baby. There were also lectures on languages and modern politics, and physical education. All trainees were then dispersed to hospitals around England. Hick was sent to St Alfege's hospital in Greenwich to work as a ward orderly dealing with bedpans and bottles, and taking temperatures and pulses.

After three months at St Alfege's he was deployed to the Edinburgh Royal Infirmary to receive training as a laboratory technician. Initially he looked after guinea pigs and did some portering work, which included taking corpses from wards to a storage area. Hick recalled no outright hostility to his position from the people he worked with, although there were some 'hostile stares' in the street. After several months in Edinburgh he was chosen to embark for the Middle East. After another spell at the Northfield Training Camp, with more advanced medical training, he sailed from Liverpool on the *Stirling Castle*, a converted liner.

By this stage Hick and his fellow FAU members were in an army uniform, with a Red Cross on the shoulder and the letters 'FAU'. Having been expected to be treated as 'the lowest form of military life', he found that, as the FAU members were technically civilians, they were ranked with the warrant officers, which meant the privilege of eating off a plate instead of from a can, and sleeping in a bunk instead of a hammock.

Upon arrival in North Africa, Hick was assigned to working with refugees, rather than supporting the RAMC units within the Eighth Army in field ambulance work. The refugees that Hick supported had fled from the fighting in Yugoslavia and were now housed in the El Shatt camp at the southern end of the Suez Canal. This brand new camp was situated within sight of Mount Sinai and housed around 20,000 refugee families in double army tents, in cramped conditions. Hick worked in the hospital, housed in a converted army mess hut, during a phase in which the patients had not been sorted by gender or categorised by disease. Hick began work in an isolation hospital and then became night manager of the whole hospital provision, being supported by around a dozen Yugoslav Red Cross nurses.

Hick found the experience stressful as there were only three doctors for 20,000 people – an American, Dr Dodds, an army doctor, and an Indian doctor. As they worked flat out all day, they could not be disturbed at nights, leaving Hick to make decisions such as when to inject patients in the event of heart failure, or when to perform a tracheotomy on a child with diphtheria. He also recalled an insane patient who left the building and swam across the Suez Canal, having to be returned by the Military Police.

Due to the large number of children in camp, Hick was then appointed as Chief Education Officer, being supported by three trained teachers and some untrained ones. Hick recalled:

> we had schools in tents and one had to do everything, of course, with the aid of partisan commissars and an interpreter. Everything had to be agreed, and I did not smoke. I was a non-smoker but I received a ration of cigarettes and I used them to subtly oil the proceedings in committees. As things progressed cigarettes appeared. If they didn't progress they didn't appear. So all that was quite interesting.

Following this challenging and varied six months at El Shatt, Hick was transferred to a hospital in Cairo to be a laboratory technician. It was there that he contracted jaundice. For a month he was kept in a ward overlooking the Nile and watched the dhows sail past. Following a period of convalescence in Palestine, Hick was sent for malaria training under army jurisdiction in Damascus. Although he had learned a variety of specialist laboratory technician skills, he never got to practise them as he was sent to do work of immediate priority and was unable to insist on undertaking the work he had trained for.

It was then planned for Hick and some other FAU men to be sent to Albania. However, when Enver Hoxha, dictator of that country, learnt that a team of relief workers would be accompanied by 600 British troops, he refused them entry, so Hick went to Greece, which was then in the final throes of a civil war. Here, based in Ipiros in north-west Greece, the FAU was responsible for distributing clothes all the way up to the Albanian border. Accompanied by Peter Ure, a future professor of English Literature, Hick would set out on foot or mule for a week travelling from village to village to ascertain the current situation. Occasionally they would find the head of a village with his throat having been cut. In addition, there was widespread destruction as the retreated Germans had laid waste to many villages, often only leaving the church standing. ELAS, a communist group, was also fighting a rearguard action against the Greek government, leaving the villagers in the midst of continuing bloodshed.

Hick recalled:

> As soon as we arrived, of course, we were the first non-Greeks they had seen since the Germans a week or two before and so we were greeted with colossal enthusiasm, and so the first thing to do was to sit down with the elders and drink *oozo* with all the rest of the village standing around watching, and occasionally they put on a lavish feast. They, they killed a, a sheep and roasted it, and all that took an awfully long time of course, and the worst thing was that they offered what was supposed to be the delicacies like the sheep's eyes and heart to the honoured visitors. I usually managed to palm the eye and, you know, pretend that I was enjoying it.

At the end of the war, Hick managed to get a lift back to England on an RAF plane, and demobilised himself so he could resume his academic studies. This was against regulations, so he had to go before another tribunal, which refused him the right to do so. He appealed and the appellate tribunal upheld his decision. Hick went on to become a Presbyterian minister and Professor of the Philosophy of Religion at Claremont University.

The FAU ceased operations on 30 June 1946. Many members transferred to the Friends' Relief Service or the United Nations Relief and Rehabilitation Administration to continue their work, and many activities were handed on to other bodies such as the FRS, UNRRA and the local Red Cross.

The high esteem in which the FAU was held in society during the war was epitomised when a group of volunteers returned from a stint of work in Europe. They had been away so long that they had not actually attended a tribunal in order to be formally placed on the conscientious objectors register. Therefore, they were still provisionally registered, and so the formality of a hearing had to be organised. This occurred at Fulham and, following a successful outcome, with the men being placed on the register, the chairman, Judge Hargreaves, shook hands with them as he left the town hall.

Land work

Many conscientious objectors were directed to work on the land by the tribunals. By April 1943, there were 7,295 conditionally registered COs engaged in land work, as well as many others who had volunteered for such work without conditions. Early in the war, it had proved difficult for many COs to find land work, as many farmers and agricultural authorities were reluctant to employ objectors.

Ernest Brown, Minister for Labour and a devout Nonconformist, approached the churches and from this contact the Christian Pacifist Forestry and Land Units (CPFLU) began. The organisation was headed by Reverend Henry Carter, the founder of the Methodist Peace Fellowship. Carter's aim was to provide openings for three categories of religious conscientious objectors: firstly, those whose firms had transferred to war work in which COs felt unable to continue; secondly, those dismissed from their jobs for being objectors; and thirdly, those directed into land work by the tribunals, but who had been unable to find such work.

The first unit was formed in Hemsted Forest, Kent, and was accommodated in a large, derelict house that the six unit members had to work hard on to make habitable. Their work was overseen by the Forestry Commission, and soon there were forestry units across Sussex, Hampshire and the Forest of Dean. Sometimes units slept in tents, caravans and even disused railway coaches. For others, more sturdy accommodation was found in the form of Youth Hostels and village schoolrooms.

The units accommodated men from all the main Christian denominations, and by the end of 1940, over 400 men had enrolled and were kept informed of each others' activities via the medium of a printed chairman's letter. A sense of fellowship grew between members, living as they were in isolated areas with men of a similar outlook on life. They were also drawn together by the continuing opprobrium of many in the civilian population. Henry Carter wrote:

> The hostility of which I have spoken still smoulders, and flares up on occasion. There have been a few local outbreaks of physical violence; in more than a few places a ganger has been bullying and tyrannous; and I add with regret that some places of worship have refused offers of service in church and social activities. Where such tensions have arisen the real meaning of Christian pacifism has been tested, and often I have felt thankful for the absence of resentment and the presence of goodwill.

However, over time the units found themselves increasingly accepted. Carter continued:

> Usually, as time passes tension ceases and neighbourly relations are formed and continue. A Unit entertained in their forest quarters some army officers, 'on manoeuvres'; when on the last morning the senior officer learned that his forestry hosts were COs, he said, 'Well I take my hat off to you chaps.' Resolutions and letters of appreciations for work done by Unit members as lay preachers, Sunday school teachers and in youth clubs come now and again from Quarterly Meetings and other Church bodies in rural areas.

As members of the units became more integrated into their local communities, offers of private land work increased. As the war situation improved from 1943 onwards, many of the CPFLU men were moved into employment to prepare the country for post-war conditions.

Apart from the specifically Christian units established by Henry Carter, other COs were ordered into land work. A minority of this population resented the compulsion, and set out to do their jobs half-heartedly. This gave the right-wing press easy ammunition to attack them, as the headline in the *Daily Express* of 21 May 1944 fulminated:

FARMERS RAGE AT 'SUNBATHING CONCHIES'
THEY SPEND THEIR TIME BEHIND THE HEDGES READING
They Cannot Be Sacked for Loafing

Often the independently minded objector was forced to work in a 'gang' system whereby they were engaged in one repetitive task such as threshing over a number of days. This could lead to disobedience and revolts, which in turn led to some suspensions and sackings from land work by the County Labour Officer.

John Bishop, a CO from Luton, had left a job at engineering firm Percival's due to the fact it was producing training aircraft for the RAF. He then found employment with a Methodist local preacher who had preached pacifism through the 1930s. He was a grocer and dairyman with a milk round and Bishop worked for him for a long period. It was hinted to him that this was not congruent with the agricultural work he had been ordered to undertake by the tribunal.

Bishop then moved on to work for a dairy farmer who also had a milk round. This work involved being up at 5.00 am seven days a week, fifty-two weeks a year, causing Bishop's spirits to became low. He later reflected:

I look now at the Ten Commandments, 'remember the Sabbath day to keep it Holy' and I think there is a lot of common sense in that. You will not stay sane for very long unless you have a minimum of a day off in seven and if you can have a holiday or something of that sort there's a lot to it.

He then became aware of the fact that the Great Ouse Catchment Board, who were doing a lot of drainage work across southern Bedfordshire at that time, were employing people. They had taken on some local conscientious objectors from other Nonconformist chapels in Luton. The work involved digging ditches and erecting fences, which, as well as improving Bishop's physical fitness, led him to realise that he needed to further his education in order to secure a professional career once the war ended. He therefore enrolled on some English courses that had been advertised in *Peace News*, alongside taking Methodist Sunday school teacher training courses. He then found out that there was a scheme for the emergency training of schoolteachers for after the war, and that places were available for conscientious objectors. Thus for Bishop, his experience of land work was short term, with tasks undertaken grudgingly in order to fulfil his registration conditions.

Some COs had volunteered for land work in Jersey, and remained once British troops vacated the island. This meant that they lived through some of the Nazi occupation. An anonymous account appeared on the front page of the CBCO bulletin of May 1945:

MANY CHANNEL ISLAND COs FREED

What was the fate of the many British COs who went to Jersey in 1940 to help on the land when the island was in dire need of men? Some were recently repatriated from Germany; others were liberated by the Americans. This is the amazing story of one of the latter:

In May 1940 I went to Jersey to do potato-picking under a Ministry of Labour scheme, and had been there only a fortnight when British troops were withdrawn from the island, and, after a lapse of another two weeks, a small German force landed by plane and assumed control. The actual occupation was quite peaceful apart from a small bombing raid – no doubt intended to instil in the natives a proper respect for the Third Reich – and there was no attempt to resistance by the civilians left.

I was one of the 104 COs who were given an opportunity to leave for England, but who decided, partly from curiosity, partly through reluctance to scurry to safety, and partly to keep up the labour power of the island, to stay put and face whatever the future might bring.

On the whole, life in Jersey passed without major events: much of my time was occupied in scratching-out a living (almost literally true) and time hung heavily. Perhaps I was in a more favourable position than others, having no property to commandeer, nor stocks to requisition, but only the labour of my hands to contribute to the community.

In September 1942 the first batch of transportations took place; I was in the second batch, following in its wake towards the end of the month.

We were taken by boat to St Malo and thence by train to Dorsten near Essen in West Germany, where we spent six weeks. There the single men were separated from those with families, and, being unmarried myself, I was taken to Laufen in Upper Bavaria where I was held in an Internment Camp which, I imagine, was conducted on a slightly better system than the prisoner-of-war Camps. There I was to remain from Armistice Day of 1942 (the irony of fate!) until the Camp was liberated by spearheads of the American Seventh Army.

On the whole, the treatment was not unfair, and I myself know of nothing that might rank as 'atrocities' happening in this particular camp, though the German authorities were very difficult about the observance of the numerous regulations to which we were subject. When the Allied fortunes of war were in the ascendant, treatment became noticeably better. The food was poor, and only the Red Cross parcels kept us going.

It was a real thrill to make our way by car to Rheims; to board the large transport plane which awaited us at a nearby airfield, and to see low down through the side windows of the plane the vague shape that meant Home.

Conscientious objectors in the armed services

Conscientious objectors had made themselves indispensable in many areas of work that they felt were not at odds with their consciences. Providing relief for the destitute and distressed at home and abroad was, for many, clearly congruent with their Christian ethos. Similarly, land and forestry work could be seen as providing food for civilians as well as the military, and maintaining the functionality of the countryside for when peace returned. Many objectors endured danger and harrowing sights, whilst others worked themselves to exhaustion. Their renunciation of war did not equate to a renunciation of society. For many pacifists their conscience only dictated an objection to taking the life of another human being. They were willing to accept being sent for service in branches of military service in which killing was not a requirement of the role.

With this type of CO in mind, the Non-Combatant Corps had first been established in March 1916. Objectors were under the command of regular army officers and NCOs, wore army uniform and were subject to army discipline. However, they were exempted from carrying weapons or participating in battle. Members provided physical labour but were not compelled to load or unload munitions. Churchill categorised NCC members as 'soldiers, and not as conscientious objectors', with the NCC being 'entirely composed of men whose conscience permits them to serve as British soldiers, though it does not permit them to take human life'.

They received approbation from some sections of the press, who dubbed them the 'No Courage Corps', and their existence was opposed by the No-Conscription Fellowship. The NCC was reconstituted in April 1940, consisting both of

conscientious objectors directed there by tribunals and men deemed physically
unfit for military service. There were fourteen NCC companies, in which 6,766
men served during the course of the war, of whom 465 specialised in bomb
disposal. NCC members wore khaki uniform and were equivalent to the rank
of private.

NCC members performed a wide range of duties including hedging, ditching,
limestone quarrying, road building, laying railway tracks and loading and
unloading supplies. Some undertook rescue and reconstruction work in the Blitz,
whilst others served as fire-watchers. There were six categories of employment
that regulations permitted members to undertake:

(a) Construction and maintenance of hospitals, barracks, camps, railways,
     roads and recreative grounds
(b) Care of burial grounds
(c) Employment at baths and laundries
(d) Passive air defence
(e) Quarrying, timber-cutting, filling in of trenches
(f) General duties, not involving the handling of military material of an
     aggressive nature.

Although innocuous looking enough, some of these duties could come very
close to active engagement in the killing process. For example, making roads on
an anti-aircraft site, or laying railway tracks for the supply of a military arsenal,
or repairing runways for RAF bombers under category (a) could have led to
complaints from those who had seen themselves undertaking more routine tasks.
However, there was generally little effective protest from Corps members. Some
even built machine-gun nests under orders, although a few did register their
dislike of such tasks.

There were occasional demonstrations of dissent, such as when No. 6 Company
was put on fire-watching duties at warehouses in Liverpool in 1941. Having been
assured that the buildings contained only goods to be consumed by the civilian
population, it was later discovered by Michael Hewlett, one of the COs, that one
of the warehouses contained shell cases. He lodged an immediate protest and,
alongside two other men, Wynyard Browne and Alistair McManus, refused to
fire-watch in that area. The trio were placed under charge and court-martialled,
accused of not undertaking section (d) of the list of permissible duties – passive
air defence. Hewlett's solicitor maintained the order contravened section (f), the
handling of military material of an aggressive nature. Hewlett was found not
guilty, and the cases against the other two men were dropped.

One NCC recruit was Harold Hitchcock. (Plates, page 14) Before the war, he had joined the Communist Party due to his disgust with fascism. Just before the outbreak of war he moved to Camden Town and started to work as a commercial artist for Universal Publicity producing lithographic silkscreen posters. As a pacifist he became a conscientious objector and enlisted in the Non-Combatant Corps.

On the outbreak of war, his firm decamped from London to Lewes, Sussex, and Hitchcock was accused, along with a friend, of being a Fifth Columnist. Hitchcock later recalled that, although he could not bring himself to kill his fellow man, he felt guilty about not helping with the war effort, hence his volunteering to join the bomb disposal squad – dangerous work for which there was no coercion to undertake. Hitchcock enjoyed the privilege of not having to wear a uniform or undertaking parade duties, and was afforded much free time in which to continue his painting. He would meet with fellow pacifists to share ideas and interests and described himself as a 'spiritual seeker'.

Not all members of the public approved of the existence of the NCC. The *Rugby Advertiser* of 12 October 1943 reported that, although NCC members stationed at Long Buckby had been generally well received by the villagers, they had been banned from the working men's club. A chalked notice had been erected that stated, 'This club is out of bounds to members of the Non-Combatant Corps. Rule 4b cannot apply to them. The Committee.' It was explained by the club steward that Rule 4b allowed admission to members of the fighting forces, and could not apply to non-combatants.

Many pacifists were able to accept being directed to non-fighting services such as the Royal Army Medical Corps, the Army Dental Corps and the Pay Corps. One such young man was James Driscoll, a recently married Christian from London. Having registered as a conscientious objector, he was ordered to appear before the South-East Local Tribunal on 19 March 1940, at which he stated, 'I refuse to have any part in the killing and maiming of my fellow beings because it is incompatible with my Christian faith. I am, however, willing to do purely non-combatant duties in the Medical Corps.' Driscoll preferred the RAMC to the Pay Corps as he could not bear the thought of sitting behind a desk in a warm office whilst others were fighting and dying. However, the tribunal directed him into agricultural or forestry work, possibly because he had no first aid training. Driscoll therefore lodged an appeal for which he made a written submission: 'I did not object to non-combatant duties in the Medical Corps. Indeed, I believe my Christian duty in the present emergency is to help alleviate the sufferings caused by the hostilities.'

The appeal was heard on 6 August 1940 and Driscoll was accepted into the RAMC. In his later years, he reflected on the different experience he would have had as a conscientious objector in Germany, where they frequently faced death by firing squad, hanging or beheading. Driscoll had been provided with travelling and subsistence expenses for his appeal. But not all of society was as humane and tolerant as the tribunal system for him. He was dismissed from his job at the Northern Feather Works in London, a manufacturer of pillows and cushions.

Driscoll's conscientious objection was not the only thing that set him apart in the army. As a devout Christian, he had been advised to kneel down at his bedside to pray every night before lights out. Driscoll feared that this might bring ridicule, but in fact this brought forward two other Christians with whom he became close. He was sent to North Africa as part of the 131st Field Ambulance, having been trained as a nursing orderly. One of the roles he was assigned to was the performance of emergency operations in the field without the use of blood transfusions.

During the Battle of El Alamein in October 1942, which was, for Churchill, the pivotal point in the war, Driscoll responded to an appeal for stretcher-bearers to go onto the battlefield to retrieve casualties under heavy shellfire. During one intense moment, a box barrage opened up as he and a colleague lay exposed in the field. 'I remember lying tense while the perspiration ran from under my steel helmet to drop off my nose onto the sand, and all the while contemplating that the next moment could be my last.'

Recalling his tribunal statement about wishing to relieve the suffering of his fellow humans, Driscoll volunteered for the dangerous task of accompanying battle casualties being transported by air across the extended supply lines in North Africa. He later witnessed the disinterment of the bodies of half a dozen Italian partisans who had been executed by the Germans, in order that they could have a Christian burial. In 1944, Driscoll landed in Normandy, and his ambulance unit was shelled, resulting in him having to bury his dead comrades.

Eventually, the CO of 1940 was, in May 1945, chosen to take part in the victory parade through Berlin, saluting Winston Churchill and Field Marshal Montgomery. His good work was recognised when a Polish doctor in charge of the 105 General Hospital in Belgium recommended Driscoll for promotion to lance corporal. However, this had to be revoked due to a ruling that COs could not rise beyond the rank of private. The testimonial on his army release document demonstrated the service that he had given to the military:

Military Conduct: Exemplary
   Testimonial: A willing and conscientious worker who has given very satisfactory service. Has common sense and works well without supervision. Is of good appearance, honest and amenable to discipline and is popular with his comrades.

Another CO who found his way into the RAMC was David Briggs, a schoolteacher. He recalled the experience of landing on the Normandy beaches on D-Day, 6 June 1944, during an interview to mark the seventieth anniversary:

> The thing that has always stuck in my mind was the sound of nightingales, the most beautiful sound, which drifted across the water into our boat. Every night we'd hear these wonderful songs from the nightingales and it was very, very peaceful. And it was the contrast between that and D-Day that has stuck in my mind.

Approaching the beach, Briggs remembered a lot of air activity and the constant fear of being torpedoed. Upon landing at about midday there was an 'eerie quiet on the beach'. The first thing he saw was a dead Canadian lying in the water.

> The landing craft was relieved of the tanks. The tanks rolled out onto the beach and then all the space that was left … we had brackets coming out of the walls to hold stretchers. Our job as medics was to go onto the beach to rescue the wounded of all nationalities, German as well as English, and ferry them back to the UK. And then that job was finished and then we were discharged from the boat. We were told later that the boat was torpedoed and sunk.

Briggs's objection was borne out of his Christian faith. He had attended Marlborough School, which had a military ethos. All pupils joined the Officers' Training Corps (OTC) for two years and then at sixteen there was the option of remaining with them or joining the Scouts. He chose the latter, and it was around this age that he came to the conclusion that Christianity and war were totally incompatible. Briggs's close friend Frank Sadler engaged in in-depth discussions on the rights and wrongs of military service. Both detested war, but when conscription was enforced Sadler joined the services. Briggs registered as a CO and was initially posted to the Army Pay Corps. However, he did not feel that he was sharing the sufferings and privations the rest of his generation were experiencing and requested a transfer to the RAMC, reflecting, 'I wanted to be a part of everything … not to chicken out of anything … to experience the dangers that other people had. But I was not prepared to carry arms. My role was purely humanitarian and saving life.'

Briggs remained convinced of the morality of his position:

> I never wavered in my conviction. I was in the minority. I accept that. But I was true to myself. I do feel that I did my share which is what I wanted to do.

> My greatest grief was the loss of my dear friend Frank. ... He really hated the
> war ... he was killed in action in mid-June 1944. I have a very firm faith that
> this life isn't the only life. That helps me to explain all sorts of tragedies.

One renowned piece of work done by COs in the army was that undertaken by
medics in the 6th Airborne Division during the Normandy invasion. One of their
number was Arthur Marsden. He was an active member of a Methodist church in
Hull, and, on registering as an objector, was posted to the Non-Combatant Corps.
Marsden was posted to London with the Pioneer Corps, where he did manual
labour such as the erection of corrugated iron huts. He had met up with fellow
Christians, and a group of five held frequent prayer meetings and Bible readings.
Marsden and his friends then volunteered for the bomb disposal squad during
the London Blitz.

The same group then volunteered for service in the Parachute Brigade and
were accepted as medical orderlies in the 6th Airborne Division. After undergoing
rigorous physical training, the group was dropped behind the German lines
during the early hours of D-Day. In fact, they were released 10 miles from their
planned drop zone and became separated. Three of them met up and lived in a
ditch for three days on their iron rations, still carrying their medical equipment.
In addition to the physical sustenance provided by their rations, the trio drew on
their faith by reading their pocket testaments and praying.

Marsden and his comrades were captured by the Germans and put in crowded
railway trucks to be sent to Germany. However, they found themselves called
upon to serve in German field hospitals treating men wounded during the British
assault on Caen. Following this they became prisoners of war in Germany and had
to serve out the final year of the war in a camp.

The broad tolerance shown by the authorities towards the consciences of those
who refused to fight meant that men could find roles that they did not find morally
repugnant. For some, this meant social work within communities in Britain and
elsewhere, whilst for others it meant alleviating the distress caused directly by the
war. Many COs served in active war zones in Europe and the Far East, either in
organisations such as the Friends' Ambulance Unit or more directly in the army
as bomb disposal operatives, labour hands or medics. For these groups, a refusal
to engage in the direct act of killing, rather than the conduct of war per se, guided
their actions. What is in little doubt is that many lives were enhanced due to the
varied work done by conscientious objectors during the war.

Chapter 8
Human Guinea Pigs

In a secluded villa in a leafy suburb of Sheffield, members of one Pacifist Service Unit underwent some remarkable scientific experiments. This work was the brainchild of Dr Kenneth Mellanby, a biologist at the University of Sheffield who was in a reserved occupation due to his status, with the idea that his skills would be used for some scientific work considered of national importance. However, the army at that time had no direct use for biologists and had no suggestions for any functional role for him. For Mellanby, this was a 'curious position', leading to frustration due to his inability to contribute to the war effort. He held the post of Sorby Research Fellow of the Royal Society, and was working on problems of insect physiology. He felt that this research should be postponed and that he actively needed to find something more useful to do.

Mellanby had noted a great outcry when many city children had been evacuated to rural areas, the most serious complaint being that a lot of them were lousy. Head lice were common, but the official figures of the School Medical Service were very different from those reported by those who had to receive evacuees from cities, particularly Liverpool and Manchester. Mellanby approached the Deputy Medical Officer at the Ministry of Health, Sir Weldon Dalrymple-Champneys, with the suggestion of recruiting a number of human volunteers and housing them in one place in order that experiments could be performed on them to discover more about the prevalence and spread of lice and scabies. Mellanby found it surprising that the Ministry immediately agreed to his proposal, even though 'no learned committee' had suggested it and he being 'one very junior scientist'. Dr Mellanby took over 'Fairholme', 18 Oakholme Road, Broomhill, Sheffield, in which to undertake his work. (Plates, page 14) He chose conscientious objectors as his subjects as they tended to be healthy and young. In addition, they were unlikely to be removed from the institute for any military purpose, a loss that would have severely disrupted his experiments. Mellanby later recalled:

> The idea of using Conscientious Objectors had been growing in my mind for some time, and I knew that at this time there were many individuals who felt that they could not take part in the war as combatants and who at the same time wished to serve humanity. In the summer of 1940 the number of outlets for such service was small, and many pacifists appeared to think that the duties

which they were performing, or to which they had been directed, were very unimportant. Preliminary discussions had suggested that there would be a good response to an appeal for volunteers to serve as subjects for medical research, provided that it could be shown that this would be likely to be of value in alleviating suffering, and provided that it was not solely directed to improving military efficiency.

Mellanby and his team took over Fairholme on 1 December 1940. The property was a largish Victorian villa with a small but usable garden. Although the city of Sheffield continued southwards and westwards for another couple of miles, views of open fields could still be seen. Broomhill was then, and remains to this day, a pleasant suburb, and Fairholme now forms part of the accommodation for the Stephenson Hall of Residence of the university. The house had not long been vacated and was in an excellent state of repair. The rooms were large and light, providing a sense of space, which Mellanby compared favourably to a modern laboratory.

The first task was to equip the house with furniture to accommodate a dozen or more residents and the scientific equipment that would be required for Mellanby to be able to carry out his experiments. This took just under a fortnight. Bedding and towels were purchased from local shops, whilst furniture had to be sourced from second-hand sale rooms. Mellanby had to visit half a dozen of these, spending around £300 in the process. This provided enough beds, chairs and tables to accommodate up to twenty people.

Mellanby then contacted the headquarters of the Pacifist Service Units to seek volunteers, and this organisation was sympathetic to his scheme:

> [The PSU] took a refreshingly realistic attitude to their members, and made no pretence that just because a man called himself a Conscientious Objector he was therefore a paragon of all the virtues – in fact they warned me that I was taking on a very difficult set of human problems.

He was also placed in contact with local Sheffield residents who were pacifists. The first arrival from outside of Sheffield was Walter Bartley, who had travelled from Brighton. Bartley, who acted as a laboratory assistant throughout the experiments, had left school at 15 to work as a laboratory technician. At the outbreak of the war, he was employed by the Brighton Technical College but, due to his pacifist convictions, he was dismissed from his post. Therefore, Bartley was to fulfil a dual role of technician and guinea pig. Bartley was one of twelve volunteers recruited initially, a number that eventually grew to thirty-five, including three women.

The first local recruits to arrive were a maths teacher and a fine arts graduate, followed by a ladies' hairdresser, a milkman and an electrician.

All the volunteers were young. For example, the nineteen men and one woman who would take part in the vitamin C experiment were aged from 17 to 34. Some volunteers had regular jobs outside the programme whilst the rest were expected to carry out domestic tasks in the house, as well as being given duties to perform for the experimenters such as collecting data.

One of volunteers was Norman Proctor, a baker from nearby Ranmoor. Despite being in a reserved occupation, Proctor was dismissed from this job as his colleagues refused to work with him due to his conscientious objection. He joined the Sorby Institute in December 1940. (Plates, page 11) Proctor recalled the admiration his work drew from those in the military. 'One of our jobs was examining soldiers for scabies at an army medical centre,' he said. 'Most people were hostile to conscientious objectors, but these soldiers said they'd rather be in the army than do what we were doing.'

Bernard Hicken had originally been struck off the CO register. His case was reported in the *Halifax Courier* of 2 December 1939:

> An Ogden youth was struck off the list of Conscientious Objectors without qualification by the Yorks Tribunal in Leeds on Tuesday.
>
> He was Bernard Henry Hicken, aged 22, audit clerk, with a firm of Halifax accountants, a single man and only son living at home with his parents at 8 Upper Brockholes, Ogden, Halifax. He said he was a Methodist and on religious grounds he objected to war.
>
> To this the chairman (Judge Stewart) retorted 'So do most of us. But there is a war, and you and I cannot help it now.'
>
> Hicken: Yes we can, by refusing to accept the position brought about by war.
>
> The Chairman: What do you mean? You would have to impose your will on a lot of people who would not agree with you. Would you call the war off?
>
> Hicken: It is the only thing that can be done.
>
> The Chairman: I won't ask you how, but, assuming you could, you would have to be as complete a dictator as is Hitler in Germany.
>
> Hicken added that he had been a member of the Peace Pledge Union since the outbreak of war. He would perform no service caused by the war and contended that he was rendering service to humanity by refusing to help to destroy another nation.
>
> When the chairman suggested that Hicken was apparently living in a world of make-believe, Hicken replied, 'Missionaries have been able to convert the

cannibal without the use of arms, therefore we should be able to convert civilised people like the Germans without the use of arms.'

Another of the volunteers, Richard Wodeman, was sentenced to three months' imprisonment for his refusal to have his conscience examined before a tribunal. This was despite the fact that he had already performed valuable service at the institute. The tribunal argued that it had no choice, as it had no grounds on which to judge his conscience. Therefore he was liable for military service and, after refusing to attend a medical examination or pay a subsequent £5 fine, his case went before the Sheffield Magistrates Court. The *Sheffield Telegraph* ran a headline, 'CO Praised by JP Who Jailed Him'. The chairman stated that he was sure Wodeman was doing useful work and the prosecuting lawyer agreed. This angered Mellanby, and his anger was reflected in the press. *Reynold's News* thundered:

> Richard Wodeman, for a soldier's pay, does the job of a human guinea pig. He has been inoculated with dangerous germs. He denies himself food and water as part of an experiment to aid shipwrecked sailors. He is a hero with a conscience which commands respect.
>
> Unfortunately, the military authorities do not share the public's respect for conscience. Because Wodeman objects to military service he has been sentenced to three months' imprisonment in defiance of his record and of the government's clear pledge that such men will not be the victims of stupid officialdom. This sentence should be quashed.

Cecil Wilson, MP for Sheffield Attercliffe, asked Ernest Brown in the Commons:

> Why a man who was undergoing an experiment for alleviating sufferings was arrested during the course of the experiment and prosecuted; whether it is intended to prosecute others of the forty-seven men who have been undergoing the experiment; and whether he can make any statement about Richard Wodeman, who was sentenced by Sheffield Court to three months' imprisonment for refusing to undergo medical examination.

The campaign had an effect as, despite again refusing to attend a tribunal, Wodeman was released from prison after a few weeks after intervention by the Home Secretary, and allowed to return to the institute.

Mellanby had to be wary of conducting any experiments that would have an exclusive application to the military, as this would have offended the consciences of some of his subjects. Therefore, he took care to point out that the work was worthwhile in civilian application too. 'It is essential not only to explain scientific details to this kind of volunteer, but also to respect and be tolerant of his beliefs. I even found myself developing a "conscience" regarding the sort of experiments we should, or should not, carry out,' he recalled in his account of the programme, *Human Guinea-Pigs*.

Hans Krebs (Plates, page 12), who assumed the directorship of the Sorby Research Institute when Mellanby left to join the Royal Army Medical Corps in 1943, outlined the factors that had to be taken into account when managing a long-term dietary based experiment with participants who were living in close proximity to each other, and whose morale and commitment to the project needed to be maintained:

> The success of nutritional experiments on human volunteers depends on the whole-hearted co-operation of the subjects, for it is obviously impossible to impose by force a restricted diet upon human beings for long periods. Co-operation, in turn, depends on morale. In a group of people living as a community, morale largely depends on management.

Obviously, restricting aspects of people's diet over a long period of time could lead to mood changes, which could then affect the morale of other volunteers. Krebs continued:

> The management of this team of volunteers was complicated by the circumstances that some of the customary methods of maintaining morale were not expedient. It would have been impracticable, for instance, to eliminate a troublesome person for disciplinary reasons halfway through the experiment, as this would have entailed a serious loss to the investigation. A special problem was that of avoiding irritability in a small community with people living in very close contact with one another for a long period. The Armed Forces deal with this problem to some extent by moving people about at frequent intervals, but this method was, of course, not applicable to the team of volunteers.

The technique of managing the volunteers evolved over the years that the Sorby Research Institute was in operation. Krebs outlined the four key features:

1. <u>Care in selection of volunteers.</u> It was found to be a great assistance to invite a new candidate to reside in the community for several days before a decision was made on either side. This gave the applicant an opportunity

of meeting the volunteers and learning something of their work and life; at the same time the older members of the team were able to form an opinion as to whether he was likely to fit in with the somewhat unusual community.

2. Participation of the volunteers in the management. The volunteers were given the greatest possible share in the responsibility of running the community as well as the experiment. They were encouraged to function not merely as passive guinea pigs, but to take an intelligent and active part in the work, and to regard themselves as partners, equal in importance to the team of investigators. Many routine duties, especially in the domestic sphere, such as cooking and cleaning, were discharged by the volunteers and everyone was expected to play his part. The most important part of the routine work in such a nutritional experiment, is the cooking. Whilst the ingredients to be used, as well as general instructions about the dietary and standard recipes, were laid down by the team of investigators, the actual preparation of the meals was the responsibility of the volunteers themselves. One of them, a professional baker and confectioner [Norman Proctor], was in charge of the general supervision of the kitchen, whilst the bulk of the routine cooking was in the hands of a rota of volunteers. Kitchen duties changed weekly and all the volunteers who were not employed on work outside the Institute were on the rota. The method of change the cook introduced some variety of style and, what was more important, greatly reduced the formulation of grievances against him. In a long-drawn-out nutritional experiment with a monotonous diet, the cook is liable to be the first target for grievances. By making the volunteers themselves responsible, in turn, for the preparation of the food, food was virtually eliminated as a source of grumbling. The prospect of taking their own turn of cooking duties, and especially the existence of a high degree of esprit-de-corps, induced the volunteers to put up cheerfully with the shortcomings of the food. Other routine work in which the volunteers took a responsible share was laboratory work, record keeping and clerical work.

3. Regular occupation. The routine work at the Sorby Research Institute was not sufficient to occupy all the 23 volunteers. Those who were in a position to carry on in their ordinary occupations were therefore encouraged to do so. This applied to 9 of them. Others, who had special experience in the diagnosis and treatment of scabies, took part in a scabies survey conducted by K. Mellanby in schools and mental hospitals. The remainder filled

in some of their spare time on a vegetable garden, though the dietary restriction prevented them from partaking of much of the produce.

4. Holidays. When it became obvious that the experiment had to be continued for a very long period it was decided to allow the volunteers leave of absence from the Institute. The restricted diet was maintained during the holidays and the volunteers were given detailed dietary instructions. Certain foods such as bread (except during the period when the special white flour was in use), meat, tea, sugar and vegetables such as potatoes, white turnips or white beans, they could buy in the shops; other items such as dried skimmed milk, jam, white margarine, they took with them from the Institute. The refreshing break of holiday time, even though it meant no relaxation from the monotony of the diet, considerably helped in making the prolonged restrictions endurable.

The Scabies Experiment

The first experiment began in 1940 with the volunteers who had been recruited via the Sheffield Pacifist Service Unit, their interest drawn by the opportunity to take part in research that would benefit humanity and being able to share something with an equivalent risk to military service. At first Mellanby was free to undertake any experiments he wished, and his first investigation was into scabies. Mellanby had an interest in head lice infestation and scabies was thus a natural area of research for him.

In the study aimed at discovering the mode of transmission of scabies, it was found very difficult to achieve the passage of the mite from one man to another. Wearing the used underclothes from an infected person was found to be successful on some occasions, although it took two or three weeks before a gradually increasing irritation was felt. The itching experienced by the infected men was described as almost intolerable. One of the volunteers, Norman Proctor, recalled, 'We had to put on soldiers' dirty uniforms and underwear – this was hard for some volunteers. Then we had to share beds, trying to pass the scabies among us.' Proctor did eventually contract scabies when five mites were put onto his wrist. They burrowed into his skin and laid their eggs in his arm:

You could see the burrows under a microscope and a little lump were the eggs. It was extremely itchy. At night the men would get out of bed and walk around naked in the cold to stop the itching. The cure in the early days was awful. Another volunteer held you down in a very hot bath, then they rubbed

you with sulphur ointment. It caused impetigo and other skin troubles. Later
Dr Mellanby treated us with Benzyl Benzoate. My five mites had multiplied
to 59 before they were cleared off. They were over my body. The results were
published by the Medical Research Council. In those days many scientific
things had still to be proven.

Mellanby recognised the discomfort of his subjects:

This experiment was very unpleasant for the participants. ... Some kept
rough brushes to rub over the skin to relieve the irritation. On cold nights
some would rise from a sleepless bed and walk naked through the house, as
when the skin was chilled the itching temporarily subsided and sometimes, if
sufficiently tired, it was possible to fall asleep before the skin got warm and the
irritation returned. Certain volunteers were reduced to sleeping naked as they
scratched so vigorously in their sleep that their pyjamas were torn to shreds.

The constant scratching frequently damaged the skin and allowed the entry
of sepsis-producing bacteria, giving rise to secondary infections. Sometimes
Mellanby was forced to terminate the infection to avoid permanent damage being
done to the volunteers, even though they expressed a willingness to continue with
the experiment. Mellanby published his findings in a small book, *Scabies*, which
formed part of the Oxford War Manuals series. The general editor of the series,
the Right Honourable Lord Horder, commented in the foreword:

If any good is to emerge from the evil which confronts us today, it will be salvaged
in the form of medical progress accelerated through intensity of experience.
Vital to the future stability of this hoped-for gain is the adequate documentation
of that hardly-won experience which the Oxford series aims to encourage.

Mellanby paid tribute to the work of the volunteers, thus highlighting their
contribution at a time in which many conscientious objectors were still facing
taunts, insults and discrimination:

The investigation could only have been carried out with the aid of human
volunteers; nineteen such volunteers, all of whom are pacifists, have voluntarily
given their services and have been infected for periods of many months.
A further thirty-five volunteers, pacifists and others, have suffered infection
for shorter periods. In addition to being volunteers, some of these people have
given valuable assistance in other branches of the investigation.

Water and vitamin deprivation

Another early experiment at the Sorby Institute considered the effects of water deprivation on shipwreck survivors in lifeboats. This experiment was regarded by the volunteers as the most unpleasant, and for this Dr Mellanby and an army major also joined them in their thirst. It was designed to study the minimum requirements for water of shipwrecked sailors. As part of the study they were allowed no fluid at all for three and a half days, with a diet consisting of the types of dried food that were packed in lifeboats for shipwrecked sailors: ships' biscuits, dried pulverised meat, malted milk tablets and plain chocolate. Triallists were then allowed a few days of normal food and drink, before a month of very low water intake. Norman Proctor recalled this experiment: 'We had no water for three days. We lived on dried meat, ships' biscuits and chocolate. I got a bad headache. One man had to stop as he got a high fever but these experiments saved lives – lifeboats now carry more water and less food.'

However, the most important work of the Institute was in nutrition, particularly vitamin deficiency. In 1942, Mellanby approached Dr Hans Krebs about the possibility of conducting some nutritional experiments on the volunteers. Krebs was an eminent German scientist who, in 1933, was working at the Medical Centre of the University of Freiburg. However, his Jewish ancestry meant that he fell foul of the Law for the Restoration of the Professional Civil Service, which enabled the removal of all non-Aryans and anti-Nazis from professional occupations. Krebs had received official notice of dismissal from his job in April 1933, and his service was terminated on 1 July. An admirer, Sir Frederick Gowland Hopkins of the University of Cambridge, found him a post in England, and Krebs left Germany with only his personal belongings and research samples. In 1935, the University of Sheffield appointed him Lecturer in Pharmacology, and he became the first head of the Department of Biochemistry in 1938.

The conscientious objectors had expressed some enthusiasm about nutritional research, so Krebs agreed to direct the project, subject to the government taking the decision as to what form the research should take. In a period of severe rationing in Britain, it was important for the authorities to know what the consequences would be of prolonged absence of certain vitamins. Therefore, the work was commissioned by the Medical Research Council at the request of the Ministry of Food. As Mellanby left the institute in late 1943 to take up a commission in the Royal Army Medical Corps as a specialist in biological research, the experiments were overseen by Krebs, who succeeded him as director.

The first vitamin test examined the effect of prolonged deficiency of calcium. There were six conscientious objectors who initially underwent this, taking

100 mls of milk and 1½ lb of national wholemeal bread daily, with cheese being entirely excluded from the diet. After twenty weeks the volunteers were low in calcium, indicating that a prolonged exposure to the diet would cause a softening of their bones, nails and hair. By doubling the daily allowance of milk, they were able to return to normal levels within two weeks. Therefore, the Ministry of Health was able to conclude that a ration of two pints of milk per week, supplemented by cheese, was sufficient to maintain normal levels of calcium.

For another experiment it was decided to study high extraction (65 per cent) wheatmeal, which later became known as 'national wheatmeal', and to compare its digestibility to conventional wheat, which had a 75 per cent extraction rate, and its effects on calcium absorption. This was due to the fact that wheat was a staple of the British wartime diet, with much of the wheat having to be imported via the dangerous Atlantic convoys. U-boats were a constant menace, and many thousands of merchant seamen were losing their lives in trying to maintain supplies. Therefore, any means of making the existing wheat go further in the diet would be valuable. The volunteers were given diets containing 500g and 700g of either high extraction wheatmeal or wheat flour, and the dry weight and nitrogen content of the faeces were measured, the volunteers having to collect their own samples. It was found that a high proportion of the extra meal extracted proved to be digestible and its nitrogen largely utilised, making the experiment a success.

A further experiment examined the effects of vitamin C deficiency. The twenty volunteers taking part in this experiment were put on a diet that excluded all foods containing that vitamin for six weeks, but included a daily supplement of 70mg ascorbic acid. Then three of them continued on the supplement of 70mg ascorbic acid daily, seven a supplement of 10mg daily, and ten were given none. John Pemberton was responsible for not only the clinical examinations that involved recording the known and suspected signs of scurvy as they appeared, and the occurrence of any other illnesses, but also carrying out some minor surgical operations. The volunteers agreed to having a 3cm incision into one of their thighs under a local anaesthetic and closing the wound with five sutures. The healing and breaking strength of the wounds was studied by excising the wounds at various stages, including the stage when scurvy had developed, and the stages of recovery.

All ten of the volunteers deprived of vitamin C developed the signs of clinical scurvy in six to eight months. These included haemorrhages in the skin round the hair follicles, bleeding of the gums and, in one case, effusions into the knee joints. The wounds in this group tended to break down and bleed readily and their breaking strain was much reduced. One man who had developed scurvy after thirty-one weeks on the depleted diet complained one morning of severe pain in the lower sternal region. His pulse became rapid and his blood pressure fell alarmingly. He was given 1g of ascorbic acid intravenously and recovered in a few days. He was thought to have had a haemorrhage into his heart muscle.

One major investigation undertaken at the institute was into vitamin A deficiency, the results of which were written up in 1946 by Dr Krebs and his assistant Miss E.M. Hume, and published in 1949 having been peer reviewed. Again, some of the objectors played a greater part in the experiment beyond acting as 'human guinea pigs'. H.A. Garling prepared the graphs and tables in the published report. Mellanby's original choice of 18 Oakholme Road for the Sorby Research Institute was fortuitous when it came to the dietary experiments, as it had a large kitchen for food preparation to which had been added laboratory facilities, which included dark rooms for dark adaptations measurements and an office for administrative work.

The experiment was carried out by a team of workers, of whom members of the Vitamin A Sub-Committee formed the nucleus. The members of the team met at regular intervals in Sheffield in order to plan and modify the course of the experiment and to utilise new opportunities whenever these might arise. Walter Bartley was once again central to the smooth running of the process, as he attended the committee meetings to represent the point of view of the volunteers. In such a long-running experiment, which for some volunteers lasted for two years, regular meetings between them and the researchers were crucial. This gave the latter a chance to ask questions and the former to communicate any important changes to the experiment. One further indication of the mutual respect between the scientists and the guinea pigs was the publication of the volunteers' names in the final published report. This was a radical departure from traditional medical practice of the time, but, as Hume and Krebs pointed out, in accordance with new tendencies discussed by Dr D. Guthrie in his 1945 paper '"The Patient": A Neglected Factor in the History of Medicine'. The volunteers, twenty men and three women aged from 19 to 34 years of age, were as follows:

Name	Sex	Age when starting experiment (yrs, mths)	Occupation prior to experiment	Occupation during experiment
Bartley, M	F	23.6	Office clerk	Office clerk
Bartley, W.	M	26.6	Laboratory assistant	Laboratory assistant
Bloomfield, H.	M	28.1	Various	S.R.I.
Broderick, J.	M	23.0	Draughtsman	Draughtsman
Brown, L.	M	28.3	Shop Assistant	S.R.I.

Name	Sex	Age when starting experiment (yrs, mths)	Occupation prior to experiment	Occupation during experiment
Drabble, H.,	M	23.0	Student	S.R.I.
Drake, G.	M	30.9	Traveller	S.R.I.
Garling, H.	M	27.1	Income tax clerk	S.R.I.
Garnett, C.	M	22.2	Civil Defence worker	Civil Defence worker
Golding, A.	M	32.5	Insurance clerk	S.R.I.
Hicken, B.	M	24.9	Audit clerk	S.R.I.
Proctor, N.	M	31.0	Baker	S.R.I.
Russell, E.	F	29.9	Social Worker	Social Worker
Saunders, P.	M	21.4	Commercial artist	S.R.I.
Stuart, S.	M	25.2	Bank clerk	Bank clerk
Thompson, W.	M	28.4	Schoolmaster	Schoolmaster
Tridgell, L.	M	20.11	Clerk	S.R.I.
Watson, C.	M	25.3	Architect's clerk	Student
Whitehead, A.	M	29.9	Pharmacist	Pharmacist
Whitehead, D.	F	29.3	Housewife	Shop Assistant
Williams, D.	M	22.1	Cleark	S.R.I.
Wodeman, R.	M	32.3	Various	S.R.I.
Woodhouse, J.	M	23.10	Clerk	Clerk

The vitamin A deficiency experiment had been inspired by the Ministry of Food's desire to plan food policy from 1942. More information was needed on the vitamin A and carotene requirements of adults, so a group of volunteers was needed to undergo prolonged exposure to a diet low in these components. They lived on such a diet for periods ranging from six and a half months to twenty-five months. The volunteers had blood samples collected, and these were sent to laboratories in Cambridge, Liverpool and Oxford every fortnight. The composition of hair follicles was also recorded.

One volunteer was Ethel Russell (later Stuart) from Grenoside, north Sheffield. She took part in the vitamin A deficiency experiment while continuing to live at home with her parents. She recalled, when aged 90, 'It was a strict diet but wasn't difficult to stick to, except for cutting out chocolate. I went into the institute for blood and eyesight tests. It took a long time for signs of deficiency to show up. They expected the effect to be much worse than it was.' She reflected in 2006, 'I feel the experiments were important and worthwhile – I would take part again if it would help people.'

Norman Proctor became totally night blind due to the same experiment. 'I got it back when I came off the diet. But two volunteers got TB, one almost certainly due to the experiment,' he said. Interviewed in 2006, Proctor still had scars on his legs from experiments on wound healing. 'The scientists took pieces out of my thighs. I had a local injection, then they cut an incision over the muscle. When I saw blood I passed out. After a few days they cut around the scar, lifted it and tested it for healing.'

Bernard Hicken described the effect of the vitamin A deficiency on his health:

> After eighteen months of this diet I suppose nature caught up with me and I had to be taken into hospital and given massive doses of Vitamin A and I was six months in hospital with a pleural effusion. ... When I came out of hospital I was like an old man.

Hicken's wife, Una, later gave further evidence of his health problems to the BBC People's War archive:

> He went to the hospital and they found that he had a TB abscess on his chest due to the experiments he'd taken part in. I don't think they expected him to pull through. There was this empty bungalow available at the seaside and my mother told us to go there to help him get better. This [abscess] on his chest had to be bandaged because it was suppurating all the time but an osteopath in Sheffield said if he took the bandages off and lay in the sun, the sun would help him get better.

As news of the work of the Sorby Research Institute spread, it attracted attention in the press, and many letters of encouragement were received at Fairholme. There were also concerns raised about the ethical implications of the work. On 14 May 1942, Mr C.H. Wilson MP, a committed pacifist, challenged the Minister of Health, Ernest Brown, about the experiments. Wilson asked:

> whether he can give any information regarding the investigation of scabies by Dr Kenneth Mellanby; how many persons were infected with the disease; how long the period of examination lasted; what results were obtained; how many of the persons infected were conscientious objectors; whether it was a condition of registration that they should undertake his experiment; and whether there were any temporary or permanent dangers attaching to it?

Brown replied:

> This investigation began at my instance, but is now being continued under the
> auspices of the Medical Research Council. Its object has been to obtain more
> knowledge of the parasite, the means by which scabies is spread, and the best
> methods of treatment. For this the services of human volunteers were essential.
> Forty-seven volunteers have been infected. They have remained under
> examination for varying periods up to eighteen months. The investigation is
> still in progress, but preliminary results are to be found in the White Paper
> now available regarding scabies. Of the volunteers infected, the majority (and
> all who are infected for more than one week) are conscientious objectors; none
> of them has been directed to this duty by a tribunal, though some who were
> already engaged in it when they went before a tribunal were exempted from
> military service on condition that they continued in the work or took up first
> aid duties. They have suffered discomfort rather than danger, but I am advised
> that they have not been free from risk of some prolonged disability.

Wilson retorted: 'Was there a medical examination before these people underwent this
experiment, and has there been a medical examination since and with what result?'

Brown reassured him that the Medical Research Council was overseeing this
'valuable work' without directly answering the question. Wilson's concern was,
on hearing of the work of the institute, that people were being compelled to
take part in the experiments. In order to put his mind at rest, he was invited to
visit Fairholme, and was able to provide assistance to Mellanby from this time
onwards.

It seems unlikely that many of these experiments would be allowed to be
repeated under modern ethical guidelines. Some were dangerous for the
volunteers, although none of them suffered any permanent disability as a result.
In 2006, John Pemberton, who had worked at the institute, attempted to trace the
surviving volunteers to solicit their views on the work. Only four still living could
be found – Norman Proctor, Joe Woodhouse, Ethel Stuart and Harold Garling –
and all said they thought the work was 'worthwhile' and that they would have
volunteered again if asked. Pemberton acknowledged that, despite there being no
long-term ill effects, the volunteers 'often underwent considerable discomfort,
pain, and, in a few cases, danger to life'.

In addition to the benefits to wider society that the experiment brought, and
the enhanced self-esteem that the objectors felt in undertaking work of benefit to
humanity, the scientists themselves learnt much from the process. Hans Krebs
recalled:

My work with conscientious objectors taught me a good deal about how to get on with people who hold strong views. Conscientious objectors are non-conforming individualists; some indeed are eccentrics who object not only to making war but also to many other things. For the first time in my life I was in charge of a group of people from a great variety of backgrounds and of widely differing attitudes. My research team had always been small, with the orientation of all its members in the same direction. As a physician, of course, I had been in contact with every kind of person, but the relations between doctor and patient are very different from those which exist between a team leader and the members of a heterogenous group such as our volunteers.

In Krebs's first encounters with the volunteers he had not been properly awake to all of their sensibilities and admitted to having blundered. When trying to explain the importance of exploring the qualities of high extraction flour, Krebs mentioned that if it proved satisfactory for human consumption, its use would save shipping space, since the same tonnage would result in greater nutrition through a fuller use of its cargo. The objectors interpreted his word to mean that saving shipping space would allow for the importation of more arms. This faux pas caused a temporary storm. After a short time, however, Krebs began to win the volunteers' confidence and was to keep it throughout their four-year association. He was surprised, on Mellanby's departure, that the volunteers expressed the wish that Krebs should take over the administrations of the institute, although alternatives existed.

Krebs thus realised, for the first time, that he was acceptable as a leader of a large and potentially difficult group of people:

> I can only think their confidence in me had something to do with the fact that I have constitutionally a profound respect for every person – whatever his views – as long as he is honest with himself and others. In the course of my association with the team, many problems of human relations came up and I learned how to cope with them.

Fairholme was far from being any sort of isolation unit, with many people from the military, education and health professions paying a visit. A visitors' book was kept, which is now housed in the University of Sheffield's Library Special Collections. Some visitors were troops, who were sent for treatment, whilst others seem to have visited in order to glean medical knowledge from Mellanby and Krebs. For example, on 16 March 1942, Robert C. Hardin and Russell O. Gee of the 109th Medical Battalion of the US Army Northern Ireland force signed in. There were visitors from the Ministry of Supply, an RAF base in Rotherham, RAMC Field Ambulances, the Ministry of Health, the Canadian Field Ambulance and J.B. Sneddon, a lieutenant from the Royal Naval Volunteer Reserve based at the Royal Navy hospital at Chatham. There were visitors from a nutritional laboratory in Cambridge, probably to collect samples to study for the vitamin deficiency experiments, and an M.J. Kalapesi, a representative from the Indian government.

One of the bedrooms at Fairholme had been turned into a military wing during the scabies experiment. This led to pacifists and soldiers living in amity under one roof, with the pacifists waiting on the needs of their military guests. Mellanby claimed that the soldier patients seemed to enjoy their stays as they got a proper bed to sleep in with real sheets. Due to limitations of space the institute could only admit eight external patients at a time. Therefore, a second hospital was established in the Broomhill area with twenty beds, staffed by RAMC medical orderlies. Soon as many as 150 patients per week were being treated by the Sorby Institute, and Mellanby was able to run a series of courses on the subject of scabies for the Royal Canadian Army Medical Corps, and was invited to speak to the American forces stationed in Northern Ireland on the dangers of the disease, as it was infrequently experienced in the US.

Mellanby also paid tribute to the work of the conscientious objector volunteers:

> They have become more than simple passive guinea pigs … for they have taken an active part, co-operating with the work and this making possible experiments which have often been considered impracticable.
>
> I myself am not a pacifist, but for three years I have lived and worked with these volunteers and I think it is possible for me to give a fairly detached view of them and of the contribution they have made to research and medicine. It will appear that the volunteers, except for their views on war, were a fairly normal selection with perhaps rather more virtues and rather less vices that the average members of the population, but for the most part they were in no way either saints or 'cissies'. Some were diligent, a few were bone idle. Most of them were of more than average intelligence. But in addition to their pacifist views (and these were by no means uniform) they had one thing in common throughout the long period through which they served as human guinea pigs. They co-ordinated the experimental work with complete trustworthiness and loyalty. … I think that this was a remarkable achievement on their part which deserves the highest praise.

Mellanby reflected that the main complaint of the volunteers was that, though some did now suffer much discomfort, they would nevertheless have liked to have done more if that had been possible. His view was that the vitamin deficiency tests 'must have been the most tedious experiments ever performed. They lived for years on very restricted diets, they could only eat the foods provided, they had to collect their excrements for analysis.'

For Mellanby, the most remarkable thing about all these investigations was the loyal and co-operative behaviour of the volunteers. However, reflecting over four decades later, he opined, 'It is perhaps unfortunate that such experiments can only be carried out in wartime, for today workers would find themselves prevented from doing most long-term experiments by litigation and red tape.'

The objectors' work caused advancements in medical knowledge and the public saw them as willing to put themselves at risk and undergo physical hardship for the good of others. In addition, for those who lived permanently at 18 Oakholme Road, they were part of a community of like-minded souls who could provide mutual affirmation for both their wartime stance and the importance of their role. For the generations of students who have walked past this impressive house on their way to and from lectures, or to enjoy the social aspects of university life, in the decades since the Sorby Research Institute experiments, few would have been aware of the work that occurred within its walls during the war. That was certainly the case for this author, who spent an enjoyable year as a resident of Stephenson Hall in 1988–89. It is therefore with a sense of appreciation to the volunteers and scientists that their story is included in this book.

Chapter 9

Female Conscientious Objectors

Since the beginning of the war, feminist organisations had been agitating for equality with men in terms of national service. However, across the nation there was a reluctance to conscript women, whilst men in the forces expected their wives to be adequately looked after while they were on active service. Therefore, the government reached a compromise. On 2 December 1941, Winston Churchill brought forward a motion in the House of Commons 'that the obligation for National Service should be extended to include the resources of woman-power and man-power still available'. All single women aged from 20 to 30 could be compelled to join a range of military or industrial organisations. This could include work in the Women's Land Army or domestic service in hospitals as it was thought that no serious conscientious objection could be raised to those fields. In addition, the age range for men was extended to 18 to 51.

The National Service (No. 2) Act came into force on 18 December 1941, allowing for the conscription of single women. Crucially, the same arrangements for female conscientious objection were to be in force as those that had applied to men since 1939. Women could be called up to the Women's Royal Naval Service (WRNS), the Auxiliary Territorial Service (ATS), the Women's Auxiliary Air Force (WAAF) and Civil Defence forces, and those who objected on the grounds of conscience could register to do so. Denis Hayes of the Central Board for Conscientious Objectors articulated concerns held at the time that 'not only were women on the whole less able to express themselves than men but they were also more emotional and more easily upset by tribunal questioning.'

One woman who voiced the feminist objection to conscription was Constance Braithwaite. Writing in *Peace News* on 24 April 1941, she stated:

> Most women have a particular concern for the rearing, preserving and enriching of individual life. It is therefore particularly outrageous to compel women to participate in the prosecution of war, that is, in the wholesale and indiscriminate slaughter of individual life. Industrial conscription involves not only this but also the encouragement of many women to neglect their own children.
>
> It is tragic that one of the results of political equality in this county is that women should participate equally in the most stupid of men's convictions – war. Violence is not women's method: they have often suffered from its use and rarely profited from it.

Convention has in the past recognised that women should not be required to fight, partly due to concern for the preservation of the race. But it is also due to the fact that men have expected a higher moral standard from women than they have expected from themselves.

In order to address these concerns, a new order was issued that stated, from 22 January 1942, tribunals were to consist of six members, including two women. In all, the CBCO recorded that 1,074 women had registered as COs by 1948, with a mere sixty-nine, or 6.4 per cent, receiving unconditional registration. The majority, 689, or 64.1 per cent, were conditionally registered, thirty-eight were directed into non-combatant duties in the armed forces, whilst 278 were removed from the register, having failed to satisfy the tribunals of their sincerity.

There were, in addition, an unidentifiable number of women who refused to comply with the necessity to register. Some were tracked down and pursued through the system but others were not. Winifred Rawlins outlined this line of thought in *Peace News*:

> I am aware that if I were to register and state my pacifist principles I should probably be given the opportunity to do some work which, in itself, I could take no objection. It is the fact of conscription with which I am concerned, not whether I can avoid work.
>
> The greatest evil in the conscription of women lies in the fact that thousands of women who have not reached the point of any kind of resistance, many of them inarticulate working women of immature age, are by means of it drawn into work which outrages all the deepest and womanly instincts in them, work which they would shrink from were it not placed before them as an unavoidable duty to the State.

It was not until 2 April 1942 that the first female conscientious objector appeared before a tribunal. She was Miss Joyce H. Allan of East Horndon, Kent, a member of the Peace Pledge Union. She was registered on the condition she continue her work as a schoolteacher, although towards the end of the war she transferred to the Friends' Relief Service in Liverpool. In 2005 she recalled some of her experiences:

> I asked to be registered as a conscientious objector. I knew I was the first woman to come before the Bristol tribunal, but it wasn't until fifty years after the war that I learned that I'd been the first one in the country. I was very much against the war and I wanted to take any opportunity of making a point about it.

I got there at a very good time and sat through two men's tribunals. It was pretty kindly. Nevertheless, they gave me a good grilling. I didn't get the feeling that I was treated any differently from the way they treated the men. I wasn't awfully conscious of being a woman conscientious objector. It didn't impinge on my thinking a great deal.

I got all these letters from men in the air force. These chaps were frightened. They hated what they were doing and they were scared. What they were doing must have been fantastically scary, and I think it had driven them to write. I was absolutely staggered.

I was teaching at a boys' boarding school in Somerset. There was quite a little bit about it in the newspapers: 'Girl conchie teaches boys'. One of the headlines in the paper about me was headed 'Girl Conchie Criticises the British Constitution', when actually there isn't a British constitution.

I went up to Liverpool at the end of the war to work in what had been the Friends' Relief Service (FRS), although by that time it had been taken over by a local Quaker committee. We had this old baker's premises. We all lived there. One of the things I did was I had a large pram and I collected babies – four babies and one trotting by the side of me – and took them to a nursery so the parents could go to work and not keep the older children home from school.

Some of those people who enjoyed the war look back at it for the camaraderie. Of course, the COs got that if they were in the FRS or in the Friends' Ambulance Unit; they got the feeling of all living together. And some of the people got that in the army or in the air force. When they're marching along proudly with their medals, they're remembering those happy times, and the sad times too, I think. But I just can't understand their mindset, because since I was 13 I've felt that war was wrong.

Some tribunal members did not alter their aggressive style for women COs. Miss Hazel Kerr was told that if her arguments were carried to their logical conclusion she would starve herself and that 'might be the most useful thing you could do'.

Constance Bolam was the first female CO to go to prison, having been told by Northumberland and Durham tribunal Chairman Judge Richardson, 'You must recognise that we on the tribunal have some common sense, and you have none. It is no good talking rubbish to us like that.' This led to derisive clapping from about forty of Bolam's supporters, causing the hearing to be suspended and the police called. Bolam, from Newcastle upon Tyne, was 21 years old at the time of her call-up, a housemaid to a Miss Kitty Alexander. She had been directed to work as a ward maid at the local Eye Infirmary, but told the magistrate court on 7 January 1942 that she disagreed with war in any shape or form and would not take up any work she was directed to do. Hospital work was there for the execution of the war, she said, and she would have not been expected to take up the post under peacetime conditions. She was fined forty shillings but refused to pay, so she was sent to Durham Prison for a month. One of the tasks she was given was to knit socks for soldiers in her cell, which she refused to do. Miss Kitty Alexander, Bolam's employer, even refused to register as a CO. Her case was brought before the Northumberland Petty Sessions on 2 December 1942, where she entered a plea of 'technically guilty but morally not guilty'. She was fined £5, which she refused to pay, and was given a month's imprisonment instead. This cost her her job as a cashier in a local insurance office, although after the war she regained employment with an architect and joined the Campaign for Nuclear Disarmament (CND). On leaving the court she was grabbed by the arm by a policeman and she told him, 'You take your hands off me or I'll have you for assault.' Both women received a large volume of post from well-wishers, with Constance Bolam eventually marrying one of her admirers.

Women could also be directed into industry via the Defence Regulations, and in these cases were not permitted to a tribunal hearing. Mary Cockcroft of Sowerby Bridge, Yorkshire was a 19-year-old Quaker who was directed to leave her post with the local Co-operative Society and to report to the Victoria Hospital, Keighley. She refused and was fined £10, which an anonymous donor paid on her behalf. Another direction to the hospital was then issued, which she ignored, and she was then fined £20 or two months in prison. Cockcroft chose the latter. Her case was raised in the House of Commons by Labour MP Cecil Wilson on 22 October 1942. By an accident of birth, she did not fall into the 20–31 age range for registration as a CO under the National Service Act and was thus not able to state her case to a tribunal. Wilson asked the:

> Minister of Labour whether the Proclamation of 23rd July is still in force whereby only single women between the ages of 20 and 31 are liable for military and industrial conscription and that only such women between these ages have the right to register provisionally as conscientious objectors; and why Mary Cockcroft, of Sowerby Bridge, who is not yet 20 years of age, has been twice prosecuted for failing to comply with the direction of the Ministry and is now serving two months' imprisonment, although she had no opportunity of appearing before a conscientious objectors' tribunal?

On 2 March 1943, the Duke of Bedford spoke in the House of Lords about Cockcroft's case:

> I have seen this girl. She is a mere child, a simple and sincere person, and again I saw that such a prosecution, especially of a member of the Society of

Friends, is iniquitous. ... The only adequate remedy for this state of affairs is
the recognition of conscientious objection to industrial conscription.

The case against Mary Cockroft was not pursued any further by the authorities.
Eventually the Ministry of Labour agreed that men and women could register
for military service ahead of their age requirements, and thus be placed on the
register of objectors.

From 19 September 1942, women aged from 20 to 45 could be directed into
fire-watching activities at their workplace, unless they were expectant mothers
or had children with them. One of the first prosecutions of a woman refusing
to do so was that of Elsie S. Hunt of Scarborough, who was fined £5 for failing
to register for duties. On 11 November 1942, Hilda Marshall, a clerk at the City
Treasurer's Department in Leeds, was sent to prison for a similar offence. The
Yorkshire Evening Post of that day reported:

Hilda Marshall (33), lodging in Town Street, Armley, a clerk in the Leeds
City Treasurer's Department, pleaded guilty in Leeds today to failing to
register for Civil Defence duties, and was sentenced by the Stipendiary
Magistrate (Mr Horace Marshall) to three months' imprisonment in the
second division.

Mr G. Goodhart, Town Clerk's Department, who prosecuted, said the
defendant was allowed to register through the chief clerk of the department in
which she was employed. When given a form to fill up she left it with a note
stating: 'I am not registering for fire-watching as I have no intention of doing
anything to help the war. I am a conscientious objector.'

The Stipendiary: You mean to say you won't move a finger to help your
country in the war?

Defendant: Not to help the war effort, no.

The Magistrate: Are you not going to do anything at all?

Defendant: No I can't.

The Magistrate: Is she still employed by the Corporation?

Mr Goodhart: Yes she is, sir.

The Magistrate (to the defendant): I shall send you to prison for three
months in the second division.

Later the defendant was again brought before the Court and asked by the
Stipendiary Magistrate: 'Why don't you register and do your duty?'

Defendant: Because I follow Jesus Christ. Fire-watching is part and parcel
of war work.

The Magistrate: Either you are insane, or you are a malingerer. I don't know which it is, but as you are working for the Corporation I should imagine you are not insane. I think, therefore, you are a malingerer, and nothing else.

Defendant: I don't know what that is.

The Magistrate: It means a person who puts up excuses and won't do his or her duty. Will you register? If you don't, you will have to go to prison.

Defendant: I shall have to go to prison then.

The Magistrate: Very well, you will go. I think you are a humbug.

Another woman jailed, in this case on three occasions, was Florence Haynes of Ruislip, as were mother and daughter Mrs G.E. Silver and Miss G. Silver of Burnt Oak. Three members of another family were sent to prison for refusal to fire-watch, as reported in the *Surrey Advertiser* of 6 March 1943:

FIRE-WATCHING ORDER IGNORED

Three sisters, who said they were children of God and refused to have anything to do with the war effort, were sent to prison for a month each at Camberley Police Court on Thursday for failing to comply with an Order to attend for training as fire-watchers. They refused the alternative of paying a £5 fine each.

They were Lilian Barbara Dungey, Cicely Idena Dungey and Rachel Dungey, all of the Deborah Café, Frimley Road, Camberley.

Mr Alan Bradley (Clerk to the Urban Council), who prosecuted, said that the women registered in September and intimated that they desired to apply for exemption because they had a conscientious objection to participating in hostilities on any account. They were told that conscientious objection was not a valid ground for exemption, and were duly enrolled.

Colonel R.D. Beadle, Fire Guard Officer, gave evidence of enrolling the three sisters and serving them with notice to train for fire-watching. They did not attend.

Lilian Dungey made a statement in which she said that the magistrates must do whatever they thought right and just, but she must say that, as children of God, they could not take part in anything to assist the war machine.

The Clerk (Mr W.H. Hadfield): But this is fire prevention and the preserving of life. Does your conscience permit you to withhold such assistance?

Yes; because it is in connection with the war. If there were no war there would be no need for this fire prevention.

Cicely Dungey said she agreed with her sister. 'We shall utterly refuse,' she said, 'to do anything to assist the war.'

Rachel Dungey said: 'I also refuse.'

When told they would be fined £5 each or go to prison for a month, Rachel Dungey said, 'We refuse to pay.' The other sisters agreed. They were told they could have seven days to think it over, but still said they would not pay.

The trio were back in court on 9 December 1943 for the same offence. They repeated their reasons for refusal on religious grounds and were again fined and sent to prison. In all, the CBCO recorded eighty prosecutions of women COs for refusal to undertake fire-watching, a low number caused somewhat due to the reluctance of local authorities to prosecute women.

Nora Watson, from Walthamstow in Essex, had first become interested in pacifism during the 1930s. Her father had served in the Royal Naval Air Service (RNAS) during the first war, and her two uncles had been killed in France. Nora attended a Methodist Sunday school as a child, and recalled some people wearing white poppies. She joined the PPU in 1937, having become interested in the organisation after buying a copy of *Peace News* from a street corner vendor and was soon selling the newspaper herself.

Nora believed that all humans were 'brothers', and you do not kill your brothers, no matter what country you were from. She worked for a musical instrument firm, meaning that she formed contacts with clients all over Europe, including Germany. To her it seemed illogical that you would spend years building relationships with people, only to then go and kill them because government leaders had 'fallen out' with each other. When conscription came, she joined small groups of pickets who would leaflet Employment Exchanges, where those liable to conscription had to register, with information about the possibility of conscientious objection. From 1941 to 1945, she volunteered as an advisor to conscientious objectors.

Before the war, Nora recalled that the public had had a generally indulgent 'couldn't care less' attitude to peace activists until the war actually started. There was some harassment by police, who made *Peace News* vendors and leafletters move on if several passers-by gathered for a chat at the same time. However, she and her comrades managed to keep good relations with both the public and the police in her area of London. She developed a good technique of disarming the few hecklers by answering them with a new bit of information.

With the limited extension of military conscription to women in 1941, and the tightening up of industrial conscription and compulsory fire-watching for both men and women, Nora's story became that of a conscientious objector herself. There was a particular problem in that, although there was provision for claiming conscientious objection to military service, there was no legal right of conscientious objection to industrial or fire-watching compulsion.

First, Nora was given 'direction of labour', to work in a greengrocer's shop. As an absolutist, Nora refused as it would have meant the person she replaced in the shop would have been released for military service. She declared, many years later in an interview with the Imperial War Museum, 'My attitude was not to be directed to do anything in wartime that you wouldn't have asked me to do in peacetime.' It seems that, unusually, no further action was taken. This was due to the fact that the Ministry of Labour and National Service had so many people to chase up for the war effort that some cases were overlooked.

However, Nora was then caught by another regulation: 'I was in a fire-watch team in our road and I took my turn stopping up all night. Then we were directed to register for fire-watching ... I wrote and told them I had not registered because I did not believe in conscription.' Therefore, the objection was not against the work per se, but against the official compulsion to undertake it. She had to appear at the magistrates' court in Tottenham, North London, and was sentenced to fourteen days' incarceration in Holloway female prison. Nora was driven off to prison in a Black Maria on 15 January 1943, saying to herself, 'I must carry it through.'

After being taken down to the cells, she and the others under sentence were allowed to receive lunch from some women who had attended the court. She says that the women jailers were helpful and actually waved them off as they departed in the Black Maria. In this, her experience varies greatly from many other women conscientious objectors, who were humiliated and verbally abused during their hearings and afterwards. Nora served her fourteen days at the same time as Kathleen Lonsdale, the eminent Quaker scientist, who was also serving a month for refusing fire-watching registration. They never met, but Nora recalled that it was 'nice to know someone with a big name' was in prison with her.

Kathleen Lonsdale was a crystallographer who developed several X-ray techniques. This work, plus other contributions to chemistry and physics, later earned her a Fellowship of the Royal Society. As a married mother of three children under the age of 14, she was exempt from registration, but she chose to register then refuse to do war work on conscientious principle, becoming the first Quaker woman to be jailed as a conscientious objector. She declared that she had no objection to fire-watching, but felt that the issue of the war itself and the infringement of civil liberties inherent in compulsion were more important. While in Holloway, Kathleen held a Quaker meeting every week, protested to improve the poor conditions, and generally helped to keep up the morale of the other prisoners in her block. After her release she wrote a memoir of prison life, detailing the deprivations experienced by prisoners and examining the medical treatment and issues that arose from that.

Ivy Watson, too, had a gruelling experience. Having refused to register for employment, she appeared before the magistrates at Stratford, London on

22 December 1943. She was ordered to pay a £25 fine or face three months in prison. After choosing prison, after four weeks her health was so impaired that she asked her family to pay the balance of the fine so she could be released. In an account published in the CBCO bulletin, Watson told of how the prisoners had only one small cake of soap per month, one pair of stockings, no handkerchief, no coat, and no toilet paper. Like others, she used a dirty blanket as a wrap against the severe cold and tore up her Bible, the only source of paper, for toilet wipes. Watson also suffered unethical treatment. She had asked for a Nonconformist minister to visit her, and he came on the appointed day. But the prison authorities told him that she didn't want to see him and he went away in bewilderment.

Joan Williams (née Locke) was an assistant in Shoreditch public library who left a chronicle entitled *Experiences of a Woman CO 1939–43*. She was required to register in August 1941 along with all those in her age group, then 26. She refused, and wrote to the Minister of Labour saying so. Having had no response to her letter, she heard nothing further on the matter until June 1942. She then received another demand to register, which she refused. Locke was then summoned to appear at Clerkenwell Magistrates' Court in March 1943. She was remanded in custody for two weeks to be given time to reflect on her position. During her reappearance in court, the following interaction took place:

> Locke: I recognise that the country has been very generous in its treatment
>   of conscientious objectors, but there is no conscientious clause in the
>   industrial conscription act. It is to the principle of the act that I object.
> Magistrate: You object to the law?
> Locke: Because it is the organisation of the country for war purposes, and
>   I feel I cannot take part in it.
> Magistrate: Do you refuse to have the direction? Otherwise you will have to
>   go to prison.
> Locke: I would rather go to prison.

She was sentenced to two months, later commuted to six weeks. Her account of prison life in Holloway highlights the high proportion of religiously motivated female conscientious objectors. Locke encountered four Jehovah's Witnesses, a Methodist, a Quaker and someone of no denomination. During exercise period the group was able to have short conversations and receive visits from Quaker workers. Prison work was also expected, with Locke working in the library. Following her release, despite receiving more notices to register for war work, no further action was taken against her. It appears that the authorities had realised that it was not worth the time and effort enforcing these regulations for a tiny handful of the population, many of whom were already undertaking useful work, just for the sake of demonstrating that compulsion was possible.

Another account of life behind bars was written by Stella St John, an employee of the Fellowship of Reconciliation, who was imprisoned at Holloway in 1943. The depravations she described meant that it was published by the Howard League for Penal Reform as *A Prisoner's Log*. St John described the impersonal nature of their welcome:

> On arrival we were taken into a room where an officer took down particulars of our sentence, age, religion. We were then taken upstairs and locked into a kind of little metal box with wire on top, these were about 4 ft x 4 ft.

During her first day, St John was seen by an Anglican prison chaplain, whom she found to be 'not fond of conscientious objectors', taking a view often expressed in contemporary Christian culture that Hitler was the Antichrist, but going further to state that 'all Germans should be shot as mad dogs.' They did, nevertheless, share a short prayer together. St John was put to work in the laundry, a notoriously unpopular work detail.

> The first few days were extremely unpleasant. Several of us who were new had no idea what to do, when we asked we were told: 'Don't ask me I'm too busy to bother with you.' We then just stood doing nothing and got cursed for that! The prisoners in the laundry are tough, no first offenders are supposed to be put there. ... The language is really appalling and used all the time; the officers don't seem to take any notice.
>
> On receiving a red tie as a first offender, I was automatically withdrawn from the laundry and put in the work room where the other two COs were working. ... We worked on pants for men prisoners as we could not do war work. Other prisoners were making kit bags for the army, aprons for the Navy, Army and Air Force Institutes and sheets for the prison.

St John came across an old prisoner, 'Maggie', who during her frequent stays in prison was the workroom cleaner. She found her to be 'a great source of entertainment' and on returning from one of her short periods of freedom, was furious because the cleaning had not been done to her usual standard. Maggie's language was tactfully described as 'slightly indelicate' with 'nothing is left to the imagination'. It did not stop there, as on one occasion another prisoner had to have three stitches after having been hit on the head by Maggie's broom handle. St John concluded, 'Leave Maggie alone is the best policy, followed by officers and prisoners alike.'

St John described the various punishments used at Holloway, including loss of remission, solitary confinement, a restricted diet of bread and water (although no more than three consecutive days were allowed on this diet). She described other prisoners as having sympathy for those held in the punishment cells. Frequent searches took place when the prisoners were at work. Their beds were searched for stolen items or things that had been smuggled in against prison regulations, including extra clothes, pieces of rag that could be used to effect an escape, pencils and other people's library books. Every three months there was a strip search.

Hygiene was a problem, with the soap ration being extremely small, at 2 inches by 1 inch, this bar having to last for three weeks. This was another item that was frequently stolen, and many prisoners carried theirs around in their pocket. Having had a bath upon reception into the prison, the women then had a weekly bath. St John admitted that the baths were 'quite decent' and the water was usually hot. However, as they were not compulsory, many women never took one. She stated, 'Keeping yourself clean is not a thing encouraged by the authorities.' Despite these deprivations, many women did take the time to keep up their physical appearance. 'A great art in the beauty line is the accomplishment of plucking eyebrows with a couple of buttons off the frock, it took me nearly two hours to get out one lash and it was the wrong one then! But some people with experience attained wonderful results.'

St John found that the attitude of the officers varied tremendously. Some were 'very decent and kind-hearted' whilst others had definite sadistic tendencies, and were in an environment that, according to St John, gave them ample scope to exercise these tendencies. She noted that prison, far from being a place for the reformation of character, encouraged the spread of the art of crime. She was surrounded by shoplifters, and Saturday afternoons were spent sitting in the cells while these women compared notes on their different techniques. St John felt confident that, if she wished to, she could now walk into Selfridges and 'lift' a pair of stockings. Another aspect of her fellow prisoners was a generally tolerant, if slightly puzzled, attitude to conscientious objection.

> The prisoners are usually amazed when you say you are in for conscientious objection. On the whole they are very tolerant about it, some even being sympathetic to the point of saying, 'Good luck to you, I don't hold with this war, but I wouldn't get put in here for it.' Others merely look at you as if you were mad.

St John found a great sense of loyalty between prisoners, with all being treated as fellow-sufferers. Although she was initially placed with women serving long sentences, she was struck by their kindness in 'showing me the ropes'. Despite finding some acceptance of her views within the milieu of her fellow inmates, some family members were less tolerant. Her aunt wrote to an FoR staff member:

> To my mind her views on the war are absolutely lacking in sense – if all Englishmen took that line you, Stella, myself and all helpless people, would by this time have been raped, tortured, hanged or even worse. There would have been nothing to stem the awful tide of devilish brutality and the world would be hell on earth. ... I do admire her with all my heart. It is not that she wants to lead a lazy life like so many COs, she does such splendid work ... I know she has gone to prison for conscience sake. It is grand of her – but as I say, I can't imagine how she can hold such mistaken views. It is a pity.

After her release, St John qualified as a veterinary surgeon and after the war worked with another peace campaigner, Donald Soper, in relief work at the West London Mission.

Kitty Alexander, whose case was mentioned above, also left a record of her imprisonment, this time in the shape of an oral interview given in 1999. She recalled the food as being 'absolutely appalling' in Durham Prison, losing half a stone in weight while serving her sentence. Her bed was a straw mattress on the floor and there was no heating whatsoever, so she slept in her clothes. Alexander was only granted twenty minutes' exercise per day, during which silence had to be observed. No visitors were allowed during a one-month stay, and she was permitted to write one letter per week.

Her prison work was to repair the clothing of male prisoners, and she was given books to read once a week. Like St John, she found some warders pleasant and some objectionable, and, again similar to other CO prison accounts, found her fellow non-CO inmates protective and understanding. On 'Dickie Day', heads were inspected for lice, and prisoners were expected to stand in a long queue, which made Alexander feel she had lice even though she did not. Washing facilities were inadequate, with weekly baths, and she had to wear poorly fitting prison clothes and shoes.

Other women were pursued by the authorities over a number of years. For example, Margaret Prendergast of Liverpool was fined £3 in 1941. This was never paid, and she appeared before a tribunal in 1942 and was finally sentenced to a month in prison in 1943. Betty Brown of Scunthorpe received two separate sentences: twenty-eight days in 1942 and a month in 1944.

A further category of female conscientious objectors was those who objected to being directed in the WRNS, ATS, WAAF or Civil Defence. All single women aged from 19 to 31 were liable for this military service. However, there was a stipulation that no woman would be required to use a lethal weapon. The tribunal arrangements that applied to male objectors were transferred across to females. The first women to be called up were those aged up to 24, although those already working in certain professions or jobs could be spared registration on condition they continued with their work. These included teaching, nursing and land work. Nevertheless, some women did object to the idea of being directed to do what they were already doing, as this impinged on the freedom of the individual, so they registered as objectors anyway.

Like their male counterparts, female COs initially registered at an Employment Exchange before submitting a written statement of their objection to a local tribunal. In the case of female hearings, three outcomes were possible: unconditional registration as a CO; registration under condition on undertaking war-related civilian work; or removal from the register and direction into the forces.

If the CO disagreed with the local tribunal finding, she could appeal to the Appellate Tribunal. Of 1,000 women who appeared before local tribunals, about half appealed – a greater proportion of women than men took this step. This was due to the large number of appeals by absolutists who wanted to make a formal stand; many women in a position equivalent to men accepting conditional exemption did not appear in the conscientious objection statistics at all as they were frequently asked to attend an initial interview if they were already in jobs to which they might have been assigned anyway.

Marjorie Whittles of Liverpool was the first woman conscientious objector to be registered unconditionally, on 20 April 1942. She joined the Friends' Ambulance Unit, and later transferred to the Friends' Relief Service. In a twist of fate, she later married another conscientious objector, Michael Asquith, whose grandfather, Herbert Asquith, had been Prime Minister in 1916 when conscription was introduced alongside the idea of a conscientious objection to that conscription.

In all, the total number of women who appeared before tribunals is given as 1,056, of which fifty-nine were being prosecuted for non-compliance with conditions. In addition there were women who accepted an informal assignment to non-military work, but who in other circumstances would probably have demanded recognition as conscientious objectors. There were 430 known prosecutions of women for conscientious objection to fire-watching and industrial conscription.

Women played significant roles within the conscientious objection movement that went beyond the act of objection. Nancy Browne served as the first secretary of the CBCO, often being the first person that a CO spoke to on turning to the organisation for assistance. The last secretary, Myrtle Solomon, was also female. Although the experience of women COs was far from pleasant, there are no recorded instances of the violence that came the way of some male COs. Prison sentences tended to be of shorter duration and cases of repeated prosecutions were rare. The Ministry of Labour had learned the lesson that prosecutions only gave publicity to views that ran contrary to the general spirit of the war effort.

Chapter 10

The Campaign against the Prosecution of War

For many people in Britain, it mattered not only that the war itself was in a just cause, but that it was justly fought too. Some expressed concern about the Allied blockade of continental Europe, which caused misery and threatened famine in German-occupied countries such as Greece. However, it was the area bombing campaign that caused the greatest consternation among British pacifists and pacificists during the war.

Some people believed that any reprisal bombing just led to a cycle of retribution. One man wrote to Lord Ponsonby, the veteran pacifist, stating, 'I, like increasing numbers of others, believe that the first concern of the Government should be to STOP THE WAR before the dreadful and stupid bombing succession of London, Berlin, Coventry and Hamburg etc. destroys all chance of a better Europe.'

As the war progressed, methods of aerial bombardment caused increasing amounts of damage to civilian property and spiralling loss of life. The bombing of enemy cities became a deliberate tactic to try to break the morale of populations, and this was, naturally, bitterly opposed by those who had been against the war from its inception.

Part of the tactic of saturation bombing was to create a ring of fire around the intended target, to stop the emergency services reaching it quickly. *Time* magazine wrote, 'The objective is not merely to destroy cities, industries, human beings and the human spirit on a scale never before attempted by air action. The objective is to defeat Hitler with bombs, and to do it in 1943.'

As early as November 1939, George Bell, Bishop of Chichester, wrote an article in which he warned against the targeting of civilians in warfare. The Church of England, wrote Bell, should not fail:

> to condemn the infliction of reprisals, or the bombing of civilian populations, by the military forces of its own nation. It should set itself against the propaganda of lies and hatred. It should be ready to encourage the resumption of friendly relations with the enemy nation. It should set its face against any war of extermination or enslavement, and any measures directly aimed to destroy the morale of a population.

On 17 April 1941, as it was becoming apparent that reprisals on German cities were being undertaken in response to the Luftwaffe's blitz of Britain, *The Times* carried a letter from George Bell. Referring to the Pope's recent appeal to spare the non-combatant civilian populations of all nations, Bell highlighted the recent destruction of Belgrade and predicted further destruction of cities by the armed forces of both sides:

> The war is indeed totalitarian, fought with all their resources by whole nations against whole nations. But it is nevertheless barbarous to make unarmed women and children the deliberate object of attack. It is said that once a war has begun limitation is impossible. But, if Europe is civilized at all, what can excuse the bombing of towns by night, and the terrorising of non-combatants who work by day and cannot sleep when darkness comes?
>
> The Pope appeals to belligerents on both sides on behalf of non-combatants. Let us concentrate on the issue of night bombing. Is it not possible for the British Government to make a solemn declaration that they for their part will refrain from night bombing (either altogether or of towns with civilian populations) provided that the German Government will give the same undertaking? If this single limitation were achieved it would at least make a halt in the world's rushing down to ever-deeper baseness and confusion.

In the summer of 1941, the Quaker Corder Catchpool, who had been a long-time campaigner for peace and had served in the Friends' Ambulance Unit and spent time in prison during the First World War due to his conscientious objection, formed the Committee for the Abolition of Night Bombing. He invited Professor Stanley Jevons, T.C. Foley, Stuart Morris and Vera Brittain to join his committee. One of the first actions was to organise a petition to request that the British government give up night bombing. It gathered 15,000 signatures, including a smattering of Anglican bishops and MPs.

Some of the committee's members had personal contacts in Germany, having spent time there in the decades since the end of the First World War. George Bell had close contacts with Dietrich Bonhoeffer and Martin Niemöller from the German Confessing Church, and had been active in helping Jewish people gain political asylum in Britain before the war. Corder Catchpool had worked in Germany with the Friends' War Victims Relief Committee after his release from prison at the end of the First World War, in order to bring about reconciliation between the nations who had gone to war.

As the RAF's bombing campaign escalated, with the appointment of Arthur Harris as head of Bomber Command, the committee renamed itself the Bombing

Restriction Committee. Members of the committee set out to gather information about the legality of area bombing, to support the International Red Cross in their calls for 'sanctuary areas' in cities that should be avoided as targets, and to collect data that Bishop Bell could use to criticise area bombing from his position in the House of Lords. He received little support from his fellow churchmen, with both William Temple, the Archbishop of Canterbury, and Cyril Forster Garbett, Archbishop of York, both expressing support for the government's position. Bell's outspoken views on this issue cost him any chance he may have had of succeeding Temple as Archbishop of Canterbury in 1944.

In the final week of July 1943, the RAF launched Operation Gomorrah, targeting the city of Hamburg, creating one of the largest firestorms seen in the war; 42,600 civilians were killed and 37,000 wounded. The operation's name came from the Canaanite city of evil practices mentioned in the Book of Genesis, Chapter 19. The inhabitants of Sodom and Gomorrah had refused to turn away from their immoral behaviours, and they had been punished, 'Then the Lord rained brimstone and fire on Sodom and Gomorrah, from the Lord out of the heavens' (Genesis 19:24).

The bombing of Hamburg was incessant, with RAF Bomber Command attacking at night, and the USAAF Eighth Air Force during the day. On one night, on 27 July, 787 RAF aircraft flew over the city, creating a firestorm, a tornado of fire reaching over 1,000 feet in height, generating winds of up to 150 mph and reaching temperatures of up to 800 degrees centigrade. In all, 3,000 aircraft dropped 9,000 tons of bombs, destroying over 250,000 homes. Many thousands of factories were also ruined.

It was not just prominent public figures who expressed disquiet about the ferocity and scale of the attacks. The *Daily Telegraph* had reported in October 1943 that Hamburg had experienced at least sixty 'Coventries'. A handful of residents of that city wrote to the *New Statesman*:

Sir- Many citizens of Coventry who have endured the full horror of intense aerial bombardment would wish to dispute statements made in the *Daily Express* to the effect that all the people of Coventry expressed the opinion that they wished to bomb, and bomb harder, the peoples of Germany. This is certainly not the view of all or even the majority of people in Coventry. The general feeling is, we think, that of horror, and a desire that no other peoples shall suffer as they have done. Our impression is that most people feel the hopelessness of bombing the working classes of Germany and very little satisfaction is attained by hearing that Hamburg is suffering in the same way that Coventry has suffered.

Concerns were raised in Parliament on the progress of the bombing campaign. Richard Stokes challenged Archibald Sinclair, the Secretary of State for Air, on 11 March 1943:

> The Right Hon. Gentleman has told us something of the activities of Bomber Command and their frequent excursions over Germany. Is he able to give the House the percentage of the losses—not the actual losses—over the whole of Europe?

Stokes challenged Sinclair again on 31 March. He asked 'whether on any occasion instructions have been given to British airmen to engage in area bombing rather than limit their attention to purely military targets'.

Sinclair responded, 'The targets of Bomber Command are always military, but night bombing of military objectives necessarily involves bombing the area in which they are situated.'

In a debate in the House of Commons on 1 December 1943, Stokes asked if the policy of Bomber Command had changed, and that their objectives were now not specific military targets, but large areas. Sinclair refuted the allegation, and received support from across the Commons, with the Labour MP Manny Shinwell stating, 'while we deplore the loss of civilian life everywhere, we wish to encourage and applaud the efforts of His Majesty's Government in trying to bring the war to a speedy conclusion.'

In the upper chamber of Parliament, on 9 February, George Bell had initiated a debate on bombing policy, prefacing his remarks with this statement:

> I desire to challenge the Government on the policy which directs the bombing of enemy towns on the present scale, especially with reference to civilians, non-combatants, and non-military and non-industrial objectives. I also desire to make it plain that, in anything I say on this issue of policy, no criticism is intended of the pilots, the gunners, and the air crews who, in circumstances of tremendous danger, with supreme courage and skill, carry out the simple duty of obeying their superiors' orders.

Bell went on to point out that the United Kingdom and France had given assurances at the beginning of the war to spare civilian populations from unnecessary harm, quoted from Article 22 from the Washington Conference on Limitation of Armaments in 1922 that 'Aerial bombardment for the purpose of terrorizing the civilian population, of destroying or damaging private property not of military character, or of injuring non-combatants is prohibited.' He accepted that it was the Luftwaffe who unleashed devastation on Belgrade, Warsaw, Rotterdam, London, Portsmouth, Coventry and Canterbury, and that Hitler was a 'barbarian'. For Bell, the fundamental questions were:

1. Do the Government understand the full force of what area bombardment is doing and is destroying now?
2. Are they alive not only to the vastness of the material damage, much of which is irreparable, but also to the harvest they are laying up for the future relationships of the peoples of Europe as well as to its moral implications?

Bell gave the example of Hamburg, which, as well as being a centre of military and industrial importance, had also been the most democratic town in Germany, where anti-Nazi opposition had been the strongest. Many of the city's cultural, military, residential, industrial and religious buildings had been destroyed. The fate of Berlin, with its great art collection, Oriental and classical sculpture, and libraries of irreplaceable books, was of similar concern to Bell. With these cultural artefacts destroyed, the re-education of Germans after the war would be delayed.

He traced the tactic of area bombing back to the attacks on Lübeck and Rostock in the spring of 1942, with successive raids targeting the cities area by area, rather than precision bombing of specific military or industrial targets. Since then the destruction had spread to other cities and Bell feared its extension to attacks on Rome, which would:

> create such hatred that the misery would survive when all the military and political advantages that may have accrued may have long worn off. The history of Rome is our own history. Rome taught us the Christian faith. The destruction would rankle in the memory of every good European as Rome's destruction by the Goths or the sack of Rome rankled.

To some disagreement, which was recorded in Hansard, Bell stated that the objective of the British government was the defeat of the Hitlerite state, rather than Germany itself. Britain stood for greater ideals, and the character of the peace would be affected by the nature of the war waged to achieve it. In response, Viscount Cranborne agreed with Bell's sentiments that the bombing was not undertaken with relish, but that:

> I think … should face hard facts frankly. If [Bishop Bell] will allow me to say so, I do not think he was facing these facts, quite, this afternoon. The hard, inescapable fact is that war is a horrible thing, and that it cannot be carried on

without suffering, often caused to those who are not immediately responsible for causing the conflict. In the situation with which we are faced today we cannot expect to find means of conducting hostilities which do not involve suffering. ... What we have to do, to the best of our ability, is to weigh against each other how much suffering is going to be caused or saved by any action which we may feel obliged to take.

Cranborne also referenced the suffering happening in German–occupied countries, and the plight of the Jews, which Bell had previously raised in the Lords, stating that the best way to bring the misery to an end was to finish the war as swiftly as possible, an objective that the bombing raids were designed to achieve.

Public attitudes to carpet-bombing

Research undertaken by the social survey organisation Mass Observation showed that a significant minority of public opinion had remained opposed to retaliation bombing from 1940 to 1944. Whilst the immediate reaction to the Blitz had seldom been one of revenge, by 1944, 'nearly one person in four expresses feelings of uneasiness or revulsion' about Bomber Command's methods.

Vera Brittain (Plates, page 12) published a fortnightly letter on behalf of the committee, and in one edition she wrote, '[We] must decide whether we want the government to continue to carry out through its Bomber Command a policy of murder and massacre in our name. Has any nation the right to make its young men the instruments in such a policy?'

The committee's efforts were not generally well received in Britain. An editorial in the *Sunday Despatch* said, 'Bomber personnel, often in miserable weather, and under attack by vicious fighters, try to hit their targets. Any attempt to persuade them to worry unduly about civilians is an attempt to impair their military value.'

However, George Bernard Shaw, writing in the *Daily Mail*, opined:

We have rained 200,000 tons of bombs on German cities, and some of the biggest of them have no doubt fallen into infants' schools or lying-in hospitals. When it was proposed to rule this method of warfare out, it was we who objected and refused. Can we contend that the worst acts of the Nazis whom our Russian allies have just hanged were more horrible than the bursting of a bomb as big as a London pillar-box in a nursery in Berlin or Bremen? ... Our enemies had better know that we have not all lost our heads, and that some of us will know how to clean our slate before we face an impartial international court.

George Bell was the first to use the more forceful term 'obliteration bombing' to describe what was happening to German towns and cities, and as the obliteration continued through 1943, Vera Brittain was driven to write a book, *Seeds of Chaos: What Mass Bombing Really Means*, published in 1944 and reproduced in America as *Massacre by Bombing: The Facts behind the British-American Attack on Germany*. Brittain claimed that the Allied governments were glossing over the true extent of the suffering caused by the air attacks on Germany by using such terms as 'softening up' an area, 'neutralising the target', 'area bombing', 'saturating the defences' and 'blanketing an industrial district'. However, Brittain argued that the residents of cities 'are being subjected to agonizing forms of death and injury comparable to the worst tortures of the Middle Ages'.

Brittain then turned to the two principle arguments used to justify the bombing campaigns. Firstly, it was argued that the war would be shortened as a result. She maintained there was no evidence to justify that claim, that Churchill had described the bombings as an 'experiment'. For Brittain, this argument represented 'the downward spiral of moral values, ending in deepest abyss of the human spirit'. Although the war may have been settled within a shorter time period, the scale of killing was one that would have taken weeks to achieve using conventional ground warfare. As well as the human suffering, irreplaceable art treasures, architecture and documents were being destroyed, 'representing centuries of man's creative endeavour'. The bombing experiment had not weakened German morale, and would only create the desire for further revenge in the future, the 'psychological foundation for a Third World War'.

The second argument used to justify the saturation bombing was that it was exacting revenge for the devastation caused to English cities by the Luftwaffe. Brittain dismissed this claim, stating that it was impossible to ascribe blame to one side for the escalation of aerial bombardment, yet, 'the grim competition goes on until the mass murder of civilians becomes part of our policy, a descent into barbarism that we should have contemplated with horror in 1939.' She put forward the theory that most Britons had been not directly affected by the Blitz, leading to their 'supine acquiescence in obliteration bombing'. Brittain believed that the majority of Britain's airmen would not want to preserve their own lives by sacrificing German women and babies. Finally, by retaliating in kind and worse to the German blitz 'means the reduction of ourselves to the level of our opponents whose perceived values have persuaded us to fight'.

Brittain cited a British Institute of Public Opinion survey from 1941, which demonstrated that people in heavily bombed areas were less in favour of reprisal bombing than those who had escaped the raids. She then traced the development of Bomber Command's tactics from one of precision to area bombing and quoted some of the estimates of loss of life and devastation the new methods had wrought: 20,000 killed in Cologne on the night of 30/31 May 1943; over 100,000 killed in RAF raids on twelve German towns from April to October of that year; and nearly 7,000,000 people bombed out and evacuated. Brittain contrasted these figures with the 50,000 killed by German air raids on Britain – twenty-four times fewer than the number killed in the reprisals. Archibald Sinclair, the Secretary of State for Air, claimed that whilst 5 per cent of Coventry had been destroyed in 1940, 54 per cent of Cologne and 74 per cent of Hamburg had been demolished.

Inevitably, these huge percentages included buildings of public importance, including many hundreds of schools, hospitals and churches. Brittain called on the public to protest against such devastation. In order to make her point further, she moved on from quoting figures to providing more qualitative detail on the effects of the bombing on ten German towns and cities. For example, a report in the Swiss newspaper *National-Zeitung* gave an eyewitness account of Hamburg:

> We passed whole streets, squares, and even districts ... that had been razed. Everywhere were charred corpses, and injured people had been left unattended. We will remember those Hamburg streets as long as we live. Charred adult corpses had shrunk to the size of children. Women were wandering about half-crazy. That night, the largest workers' district of the city was wiped out.

Survivors were placed into large shelters containing up to 6,000 people, but the Stockholm correspondent of the *Daily Telegraph* reported, 'People went mad in the shelters. They screamed and threw themselves, biting and clawing the doors which were locked against them by the wardens.' Due to the great heat people died of suffocation in the shelters. In addition, the intensity of the fires sucked in oxygen from the surrounding area, thus when people did leave the shelters, they could not summon the strength to move to a safer area. The majority of the victims were women and children. The *Basler Nachrichten* reported:

> Numerous completely charred bodies of women and children were found along the outer walls to the houses; women and children in light summer clothing who emerged from the cellars into the storm of fire in the street were soon converted into burning torches.

There were also reports of women throwing their children into canals to escape the intense heat, with glass windows and metal frames being reduced to ash and cinders.

Brittain wrote of the cultural history of cities such as Münster and Nuremberg being obliterated. That the Bishop of Münster, Count von Galen, had repeatedly spoken out against the Nazis during the war was not enough to save his city from being a target of Allied bombing. Indeed, one raid, on 10 October 1943, had taken place on a Sunday morning when the churches were filled with worshippers, thus increasing the casualty rate. The city was home to no major industrial activity. Nuremberg, before its association with the enormous Nazi rallies of the 1930s, had been a medieval city, 'as priceless to Germans and all students of German culture as Oxford to ourselves'. On 29 August 1943, the *Sunday Express* recorded:

> Few towns, even in Germany, can have received so shattering a blow in forty minutes as medieval Nuremberg, the Bavarian 'holy city' of the Nazi Party, which was the target of the vast armada of bombers that roared for more than an hour over South East England late on Friday. The result was summed up in one pregnant sentence by a rear gunner on his return. He said, 'I reckon we knocked the whole place flat.'

Vera Brittain then turned her attention to the effect of the policy on the crews tasked with undertaking the raids. In her estimation, they would not dwell on the cost to civilians of their work, but in future years, once the full horror became apparent, they would find it hard to forgive themselves. Some might suffer nightmares, or even mental breakdown. Brittain switched the focus of her piece to the effect of bombing strategic targets, using the example of the Möhne and Edersee dams, made famous as the objectives of the famous Dambusters raid, led by Guy Gibson. She quoted from the *National News-Letter* of 24 June 1943 on the human effects of the breaching of the dam:

> The explosion of the Möhne dam was catastrophic. It started with a sharp tone which suddenly changed into the rushing and roaring of water which swept everything along with it through the Ruhr districts and hills. Many old historical parts of Soest were simply swept away. The water found its way into mines, and hundreds of workers were surprised by the water during the night shift. Many of them were drowned as the way out was completely blocked by the water. ... There was no drinking water available in many areas. Guy Gibson himself gave an eyewitness account of the great torrent unleashed by the bouncing bomb:
>
> A great column of whiteness rose up a thousand feet into the air and the dam wall collapsed. I looked again at the dam and at the water. It was a sight such as no man will ever see again. Down in the valley we saw cars speeding

along the roads in front of this great wave of water which was chasing them and going faster than they could ever hope to go. I saw their headlights burning and I saw the water overtake them one by one, and then the colour of the headlights underneath the water changed from light blue to green, from green to dark purple, until quietly and rather quickly there was no longer anything except the water.

The floods raced on, carrying with them as they went viaducts, railways, bridges and everything that stood in their path.

Then I felt a little remote and unreal sitting up there in the warm cockpit of my Lancaster, watching this mighty power which we had unleashed; and then I felt glad because I knew that this was the heart of Germany and the heart of her industries, the place which itself had unleashed so much misery upon the world.

Brittain admonished 'the Wing Commander' for failing to have the imagination to realise 'the woe and obliteration that he loosed upon the thousands of sleeping families, each home a shelter, up to that minute, of life made in the image of God'.

Brittain had expressed the opinion that bomber crews would find it hard to come to terms with their actions, either in the immediate aftermath, or in the years following the war. There is some evidence to support this contention. Many airmen did have tortured consciences at the time of the raids. One young radio operator wrote to RAF chaplain John Collins, expressing his horror for the carnage for which he felt partly responsible:

It was a nightmare experience looking down on the flaming city beneath. I felt sick as I thought of the women and children down there being mutilated, burned, killed, terror-stricken in the dreadful inferno – and I was partly responsible. Why, Padre John, do the Churches not tell us that we are doing an evil job? Why do chaplains persist in telling us that we are performing a noble task in defence of Christian civilisation? I believe that Hitler must be defeated; I am prepared to do my bit to that end. But don't let anyone tell us that what we are doing is noble. What we are doing is evil, a necessary evil perhaps, but evil all the same.

A draft of this lengthy piece was taken to America in late 1943 by a member of the Bombing Restriction Committee, where it was published in *Fellowship*, the magazine of the American Fellowship of Reconciliation. This was without Brittain's permission or knowledge. Reaction was condemnatory, including attacks on the article by leading Protestant and Catholic clergymen. William Shirer, the renowned journalist who had spent much time in Germany before the war, wrote in the *New York Herald Tribune* that Brittain was a mouthpiece for Nazi propaganda. First Lady Eleanor Roosevelt called the piece 'sentimental nonsense' and President Roosevelt himself had a letter sent to *Fellowship* arguing that bombing was the best way to convince the enemy to change their ways.

When Brittain's *Seeds of Chaos* was published in Britain in 1944, it drew criticism from George Orwell. Writing in *Tribune* magazine, he stated:

> Now, no one in his senses regards bombing, or any other operation of war, with anything but disgust. On the other hand, no decent person cares tuppence for the opinion of posterity. And there is something very distasteful in accepting war as an instrument and at the same time wanting to dodge responsibility for its more obviously barbarous features. Pacifism is a tenable position; provided that you are willing to take the consequences. But all talk of 'limiting' or 'humanising' war is sheer humbug, based on the fact that the average human being never bothers to examine catchwords.

Brittain responded in the pages of *Tribune*, arguing that just because the pacifist movement had not succeeded in preventing war, then it did not follow that they should 'throw in the sponge and acquiesce in any excesses which war-makers choose to initiate'.

On a visit to Germany in the spring of 1944, Orwell did admit that 'To walk through the ruined cities of Germany is to feel an actual doubt about the continuity of civilisation.' Disgustingly, some reactions were less cerebral than Orwell's, and Brittain received both hate mail and an envelope filled with dog faeces. Her reaction was that she had evidently got under her opponents' skin, which was preferable to being ignored.

Bombing of Dresden

From 13 to 15 February 1945, 722 RAF bombers and 527 from the USAAF dropped more than 3,900 tons of bombs on the city of Dresden, creating a firestorm similar to that generated in Hamburg the previous year, killing from 23,000 to 25,000 people in the process. For the first time the bombing campaign over Germany was seriously questioned in public in Britain and America. (Plates, page 15)

Richard Stokes raised the issue in the Commons on 6 March 1945, stating:

> I do not join issue on tactical questions. Where bombing is necessary for the conduct of military affairs, with military objectives, it is just too bad if civilians

and old women get their guts blown into tree tops, but there it is. That is war and has got to be put up with. The question is whether at this period of the war indiscriminate bombing of large centres of populations, full of refugees, is wise. One reads the most ghastly stories of what is going on in Dresden. I know it is a German report, but I am going to read what was in the *Manchester Guardian* of yesterday: 'Tens of thousands who lived in Dresden are now burned under its ruins. Even an attempt at identification of the victims is hopeless. What happened on that evening of February 15th? There were 1,000,000 people in Dresden, including 600,000 bombed-out evacuees and refugees from the East. The raging fires which spread irresistibly in the narrow streets killed a great many from sheer lack of oxygen.' I agree that that may be an over-statement, but one has only to read our own correspondents' reports about Cologne to see that this account is probably not far removed from what is the case.

Stokes admitted that by this stage of the war, he felt it futile to reiterate the moral issue as a case for a cessation of the bombing campaign. Nevertheless, it was the strategic issue that might give greater pause for thought:

> What are you going to find with all the cities blasted to blazes and disease rampant? May you not well find that you will simply be overtaken by your own weapons, and that the disease, filth and poverty, which will arise, will be almost impossible either to arrest or to overcome?

By now, it was not just persistent opponents of the campaign who were beginning to have doubts about its continuing efficacy. On 28 March 1945, Churchill sent a memo to General Ismay, his chief military assistant, for the benefit of the British Chiefs of Staff and the Chief of the Air Staff, writing:

> It seems to me that the moment has come when the question of bombing of German cities simply for the sake of increasing the terror, though under other pretexts, should be reviewed. Otherwise we shall come into control of an utterly ruined land. ... The destruction of Dresden remains a serious query against the conduct of Allied bombing. ... I feel the need for more precise concentration upon military objectives ... rather than on mere acts of terror and wanton destruction, however impressive.

Air Chief Marshal Harris was not impressed with the suggested change of strategy. He argued that as these attacks were shortening the war, they should not be given up, as this would mean increased Allied casualties in the long run. He stated, 'I do not personally regard the whole of the remaining cities of Germany as worth the bones of one British Grenadier.'

Men did not have to be pacifists to experience revulsion at the bombings. This extended to many tasked with carrying out the raids. Jo Capka was piloting a Wellington bomber en route to bomb Wilhelmshaven when he dropped a single bomb on an undefended German town. His immediate reaction was regret, but this was short-lived:

> I felt a complete and utter swine. I had probably wiped out innocent people – Germans, yes, but sleeping peacefully in the firm belief that there were no military targets in the town. ... Why should they sleep when I was risking death every night?

Willie Lewis told his commander that he felt uneasy at bombing Wuppertal, a city full of refugees, believing he was being asked to commit 'deliberate murder' and had a 'good mind not to come'. However, fearing a charge of Lack of Moral Fibre, he obeyed orders, although reflecting, 'we are only mean bastards taking orders from a bunch of hypocrites.'

The obliteration bombing of German cities was something that provoked a wide variety of responses from British Christians. Even before the war, the potential use of this bombing policy had caused consternation in the British Christian milieu. W.R. Matthews, the Dean of St Paul's, in a pre-war assessment of the moral dilemmas faced by the Christian in wartime, wrote:

> it is surely beyond the bounds of tolerable paradox to assert that airmen raining death and destruction on a crowded city could be doing so in a spirit of love and forgiveness, and it strikes us as little short of blasphemy when they say they are fighting in the cause of Christ.

This view of the questionable morality of the carpet-bombing policy was echoed by Sir Stafford Cripps, a devout Christian of no specific denomination, who served as Minister of Aircraft Production. At a talk at Bomber Command Headquarters in 1945, he offended senior officers by stating that a bombing mission should need to be justified on moral grounds, as well as those of military strategy and tactics.

William Temple, Archbishop of Canterbury from 1942 to 1944, altered his opinion of civilian bombing during the course of the war. Having claimed in June 1940 that there would be 'nothing left fighting for' if a policy of bombing open towns were adopted, by April 1944 he expressed the view that bombing was 'most effectively done by the total destruction of the whole community engaged in the work than by attack on the factories themselves, which can be repaired with astonishing rapidity'. The pressure on Temple, as the senior cleric in the Anglican Church, meant that, for one historian, the 'argumentative position that he was encouraged to adopt led him steadily into a dismal corner, from which he strained to discern the moral imperative.' This is a harsh judgement, as most senior clergy were in favour of the policy. Archbishop Garbett, writing in 1943, claimed that only military sites were being targeted, and that the bombing would shorten the war, saving many lives.

For some, the blitz bombing of British cities had made reprisal bombing of German cities morally acceptable. Mervyn Haigh, Bishop of Coventry, spoke shortly after that city had been devastated in December 1940: 'Nor do I believe that a nation need be morally degraded even by doing horrible things of a new kind in a war which it believes itself morally right in waging.' However, his friend and biographer, Russell Barry, Bishop of Southwell, whilst agreeing that Haigh was correct in raising the issue, disagreed with this stance, stating, 'I do not myself believe that obliteration bombing can have any possible moral justification.' George Bell, Bishop of Chichester, argued that the clergy should not play any part in condoning acts of war and called for the bombing of German cities to cease. He recognised that all the forces of the state had to be harnessed to win the war, but that the moral authority of the Church was not part of those resources. He did come in for criticism for being in favour of the principle of the war, but not its practice.

The Anglican press did not concur with the viewpoint of the Church hierarchy. The *Church Times* thundered in March 1945: 'if the German tale, that a million lie dead beneath the tumbled walls, is even one-tenth true, the Christian has cause to bend the knee and implore Almighty God's forgiveness for the wickedness of civilised war.' This was certainly the view of Bomber Command Headquarters' own chaplain, John Collins, who described carpet-bombing as 'evil'.

Collins related the contents of a letter from an RAF radio operator who had formed part of a Christian fellowship group at RAF Yatesbury. After his initial operational flight, a night raid on Hamburg, he wrote: 'It was a nightmare experience looking down on the flaming city beneath. I felt sick as I thought of the women and children down there being mutilated, burned, killed, terror-stricken in that dreadful inferno – and I was partly responsible.' Collins's correspondent went on to question why the churches and chaplains broadcast the message that the bomber crews were performing a noble task, rather than a necessary evil. The perception that taking part in bombing raids was a sinful act was one shared by Sergeant Les Bartlett, who wrote in his diary, 'I say a prayer to ask for forgiveness for the murder of so many human beings by the dropping of my bombs.'

Although not directly involved in the killing of German civilians, Stanley Johnson, a wireless technician with the Royal Army Ordnance Corps (RAOC) from a Quaker household, later came to regret the attitude he had shown during the war, saying, 'I am somewhat ashamed of the fact that at that time we gloried over the bombing of Dresden.' Of particular distaste was the 'killing of women and small children – together with irreplaceable architectural gems'. For Johnson, Britain had descended to the 'same barbaric tactics' as Hitler and was exhibiting an unchristian spirit of revenge.

The destruction of buildings as well as human life was a theme echoed by Harry Boal, a wireless operator on a Lancaster bomber. Boal was part of the crew that inadvertently dropped seven bombs on Rouen Cathedral in April 1944. He recalled that after the flight debrief, the bomb aimer looked 'pretty sick', and Boal himself still regretted the destruction six decades later. On a visit to the site in 2005, on realising that the raid was referenced in an article, he reflected, 'To stand there and know for sure that you are responsible for it is a pretty rotten feeling.' However, during the war, he did not show the same level of regret for civilian casualties as for the destruction of a Christian building. On being challenged on the role of Bomber Command by a 'very religious' aunt while on home leave, he tried to explain that the targets were military and industrial, with the aim being to foreshorten the war. Whilst agreeing that he did think of the civilian casualties being sustained, he asserted that the main battle for him was against the Luftwaffe fighters and trying to stop their missions.

Whilst some members of Bomber Command felt complete ease at the loss of life their work entailed, and other Christians could comment on the 'splendid record of the RAF', there were Christian voices that challenged the narrative of the necessity of following orders so that a war could be won. Harold Nash, a Methodist from Birmingham, was shot down and taken as a prisoner of war in September 1943. While being escorted to prison, he was offered a piece of bread by three German women from a recently bombed area. A decade after the war, a remark at a party about Christ turning the other cheek turned Nash into a committed pacifist, working for reconciliation between the peoples of Germany and Britain. He refused to condemn his comrades for the carpet-bombing, but protested at the erection of a statue to Arthur 'Bomber' Harris, as he claimed it represented approval for the decision taken by Churchill and Roosevelt to target German civilians.

Sometimes indiscriminate bombing could prove counter-productive. Ken Tout, a Salvationist, considered the obliteration bombing of Caen in 1944 in this light, as it made it harder for his tank formation to advance, leading to heavier casualties. 'With hindsight the RAF raid was too hard and wasteful to crack the nut of

Caen,' he said. In addition, in the cases of Hamburg and Dresden, 'the force used was excessive for the objective set.' Thus, Tout also saw bombing in the light of its practical results, as well as from an ethical standpoint. His conclusion that 'morally [obliteration bombing and the atomic bombs] were wrong. But so was I, firing an explosive shell into a house full of Germans' was one that sought to set the Bomber Command policy within the wider actions that needed to be undertaken in wartime.

Therefore, both the churches and the men engaged in bombing raids over Europe did question the ethical nature of the way Britain was fighting the war. Although thoughts of vengeance for the blitz of British cities were evident, the thought that they were directly responsible for so many civilian deaths troubled many men. In this instance, the failure of the churches and chaplains to provide a clear, unified and consistent message led to guilt, doubt and recriminations both during the war and in the decades that followed.

Despite the sincere campaigns both in print and in Parliament, the opposition to the tactic of saturation bombing was, eventually, futile. Martin Francis, historian of RAF culture, dismissed the most voluble MP, Richard Stokes, as an 'unpopular maverick', and suggested that contemporary perceptions of Vera Brittain would have seen her as 'self-righteous or seriously naïve'. Their views certainly found some resonance among the broader population. From mid-1944 onwards, the British public's attention was drawn towards the invasion of Normandy and subsequent land battles on the European mainland. On the domestic front, war concerns centred on the arrival of the V-2 rocket, which killed 9,000 people in the final fourteen months of the war.

In April 1945, with the liberation of Bergen-Belsen and other concentration camps, and the discovery of the affronts to humanity committed by the Nazis, it became a greater challenge to gain a sympathetic audience for the highlighting of the moral duties the Allies owed to German citizens. As philosopher Professor A.C. Grayling put it, 'Pictures of British Tommies using bulldozers to push piles of emaciated corpses into mass graves made discussion of morality in any other connection a nullity.' The post-war world was concerned with reconstruction, rather than a detailed analysis of the methodology that had brought about a cessation to hostilities.

Chapter 11

The Post-War World

For many pacifists, their opposition to war had been long-standing, and would continue following the end of the war in 1945. The notion that wars did not take place in a vacuum but in a world that was beset by inequalities was deep-seated for many in the peace movement. Therefore, in order to prevent further conflict, a new world order based on co-operation and the eradication of injustice had to emerge from the ruins of the Second World War. Thoughts as to what this world would look like were already being discussed during the latter stages of the war.

In March 1944, the National Peace Council, an umbrella group representing forty organisations directly or indirectly concerned with the promotion of peace, issued a pamphlet titled *The Conditions of a Constructive Peace*, which outlined seventeen points that needed to be addressed to achieve a war-free world. If they were not, the pamphlet warned, 'the alternatives are revolutionary peace or third world war.'

The first section concerned the basic principles of 'Positive Peace-Making'. An adjustment of human relations was needed so that contentment of the peoples would lead to reluctance to forego the manifest benefits of peace. Therefore, there should be no assignment of war guilt to one county or group of countries, as occurred at the Treaty of Versailles. There should be a 'Fellowship of Peoples', which rejected the dominance of large nations over the small, or the so-called 'advanced' over the 'backward'. Equal rights to all people without discrimination on grounds of race, colour or creed should be the order of the day. 'Creative Freedom' would mean that people should triumph over machines, and there should be religious liberty and freedom of expression. The final basic principle of the new world would be that it should have a 'Spiritual Basis' with a 'common brotherhood of mankind', with national corporate life being subject to meeting external standards.

From these basic principles flowed a number of practical policies that should be enacted to ensure a lasting peace. The first was 'Restoration and Re-settlement', with continued rationing in the victorious nations to ensure an equitable distribution of resources. Millions of refugees needed resettlement and this should include the dispelling of prejudice and hostility towards Jews. A 'New Social Order' should be established at home, with the abolition of poverty and the full spiritual, cultural and physical development of every citizen. There should be public ownership of industries and services, a social security system and educational opportunity for all. This new order should not just be confined to the UK. There should be 'World Freedom from Want' and the sharing of wealth across the world. As part of this, 'Functional Co-operation' was required to share expertise on health, education, transport and communication under the auspices of an international organisation. There should also be a 'General International Organisation' to replace the nearly defunct League of Nations, and 'Justice and Peaceful Change' with a world court to arbitrate on disputes between countries.

Germany, rather than be subjected to punishment measures as happened in 1919, should experience social reconstruction, and the termination of Allied occupation should be achieved at the earliest opportunity. There needed to be a 'More Unified Europe' based on common needs and interests, with co-operation rather than competition in economic policy. 'General Disarmament' needed to occur, and the transferring of productive power to peaceful needs. As part of this, airfields needed to be demilitarised. There should be 'Freedom for Colonial Peoples'. This would be achieved first by regulating their economies and ensuring civil liberties, thus paving the way for self-government. Of particular urgency was the issue of India, which should be granted immediate and full self-government. Finally, the pamphlet called for 'Education for World Citizenship' so young people could learn about the moral factor in world affairs and take an internationalist view. This would include the study of foreign languages and cultures, knowledge of world, as well as national, history and student exchange programmes.

Consequently, a lasting peace would require a positive policy that removed the causes of aggression by promoting the general well-being through social reconstruction and co-operation between nations. There also needed to be emergency food and medical supplies sent to people in occupied territories to minimise the barriers to establishing peace once the fighting had ended. 'The shortening of the war and the limitation wherever possible of its destructive effects must therefore be important factors in winning the peace.'

At the time of the German surrender in May 1945, there were 5,100,000 British men and women in the armed forces, while another 3,900,000 were producing equipment and supplies: a total of 9 million people. In order to permit the speedier demobilisation of as many of them as possible, it was decided by the government to continue with the policy of conscription, so their ranks could be quickly filled. This was a policy opposed by pacifist groups. However, the May 1945 edition of the CBCO bulletin warned that divisions in the movement were hampering attempts to address the issue:

A PLEA FOR UNITY

by Charles F. Carter

Let us face the facts. The PPU alone, despite its broad basis, will fail in this task. The Society of Friends alone cannot succeed; nor can the ILP nor the FoR. Yet fools that we are, we let the perfect be the enemy of the good, and because we differ in ideals, we refuse at times to co-operate in our great common purpose. The war has been won by a coalition government, because anything else would have been too weak. The peace may be lost by the division of men of goodwill.

So it is time for Christian pacifists to stop looking down their Pharisitical noses at the ILP; for the political pacifists to be ready to co-operate even with capitalist Quakers. It is time for a united defence of liberty – even the liberty of Jehovah's Witnesses. It is time to be broad-minded, and to prepare for common action. For unity is strength, and co-operations an integral part of our faith.

The atomic bombs

On 6 and 9 August 1945, the US government, with the agreement of the British government, dropped two atomic bombs on the Japanese cities of Hiroshima and Nagasaki, killing around 130,000 people immediately, and many tens of thousands more in the succeeding months. (Plates, page 16) These actions have been the subject of intense ethical debate ever since. The immediate justification from the American government was that the bombs saved the lives of many more soldiers, prisoners of war and civilians by averting the need for a protracted ground campaign. By the early 1950s, however, religious historian G. Stephens Spinks was able to detect a 'delayed sense of guilt for Hiroshima and Nagasaki'. A revisionist movement that became prominent in the 1960s accused the US of immoral acts amounting to war crimes, seeing the dropping of the bombs as unnecessary in order to win the war.

Some historians have accused President Truman of racism and the desire to prove his own masculinity. Others accuse the US of using the war in the Far East as a pretext for demonstrating to the USSR the power of nuclear technology. Far from being an ethically sound action designed to bring the war to a swift conclusion, Truman and those who supported his action have 'hammered away at the "lives saved" argument because it placed the atomic bombings in the realm of moral virtue'. From a British perspective, Max Hastings argued that critics of the atomic bombs were demanding that the US take the moral responsibility for the sparing of the Japanese people that had been abrogated by their leaders:

> No sane person would suggest that the use of the atomic bombs represented an absolute good, or was even a righteous act. But in the course of the war, it had been necessary to do many terrible things to advance the cause of Allied victory.

The social survey organisation Mass Observation gathered the early impressions of reaction in the UK to the news of the dropping of the bombs. Their File Report 2272, *A Report on Public Reactions to the Atom Bomb*, was produced in late August 1945. In it, the reactions of a middle-class family are recorded on hearing the news on the wireless. These began with murmurs of 'God' and 'Good Lord, how awful'. The family then comments on the 'frightful news', and hope that no more will be dropped and that the Japanese will surrender. Concerns are expressed that the end of the world has drawn nearer, with one sardonic comment being, 'I don't think I'll put my name down for hop-picking now – it's not worthwhile.' There was, however, plenty of opinion seeing the bomb as just desserts for the Japanese, with one respondent commenting, 'I think it's marvellous. It's just what we want, isn't it?'

The *Methodist Recorder* received a number of letters protesting against the dropping of the bombs, but the author of the 'Notes' column of 16 August 1945 observed that it was war that was wrong, and that the 'use of an atomic bomb to kill thousands is not more immoral than the use of a molecular bomb to kill hundreds'. An editorial the following week reiterated this line in arguing that 'There is no point in this arithmetic of inequity which makes an atomic bomb a hundred thousand times more sinful than a rifle bullet.' This view was not shared by all Methodists, with Donald Soper, who heard news of the bomb while sitting on a beach in Cornwall, realising immediately that the advent of atomic weapons heralded a new age of warfare. Soper went on to become one of the founder members of the Campaign for Nuclear Disarmament.

Although a more nuanced hue in recent historiography has sought to paint a less binary picture of the ethical choices surrounding the dropping of the bombs, the decision to use such a new and fearsome weapon is one that Christians have found challenging to reconcile with biblical precepts. The new power and nature of destructive capability which, in the minds of many clergy gave rise to a stark spiritual challenge that could be met – indeed, could only be met – by churchmen themselves. However, their inability to reach anywhere near a unanimous conclusion on the moral nature of nuclear weapons was an indication of the reducing influence of the Church in British national life. Alan Wilkinson, who studied the ethical issues that mass warfare caused the British churches during the twentieth century, claimed that, as in America, the British public was only too glad that all hostilities were now over and did not stop to consider the moral implications of the use of atomic weapons. For Wilkinson this was because 'consciences had been blunted by the acceptance of obliteration bombing.'

Yet one correspondent to the *Church Times*, in the immediate aftermath of the attacks, cited a widespread 'deterioration of moral standards through the war', but that the atomic bomb marked a different level of aggression with 'not one definite Christian to whom I have spoken has approved it [*sic*].' This was not a universal view, and it drew swift rebukes from other correspondents. One pointed out that the destruction of 10 million people over six years by pre-atomic bombs was not logically different to that of 300,000 (*sic*) in a matter of twenty seconds. In addition, it was argued by another cleric that as the weapon had been used by the Allies, who were 'civilized people' rather than 'German or Japanese savages', it justified the action. There was no one agreed standpoint among British Christians.

The Anglican hierarchy proved broadly condemnatory in tone. Hensley Henson, Bishop of Durham, denounced their use in a rare example of a disagreement between him and Winston Churchill over the execution of the war, whilst Cuthbert Thicknesse, Dean of St Albans, refused the use of the cathedral for a VJ day thanksgiving service. Cyril Garbett, Archbishop of York, claimed that the means for the destruction of all civilisation had been invented and that the formula for the use of nuclear weapons should be handed over to a neutral international body. The Archbishop of Canterbury, Geoffrey Fisher, referred to them as 'weapons of darkness', although acknowledging that it was a weapon not different in kind, but only degree, to any other form of killing. Bishop Chavasse of Rochester preached against their use in front of Field Marshal Montgomery, although he later came to see atomic weaponry as necessary in the context of the Cold War.

The mood of Christian Britain was not uniformly condemnatory. In the weeks following the cessation of hostilities, many clergy preached of the notion that the bombs had prevented a drawn-out war with many casualties. The Dean of Ely, Lionel Blackburne, felt indignant that those who condemned their use 'would have preferred a long drawn-out war and a hideous slaughter of fine lives while they themselves remain in security'. The Methodist minister I.G. Fogg offered prayers of thanks for a weapon that had saved thousands of lives. Eventually, apart from a few prominent voices like Donald Soper, Britain's Free Church leaders lapsed into silence and left the running to individual clergy and laymen – often pacifists who articulated views far from the denominational mainstream.

The chairman and secretary of the Congregational Union wrote to Prime Minister Attlee urging the abolition of such 'devastating instruments of destruction'. Church leaders were deluged with letters of protest, as Christians claimed that only a resurgence of moral energy for Britain and the world could overcome the unprecedented physical energy unleashed by atomic warfare. The Vatican condemned the use of the atomic bomb, a stance echoed in Britain by the *Catholic Herald*. Ronald Knox, a prominent Catholic writer and broadcaster, wrote that only an increase in the 'energy in the life of most Christian souls' could forestall the prospect of a world blighted by weapons of terror, ethical ambivalence and rampant nationalism. This energy should come from all Christians regardless of denomination or nationality.

Thus, although reaction in the higher echelons of the British churches was largely negative, further down there were disagreements. Whilst the loudest voices became those articulating the pacifist cause, those of men in the armed forces were largely ignored in the succeeding years. The evidence amongst this milieu points to a higher proportion of opinions expressing support for the decision to drop the bombs. This is hardly surprising for, in many cases, theirs were the lives saved, either through the cessation of hostilities in which they were directly involved, or by them being freed from three and a half years of brutal captivity. A Mass Observation report identified broad domestic reactions to the atomic bomb to be 'somewhat confused'. Whilst the majority of respondents felt its use was right, both in terms of ending the war sooner and as justified punishment for Japan, many doubts were expressed about the destructive power of scientific knowledge and the morality of punishing innocent civilians.

Contemporary and subsequent reactions from non-Christian military sources point towards a feeling of relief, although prisoners of war in particular would not have been in a position to know the full implications of the new technology. N.B. Gray, a steward on board the aircraft carrier HMS *Indefatigable*, which was preparing for air strikes against Japan, noted in his diary: 'A new atomic bomb dropped on Japan … News good. A little chocker.' Alistair Urquhart, a Gordon Highlander prisoner of war, felt the effects of the Nagasaki blast from a few miles away. Surveying the wreckage of the city following his release, he found it 'difficult to comprehend. Yet it would take more than this strange sight to spoil our party.' Harold Atcherley, another POW, noted in his diary his 'delight and shock of sudden, incredible, wonderful news'. Geoffrey Sherring, a Merchant Navy radio operator who was a POW in Nagasaki, was more taken with the effect of the blast on the defeathered birds of the area, a 'horrifying sight', rather than the human suffering, 'because, after all, the Japanese had scarcely endeared themselves to me. I felt they deserved it.' Leonard Cheshire, who had been the RAF's observer for the Nagasaki raid, 'said quite plainly he did not want to discuss the ethics of the thing' in a talk to the University of Oxford Air Squadron, witnessed by RAF pilot Tony Benn in 1946. This lack of sympathy or engagement was mostly evident in Christian responses too.

Religious reactions exhibited a mixture of relief, although tinged with reflection on the ethical implications of such huge blasts. At the most exculpatory end of the spectrum of responses was Brigadier General G.B. Mackenzie (Ret.). Writing in the Officers' Christian Union journal, Mackenzie saw the bombs as God's way of answering the prayer for the cessation of the war. Furthermore, Mackenzie viewed the bomb as a 'judicial act' on those who had denied his Godhead, thus equating the atomic explosions with God's judgement on Pharaoh's Egypt in the books of Exodus. A more typical feeling was one of relief, tinged with some feeling of regret that the bombing had been necessary. One officer in the Far East theatre of war, Ruggles Fisher of the Royal Norfolk Regiment, who had undertaken the second Chindit mission, recalled a feeling of relief amongst his comrades. Their next task would have been to invade Malaya and recapture Singapore, probably sustaining heavy casualties in the process. This did not mean that ethical considerations were cast aside, as Fisher considered 'all types of warfare are incompatible with Christianity, but are sadly caused by the sinfulness of mankind.'

Similarly for John Wyatt, a working-class Catholic POW in the East Surrey Regiment, it was 'an event that was to save my life and the lives of thousands of my colleagues in the Far East'. Wyatt considered that the effects of the coming winter would have killed off many thousands of prisoners, although 'I regret the tragic loss of Japanese lives in those cities but it saved the lives of many Allied Prisoners of War.' Indeed, he condemned the 'hypocrisy of the Japanese government' in describing American bombing of their cities as 'bestial' whilst undergoing horrific treatment at the hands of their camp guards. Bill Frankland, an Anglican Royal Army Medical Corps doctor, was another who considered that the dropping of the atomic bombs on Hiroshima and Nagasaki saved his life, recalling machine-gun nests being set up covering the parade ground at Blakang Mati POW camp in readiness for what the men believed to be a mass execution in the event of a ground invasion of Japanese-occupied territory.

For Hugh Montefiore, a convert from Judaism to Anglicanism, their use was a great act of moral turpitude: 'I was appalled, horrified, disgusted. Should I resign my commission?' Nearly four decades later, Montefiore reconsidered this viewpoint on a visit to Japan, after meeting an Anglican Japanese chaplain who contended that their use had shortened the war and saved tens of thousands of lives. Even with the benefit of hindsight, he concluded, 'I am still rather ashamed of what we did' – the 'we' taking upon himself the collective responsibility for decisions taken at the highest level of American military command.

Ken Tout, a tank commander with the Northamptonshire Yeomanry, echoed the view of Archbishop Fisher in that the atomic bombs were an extreme weapon, but on the same moral scale as any act of killing:

> the second atom bomb on Nagasaki was probably excessive viewing the horrors of Hiroshima. The Japanese emperor would either capitulate after Hiroshima or not at all. However, I see these as tactical errors, not as any worse morally than a bayonet in an enemy's belly.

Thus, reactions of men in the armed services to the dropping of the atomic bombs recognised the ethical implications of the events, but was naturally tinged with a sense of relief that they brought a swift end to the war in the Far East, and for many saved them from possible, or near certain, death.

These conflicting reactions to the advent of the nuclear age set the scene for the post-war pacifist movement. It might have been thought that weaponry of such magnitude could have forced more people into an anti-war stance, but the evidence presented above presents a far more nuanced picture.

One of the pressing concerns of post-war pacifists was to convince people of an even greater urgency for disarmament during the nuclear age. The Fellowship of Reconciliation issued *The Hydrogen Bomb* pamphlet, describing its 'immense destructive power', which 'has shocked the conscience of the world', bringing feelings of fear, hysteria, guilt and the belief that something was deeply wrong with the world. However, for the Fellowship of Reconciliation, the H-bomb had not taken warfare to a new ethical level but was a logical extension to what had come previously:

> We have never believed that it is possible to isolate individual weapons for condemnations or to wage a gentlemen's war in which certain methods are barred. The H-bomb is a logical stage in the steadily increasing ruthlessness of military development. If the H-bomb, which may destroy a city, were abolished, there is left the atom-bomb which may destroy one-third of a city. If the atom-bomb were abolished there is left the block-buster, which may destroy one-twentieth of a city.

It did, nevertheless, demonstrate 'unanswerable the starkly un-Christian nature of war'. The way forward lay in abandoning not just the H-bomb, but all other armaments. The first step along that road was 'for individuals to renounce war and all part in it in the name of Christ, and accept, instead, a life-service for the enthronement of love in all public and personal relationships of life'.

A further FoR pamphlet, *Is It Peace?*, asked:

> The H-bomb remains
> CAN WE RELAX OUR EFFORTS
> As long as we are relying on fear of the H-bomb to keep us out of war?
> As long as young men are still being conscripted and trained to kill, in this – or
> any other – country?
> As long as we are committed to the atomic arms race?
> As long as millions of people are starving in Asia when the money we still
> spend on armaments might feed them?
> As long as the Church of Jesus Christ makes nonsense of her Gospel by failing
> to say a clear 'no' to all forms of war?

The obvious answer to this question was a resounding 'No!'

In October 1945, thirty-one pacifists, including Vera Brittain, published an open letter to the British government asking what moral difference there was between Nazi extermination camps and the mass extermination of civilians at Hiroshima and Nagasaki. The Peace Pledge Union began a Crusade for a People's Peace. As well as the renunciation of war, the crusade called for a repudiation of all violence for political ends and the removal of racial and other forms of discrimination, which were an incubator for violence. Regular Hiroshima Day demonstrations were held in Hyde Park and Trafalgar Square during the late 1940s and early 1950s. By 1957, a Direct Action Committee against Nuclear War had been formed, and at Easter 1958, organised a march on Aldermaston Atomic Weapons Establishment. From this initiative came the Campaign for Nuclear Disarmament, which came to particular prominence in the 1980s.

Other pacifist activities in the immediate aftermath of the war included drawing attention to the plight of Germans. The composer Benjamin Britten, a PPU member, organised a 'foodless lunch' to highlight the issue. Pacifists urged the British government to send food to Europe rather than increase the food ration at home, despite the austerity the Labour government had been forced to continue after 1945. Some pacifists travelled to Germany to join work camps to help in the reconstruction of the ruined nation. They also arranged holidays to the UK for destitute German and Austrian children.

The PPU also campaigned against war crimes trials on the basis that only the victors were dispensing justice, and that those responsible for the firestorms in Hamburg and Dresden would not be forced to account for their actions. Furthermore, no action would be taken against those instrumental in the destruction of Hiroshima and Nagasaki. Most odious of all to many pacifists was the execution of prominent Nazis and members of the Japanese military for crimes against humanity. The PPU argued that war itself was a crime against humanity, so no one individual could be held to account.

Pacifists have continued to play a role in British public life through to the twenty-first century, with a demonstration against the Iraq war in 2003 attracting, according to a BBC estimate, around a million people, making it the biggest protest march in British history. This showed that pacifists could still, as they had during the 1930s, mobilise public support for major anti-war rallies. The roots of this movement can be traced back to the inter-war years and it remains to be seen what future challenges the development of warfare presents to those who wish to oppose it, and how best disapproval to war can be organised and mobilised. As political activism moves to more online and social media platforms, perhaps this is where the future Fenner Brockways, Dick Sheppards and Vera Brittains will be found.

Conclusion

The British peace movement was influential in both political and religious life in 1930s Britain. Organisations such as the League of Nations Union and Peace Pledge Union could command hundreds of thousands of followers and generate large incomes to support their education and propaganda work. Their ideals were actively supported and promoted by many leading politicians and churchmen. In addition, many literary and cultural figures lent their backing to them as well as other peace organisations. During that decade, some groups also took action to alleviate the suffering being caused by existing wars in places such as Spain, and by the oppressive regime in Germany.

Yet once the full enormity of the challenge facing Christian civilisation had become apparent by the spring of 1940, pacifist voices were increasingly in the minority, with only around 2 per cent of men registering as conscientious objectors. Pacifists on the home front turned their attentions, unsuccessfully, to campaigning for a negotiated peace and an end to the bombing operation over Germany. Young men and women who did enter the register of objectors were, on the whole, allowed to find roles within society that were in accordance with their conscience. For some this involved social work, for others it meant addressing the destruction directly caused by the Blitz. Some worked on the land whilst other adventurous souls travelled overseas to work with civilian refugees. A remarkable group volunteered to have a series of uncomfortable and potentially dangerous medical experiments performed on them. Those closest to the military machine found productive roles within the Non-Combatant Corps and Royal Army Medical Corps whereby they could feel part of the work that their generation was undertaking.

There were a handful of individuals who fell foul of the regulations, usually due to rigid inflexibility on behalf of the authorities, or within those individuals themselves. Occasionally, inhumane methods were tried to 'break' these individuals, always without success.

The range of these pacifist responses to the awfulness of war sprang from an individuality of thought and expression best summed up by Vera Brittain in 1942:

> Pacifism is nothing other than a belief in the ultimate transcendence of love over power. This belief comes from an inward assurance. It is untouched by logic and beyond arguments – though there are many arguments both for and against it. And each person's assurance is individual; his inspiration cannot arise from another's reasons, nor can its authority be quenched by another's scepticism.

Select Bibliography

Anderson, Stuart, *Refusing to Fight the 'Good War': Conscientious Objectors in North East England during the Second World War*, Tyne Bridge Publishing, Newcastle, 2017.

Barker, Rachel, *Conscience, Government and War: Conscientious Objection in Great Britain, 1939–45*, Routledge, London, 1982.

Birn, Donald, *League of Nations Union, 1918–45*, Oxford University Press, London, 1981.

Brittain, Vera, *Humiliation with Honour*, Andrew Dakers, London, 1942.

Brittain, Vera, *Seeds of Chaos: What Mass Bombing Really Means*, New Vision Publishing, London, 1944.

Brockway, Fenner, *Bermondsey Story: The Life of Alfred Salter*, George Allen & Unwin, London, 1949.

Brockway, Fenner, *98 Not Out*, Quartet Books, London, 1986.

Ceadal, Martin, *Pacifism in Britain, 1914–1945: The Defining of a Faith*, Clarendon Press, Oxford, 1980.

Gardiner, Juliet, *The Thirties: An Intimate Portrait*, HarperPress, London, 2011.

Harthill, Percy (ed.), *On Earth Peace: A Symposium by Communicants of the Church of England*, James Clarke & Co, London, 1944.

Hayes, Denis, *Challenge of Conscience*, George Allen & Unwin, London, 1949.

Hetherington, William, *Swimming Against the Tide: The Peace Pledge Union Story, 1934–2014*, Peace Pledge Union, London, 2014.

Hughes, Michael, *Conscience and Conflict: Methodism, Peace and War in the Twentieth Century*, Epworth Press, London, 2014.

Kramer, Ann, *Conscientious Objectors of the Second World War: Refusing to Fight*, Pen & Sword, Barnsley, 2013.

Krebs, Hans, *Reminiscences and Reflections*, Clarendon Press, Oxford, 1981.

Mellanby, Kenneth, *Scabies*, Oxford University Press, 1943.

Mellanby, Kenneth, *Human Guinea Pigs*, Merlin Press, London, 1973.

Milne, A.A., *Peace with Honour*, MacMillan, London, 1934.

Milne, A.A., *War with Honour*, MacMillan, London, 1940.

Overy, Richard, *The Morbid Age: Britain and the Crisis of Civilisation, 1919–1939*, Penguin, London, 2010.

Peel, Mark, *The Last Wesleyan: A Life of Donald Soper*, Scotforth Books, Lancaster, 2008.

Postgate, Oliver, *Seeing Things*, Pan Books, London, 2001.

Richards, Leyton, *Christian Pacifism after Two World Wars*, Independent Press, London, 1948.

Slack, Kenneth, *George Bell*, SCM, London, 1971.

Underhill, Evelyn, *The Church and War*, Anglican Pacifist Fellowship, London, 1940.

Weatherhead, Leslie, *Thinking Aloud in Wartime*, Hodder & Stoughton, London, 1943.

White, L.E., *Tenement Town*, Jason Press, London, 1945.

Wilkinson, Alan, *Dissent or Conform?: War, Peace and the English Churches, 1900–1945*, SCM Press, London, 1986.

Index